Joseph Niemecz, Father Primitivus
Priest of the Barmherzigen Bruder, 'cellist in the
Esterházy orchestra under Joseph Haydn, and
maker of mechanical organs which played
music by Haydn.
(courtesy of Österreichisches Institut für Kultur Geschichte,
Schloss Esterházy, Eisenstadt).

Joseph Haydn and the Mechanical Organ

First published 1982 in Great Britain by
University College Cardiff Press
P.O. Box 78
Cardiff CF1 1XL
United Kingdom

British Library Cataloguing in Publication Data

Ord-Hume, Arthur W.J.G.
    Joseph Haydn and the mechanical organ
    1. Haydn, Joseph. Organ music
    I. Title
    786.5'092'4   ML410.H4
ISBN 0 906449 37 5

The design and layout of this book
is by the author

Printed in Britain by Qualitex Printing Ltd, Cardiff

Joseph Haydn
and the
Mechanical Organ

ARTHUR W. J. G. ORD-HUME

Illustrated by the author

University College Cardiff Press

Contents

List of Line Illustrations

List of Plates

Author's Note

Whoever studies music, let his daily bread be Haydn. Beethoven indeed admirable, his is incomparable, but he has not the same usefulness as Haydn: he is not a necessity . . . Haydn the great musician, the first who created everything, discovered everything, taught everything to the rest!

Jean Ingres (1780–1867)

Introduction

There is already a great deal of literature extant on the music
and life of Joseph Haydn. Remarkably, though, very little
has ever been published on the aspect of his music with
which this book is concerned — and the majority of that which has
appeared in print was half a century ago in German.

Unlike many other composers, Haydn was intrinsically a happy
and secure man. Indeed, he had good reason to be for, other than
during a period of poverty in his early life, he enjoyed comfort,
was employed by a patron who genuinely admired his ability and
who respected him, and was allowed a measure of freedom to
travel as well as an ample salary. The most important of these
attributes was without doubt his special relationship with the
noble princes of Esterházy, no fewer than four of whom he
served, and in particular his association with Prince Nicolaus II
who was a benefactor of quite extraordinary breadth. In this
environment, Haydn had not just a comfortable home and
superabundant artistic encouragement, but he controlled his own
orchestra of hand-picked musicians.

This, however, is not just another book about Haydn. In fact,
the reader will find very little historical material on Haydn
between these covers. This is partly because there are plenty of
musical reference works which deal exhaustively with Haydn.
Nor, one must say, is this a detailed study of the musical clock or
the mechanical organ. Both instruments have already been
described in my earlier books published by George Allen &
Unwin in London. This work centres on one small yet
nevertheless fascinating facet of musical history — namely Joseph
Haydn's unusually rich involvement in the world of mechanical
music and its instruments. This resulted from the collaboration
between Haydn and a talented priest who was also on the princely
payroll of the Esterházys. A renowned patron of the arts, Nicolaus
II encouraged a unique project involving the melding of the
talents of his two servants — Haydn on the one hand and this
extraordinary cleric on the other. Brought up in Holy Orders, he
could make the finest mechanical organs of the period and when
not at work in his job as librarian, musical performer and man of

the Cloth, he spent his time crafting these small and delightful instruments which, by virtue of their clockwork motors, would play by themselves.

While the relationship between 'Papa Haydn' and the Esterházy family is well known, more particularly since the detailed researches of C.F. Pohl and E.F. Schmid in the 1930s and H.C. Robbins Landon in the past few years, very little has ever been recorded concerning this priest or his unusual hobby.

At the Esterházy palaces of Eisenstadt and, later, Eszterháza, Haydn flourished and the music flowed from his pen with ease. As kapellmeister of the Prince's orchestra he probably came first into contact with the man who was to have so interesting an influence on him when the unlikely vision of a shaven-headed, garbed monk playing the cello caught his glance. If this was no ordinary monk, then he surely earned for himself as rich a place in the history of Haydn's music as any other artist of his time. It was for this man and his spring-driven organs that Haydn produced one of his most interesting series of compositions, namely those listed in van Hoboken's catalogue as XIX: 1–32.

It was not until the 1920s that Haydn's involvement with mechanical music first came to light, although the little compositions which he had produced for the medium were known and had been catalogued, somewhat loosely, at a much earlier epoch. It was the sheer breadth of his involvement which more than half a century ago encouraged two men to look further. One was the biographer Alfred Schnerich, and the other was the scholar Ernst Fritz Schmid. Their works, published only in German, described in some detail the background to the instruments and the music but left the enquirer with almost as many questions unanswered as before. The remarkable survival of instruments built under the guidance of Haydn and playing some thirty pieces of his music provided material evidence that more work should be undertaken to examine in greater depth the circumstances surrounding these organs and their music.

The very first public hearing of any of Haydn's *Flötenuhr* music came on Vienna's radio station at 8.15 p.m. on Monday, 14 June 1926. According to the *Wiener Programm* for that date we find a broadcast called simply *Musikalische Miniaturen* which comprised an assortment of chamber music including K. Tautenhayn's air *Spieluhr*. But the closing part of the broadcast was devoted to the Haydn/Niemecz mechanical organ attributed to the year 1772. Two of its sixteen airs were played — and I doubt whether anybody batted an eyelid at the significance of the occasion.

Haydn's compositions for mechanical organ, an instrument commonly but erroneously referred to as flute-clock or musical clock, stand supreme as finely-crafted cameos of his art. But what makes these so much more enjoyable and, from the point of view of the musicologist, so fascinating, is that three of the original organs for which they were written are still in playing order. Of the thirty-two pieces he composed specially for this medium, no fewer than thirty are extant on these surviving musical mechanisms.

The purpose of this book is to try to put these pieces of music into their proper perspective in terms of the reasons why they were written. It will also provide the opportunity to describe and illustrate — in detail — for the first time in their lives — the instruments with which Joseph Haydn was so intimately concerned. My story will also serve to accord just respect to the one man who was Haydn's collaborator in making this whole episode possible. Other characters emerge in this story of music and mechanical organs — entrepreneurs, organ-builders, the noble environment of the Esterházys and their great palaces, their friends and fellow nobility.

The most detailed summary of the background to this story was published in Germany back in 1932. Frequently referred to in German literature on music, this has never been available in English. The work of Ernst Fritz Schmid of Vienna is still today a valid starting point for research and so I have taken this as the basis for my own work. But rather than offer a literal, unmodified and dated translation of this old text, I have up-dated Schmid's writings, including much new information which has come to light in recent years through my own researches and also through the detailed and extensive work of Pohl and Robbins Landon.

Schmid's analysis of the music remains as important as ever and I make no apology for having used his valuable notes and comments as published in 1932 in his original paper in the *Zeitschrift für Musikwissenschaft*. But whereas his documentation was throughout of German origin, and largely Viennese, the whole being prepared half a century ago, I have been able to draw on the considerable wealth of information which has come to light throughout the world in the intervening years. This knowledge has expanded dramatically the documentation. There is, for example, a great deal of contemporary English writing, particularly concerning the London exhibitions of associated mechanical musical instruments which are featured in the story.

It has often been suggested that the three instruments which survive and are described in this book are the sum total of mechanical organs for which the pieces of music were written, the direct implication being that Haydn wrote his set of pieces for the three clockwork organs that are with us today. How fortunate, most certainly, that these actual instruments survive. But without wishing to dispute our good fortune in this respect, the implication is somewhat untidy for while these three organs give us thirty pieces of music, variously duplicated on the three different barrels, Haydn's output for the mechanical organ totalled at least thirty-two pieces and the evidence, when examined closely and tempered with logic, leads me to suppose that these three may not be the sole Haydn-playing organs to have emerged from the Esterházy workshop of Father Primitivus Niemecz. Indeed, I am inclined to the belief that the instruments are the extant examples of a possibly much wider repertoire of instruments upon which Haydn's music was set. A degree of duplication in the music between these organs, plus a marked difference between the versions of the duplicated works, does exist. Manuscripts exist for two more compositions as yet undiscovered on any organ. There are also some tantalising references to later and apparently now-lost organs which indicate clearly that more Haydn-playing instruments from the same builder existed and may even exist somewhere to this day, awaiting discovery by the musicologist. This is indeed an exciting prospect.

Much controversy surrounds the three known organs, in particular the earliest of these which has always been referred to as the instrument of 1772. In spite of apparently water-tight evidence of dating which has come down through the years in the owner's family, I will be presenting evidence to show that the organ cannot possibly have been built as early as this, a situation now corroborated by examination of the autograph score of one of the pieces included in the repertoire of this organ.

Because confusion about clockwork organs and the proper translation of the German word *Flötenuhr* has created considerable confusion over the years, I include a section on the design and construction of these instruments and describe how the music was arranged and set upon the barrels.

I am grateful to the present owners of the Haydn mechanical organs which are the stars of this story for their help and for permission to use photographs of their instruments. I would also like to express my warmest thanks to William Malloch of Los Angeles, California, who made the initial contact with the owner of Organ Number One and who has been of great assistance in sourcing information in Germany and Austria. A particular acknowledgement goes to Dr Jan-Jaap Haspels, conservator-director of the Nationaal Museum van Speelklok tot Pierement in Utrecht who has assisted me materially as well as providing enthusiastic encouragement to this project. As well as his help in technical translation, my thanks to Ursula Becker of Koblenz and Gabi Martin of Freiburg for their translation of copious German language documentation.

It is doubtful whether this book and the study it represents would have been possible had it not been for the assistance of Grundig International Ltd. Through the good offices of managing director André Baumes and his personal assistant Jörg Lässig, I have been provided with facilities for examining and recording the organs. Besides specialised recording equipment, this company has allowed me special travel concessions without which the compilation of this book would have been infinitely harder (and more expensive). Jörg Lässig has been a tower of strength as a very active assistant in my work and has demonstrated a very real appreciation for what I believe should be not just his national composer but national instrument as well. I also acknowledge the help I have received from the Haydn-Institut in Köln, the Staatsbibliothek Preussischer Kulturbesitz, Musikabteilung in Berlin, Dr Manfred Hermann Schmid, Keeper of the musical instrument collection in the Münchener Stadtmuseum, the Südwest-Tonstudio, GmbH, in Stuttgart, Dr Friederich Berg, Keeper of the Sobek Collection at the Geymüllerschlössl in Vienna, Philips Video also of Vienna, Hannah Schaer of Paris whose fine singing of Haydn's choral works was a continual source of inspiration, and Mr Stephen Ryder of Cranford, New Jersey, who carefully read the manuscript and made a number of useful suggestions. And, of course, I acknowledge the debt to Ernst Fritz Schmid of Vienna who died on 20 January 1960.

It is fitting that in this year, the 250th anniversary of the birth of Joseph Haydn, we should pause to commemorate the part he played in consolidating the reputation and the vast repertoire of music for the mechanical organ. He added his name to the list of composers of repute who have seen automatic musical instruments not as toys or novelties, but as a real extension of musical interpretation. For the student of music today, instruments such as these serve as timeless recordings of not just performance but also style and interpretation of the past. Listening today to one of these Haydn organs is to hear the music as it was intended to be played and, indeed, as Haydn himself would have heard it.

Historians and musicologists alike have adequately recorded the work of Joseph Haydn and our undying debt of gratitude to him. His music will, no doubt, live forever. Yet history has until now overlooked the name of Primitivus Niemecz and the part which he played in preserving Haydn's music. Without the presence of Niemecz and his ability, these thirty-two delightful pieces of music would most certainly never have been written.

Above all, I hope that this book will help to sort out once and for all the confusion which exists in the minds of many — and this includes musicologists, radio announcers, programme-note producers, record-sleeve writers and lexicographers, both old and new — who translate the German word *Flötenuhr* literally instead of understanding the idiom and the instrument. The proper definition is *mechanical organ*.

Arthur W.J.G. Ord-Hume

Plate 1. Mechanical organ made in France about 1790 and contained in a mahogany *secrétaire à abattant* . . . One rank of wooden pipes comprising twenty-two notes. Among the six pieces of music on each of two interchangeable barrels are extracts from two Haydn symphonies.

Glossary of Terms

Words in bold have their own individual entries which should be consulted.

Android
An **automaton** resembling a human being. Possibly the earliest form of automaton, the concept of the android reaches far back into mythology. The creation of a 'mechanical man' is one of Man's oldest goals. Today it is a reality although the robots and automated machines which serve as mechanical men now bear little family resemblance to their creators.

Automaton
An artefact, usually a mechanism, which operates by itself using its own internal power (i.e. a spring or other integral power source). A musical automaton is a self-acting musical mechanism. Plural is *automata*.

Clockwork
A term the meaning of which has become unnecessarily complex and confused partly due to the simple fact that modern people are just not familiar with *real* clockwork. Clockwork is the term used to describe a mechanism of intermeshing toothed wheels and pinions when used to regulate motion between a power source and an end result. A prime qualification for clockwork is that it should have either an escapement or a speed regulating fan, the former providing incremental motion, the latter steady motion. The power source being regulated by this clockwork may come from the uncoiling of a wound-up spring or from the energy stored in a heavy weight wound up to the top of a case using a ratchet-and-pawl winding system via a gut line, a chain (such as a fusee), a cable or other flexible connection. Clockwork does not automatically imply a timepiece forming part of the system or that a timepiece is connected or operated by it.

Clockwork organ
A small pipe-organ having a pre-programmed repertoire of music arranged on a rotating cylinder or barrel usually made of wood and set in motion (i.e. made to play) by means of **clockwork**.

Dulcimer
See under **Harp clock**.

Flötenuhr
Mistranslated as 'toy clock', 'clockwork flutes', 'a sort of small mechanical organ', 'musical clock', 'flute clock' and similar equally incorrect terms. All the foregoing have been taken from record-sleeve and programme notes. The proper translation is very simple and perfectly accurate in every respect — a small

clockwork pipe organ. Larger instruments, often with extensive percussion capabilities, were described as **orchestrions** or, in certain specific cases, **Panharmonicons.**

Flute-playing clock

A **musical clock,** i.e. a timepiece, combined with a small musical mechanism operating flute-toned organ pipes so that a tune is played every hour or at periodic times. See also **Flötenuhr.**

Harp clock

A mechanical **dulcimer** apparently always forming part of the mechanism of a musical timepiece. The mechanism comprised a long rectangular soundboard box across which were arranged the wire strings like those of a piano. The barrel of the musicwork actuated small hammers which struck the strings. A rare instrument today since due to the need for regular tuning, many were apparently discarded. Many makers in Austria and the Black Forest. Among the composers who wrote for this medium were Franz Benda and Carl Philipp Emanuel Bach. German: **Harfenuhr.**

Harfenuhr

See under **Harp clock.**

Hurdy Gurdy

A non-automatic, manually-played stringed instrument of great antiquity sounding by the rotation of a rosin-covered wheel against a number of drone strings while the melody is picked out by stopping off different lengths of the melody strings by means of tangents. In French, the instrument is the *vielle;* in Italian it is the *lyra organizzata* (meaning the 'organised' lyre) or more commonly the *ghironda;* in Germany it is known by several names, the most common being *drehleier* (not strictly accurate) or *radleier.* Also given the Latin name *organistrum* when combined with a small pipe organ which is built integrally with the hurdy gurdy. Sometimes erroneously applied to the *genus* organette (American usage in particular).

Mechanical organ

See **Clockwork organ.**

Musical clock

A clock, i.e. timepiece, provided with a means of playing music every hour or at other periodic times by means of a musical mechanism which may be an organ, a dulcimer, a carillon of bells, or a musical-box type 'comb' of tuned steel teeth.

Musicwork

The anglicised form of the German word *musikwerke* meaning the musical mechanism of a clockwork or otherwise automatically-played instrument. Literally those parts which make the music.

Orchestrion

Literally a large mechanical or clockwork organ to which is incorporated reed stops and percussion effects so as to create the effect of a mechanical orchestra. The word is a correct and adequate generic term for a large barrel, book-playing or perforated-paper-roll-playing mechanical organ with percussion and reed stops. If the instrument incorporates as its foundation a piano, however, the proper generic term becomes *piano-orchestrion,* even if there is also a pipe or reed organ included in the instrumentation.

Organ clock   A specific type of **musical clock** incorporating a small mechanical organ.

Organwork   The anglicised form of the German *orgelwerke* which means organ mechanism.

Panharmonicon   The name which has become associated with the instruments made and exhibited by Mälzel was originally created by Haydn for the mechanical orchestra made by Joseph Gurck who was library assistant to Niemecz. Fondly and contemporarily described as a 'mechanical orchestra', it has always been assumed that only two were made and these by Mälzel, the last being destroyed in Stuttgart during the Second World War. It now transpires that the name became something of a generic term for **orchestrions** at this period and a number of large instruments produced in Vienna at the end of the eighteenth and the beginning of the nineteenth centuries carried this name. In essence, the Panharmonicon was but a precursor of the orchestrion but it is important to see it as the name which Haydn gave to Gurck and not Mälzel.

Programme   In a mechanical organ, the programme refers to the repertoire of music which the instrument can play from its own source material. In early mechanical **musicwork,** the programme could be provided from a wheel whose periphery contained various pins and bridges to control the sounding of the music, from the surface of a rotating disc where this was similarly pinned, or more commonly by means of the barrel or cylinder which, operating after the manner of an extended broad wheel, could carry a large number of pins and bridges upon its surface. Later, the programme became punched cardboard and later still perforated paper like a piano roll. The world of computers subsequently acquired the word 'programme' and with it the paper strip with punched holes, already a technique of long-standing in the world of the teleprinter.

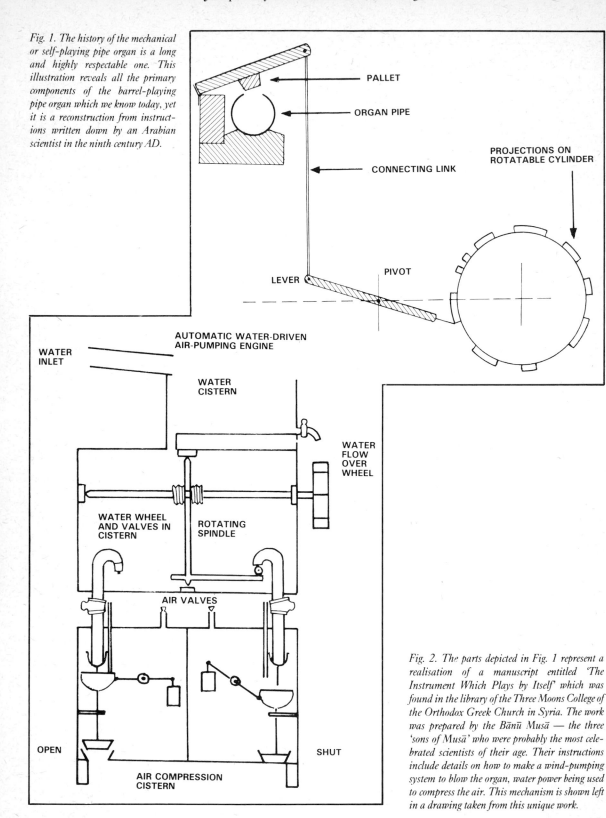

Fig. 1. The history of the mechanical or self-playing pipe organ is a long and highly respectable one. This illustration reveals all the primary components of the barrel-playing pipe organ which we know today, yet it is a reconstruction from instructions written down by an Arabian scientist in the ninth century AD.

PALLET

ORGAN PIPE

CONNECTING LINK

PROJECTIONS ON ROTATABLE CYLINDER

LEVER

PIVOT

AUTOMATIC WATER-DRIVEN AIR-PUMPING ENGINE

WATER INLET

WATER CISTERN

WATER FLOW OVER WHEEL

WATER WHEEL AND VALVES IN CISTERN

ROTATING SPINDLE

AIR VALVES

OPEN

SHUT

AIR COMPRESSION CISTERN

Fig. 2. The parts depicted in Fig. 1 represent a realisation of a manuscript entitled 'The Instrument Which Plays by Itself' which was found in the library of the Three Moons College of the Orthodox Greek Church in Syria. The work was prepared by the Bānū Musā — the three 'sons of Musā' who were probably the most celebrated scientists of their age. Their instructions include details on how to make a wind-pumping system to blow the organ, water power being used to compress the air. This mechanism is shown left in a drawing taken from this unique work.

CHAPTER 1

The Mechanical Organ

The history of the mechanical organ is a long and fascinating one. Although its detail is outside the scope of this present work, it should be emphasised that the earliest examples were the 'automatic flutes' and the self-powered water-blown organs of the Roman and Arab world. The instrument thus almost certainly pre-dated the birth of Christ. In that age when music and the arts were believed inseparable from magic, myth and devoutness, developments in engineering progressed side by side with the myth and folklore and what today we would tend to call automation. When instructions were provided for the construction of a mechanical set of bells in the eleventh century, for example, the directions were not considered to be complete unless they also described how to make an artificial person play them.[1]

While the invention of the flute goes back to Hyagnis, a Phrygian, in Asia Minor in the year 1506 B.C. (depending on which authority you consult it was either earlier or later, but still pre-Christian), the concept of the mechanical flute is likely to be almost as old. The survival of documentary material from that far-off time is minimal and much must have been lost. But besides artifacts resembling pipe organs in miniature, there is some later written evidence. Assuming from our limited knowledge of that age that the inspiration to write and record something was not one widely distributed among people and also considering that the first written evidence is in no way evidence of a first-time use, a remarkable work from the ninth century A.D. provides for us the earliest surviving instructions for making a mechanical set of flutes — a small barrel organ no less. These words and drawings were set down by an Arabian scientist and attributed to the group of wise men known as the Banū Musā.[2] There were others who contrived automatic musical instruments based on the wind-blown flute pipe at this far distant period[3] and there are clear indications that not only is the organ in its simplest form the oldest musical instrument, but even in its most primitive form it became the first to be automated so that it would play without the aegis of a skilled operator.

[1] Manuscript, Yale Medical Library (incomplete), another copy (complete) in Cracow, c.1350 (*vide The Music Box*, vol. 3, p. 200 (1967)).

[2] G.H. Farmer, *The Organ of the Ancients*, chapter 1.

[3] Donald R. Hill, *The Book of Knowledge of Ingenious Mechanical Devices*.

During the sixteenth century in Italy, organs powered by water, both as a means of rotating the pinned cylinder upon which the music to be played was set, and as a means of pumping the air to sound the pipes, were popular amongst the aristocracy. The most famous of these was the water organ in the Frascati home of Cardinal Pietro Aldobrandini and also the one in the grounds of the Villa d'Este at Tivoli near Rome.[4]

[4] A.W.J.G. Ord-Hume, *Barrel Organ*, p. 52.

By the seventeenth century, there was a thriving industry making mechanical organs as the musical component of a variety of art and craft novelties in Central Germany. An early centre for this musical engineering was Augsburg where makers such as Schlottheim, Bidermann, Rungell and others flourished. Some of their work has survived into the twentieth century although many fine pieces were lost during the Second World War. All of the remaining pieces evoke in us an awareness that great skills and subtlety must have reigned supreme amongst these workers.[5]

[5] Ord-Hume, *op. cit.*, pp. 67 *et seq.*

Indeed, although the history of mechanical music can be said to go back more than two millenia, it remained at something of an experimental state until the late sixteenth century in Central Germany and then during the eighteenth century underwent what one might term a 'quantum jump' in evolution. Because of the fact that the mechanics of the organ are extremely simple and thus the instrument is one of the easiest to build and to automate (a vast cathedral organ may indeed be a complex instrument, but it is but the development of a simple system), organ mechanisms capable of producing a very commendable performance existed quite early on. Achilles Langenbucher's 'Pomeranian Cabinet' instrument was constructed in 1617 (it was destroyed in the Second World War) yet within its ornate cabinetwork it contained a highly-developed mechanical organ which could perform music satisfactorily.[6]

[6] Ord-Hume, *op. cit.*, p. 68.

It was, however, the eighteenth century which brought the flowering of the mechanical organ as builders began to concentrate more and more on delicacy and precision of interpretation rather than the vagaries of sheer size, volume and visual novelty. This characteristic was most noticeable in the products of Central Europe and while Britain had a thriving mechanical organ industry,[7] the tone and performance of these instruments was far and away exceeded by the products of Dresden, Vienna, Augsburg and even up into Scandinavia where the work of Petter Strand, only very recently brought before a wider audience,[8] performed with a dexterity and panache and, dare one say it, musical humour, of a very high order.

[7] Ord-Hume, *op. cit.*, pp. 74 *et seq.*

[8] *The Music Box*, vol. 9, p. 277 (1980).

For sheer density of quality mechanical organ builders, though, one has to look to Germany. Here makers such as

Elffroth and Kleemayer excelled in producing instruments which were not just mechanical marvels, but were also fine decorative works of furniture or architectural art. Christian Möllinger, another member of this German enclave of eighteenth century geniuses, built very simple organs capable of performing a most impressive repertoire, the whole being housed in rich cabinetwork and usually surmounted by a symbolic statuette or similar striking decoration. Above all, these machines were all outstanding musical interpreters.

The mechanical organ, when coupled with a timepiece and arranged so that it would play at certain times, was popular with the wealthy and the aristocracy. Indeed, these artefacts were never cheap items and so only the rich could afford such items in their homes. For such a premium product, the customer could specify the music which he wanted such as arrangements of favourite operatic arias and overtures, concerti and sonatas as well as the more familiar marches and light music for dancing.

Besides having existing music arranged for its small compass of pipework, the instrument attracted a repertoire of music composed especially for it. However, unlike the music which was composed for other types of non-mechanical instrument such as

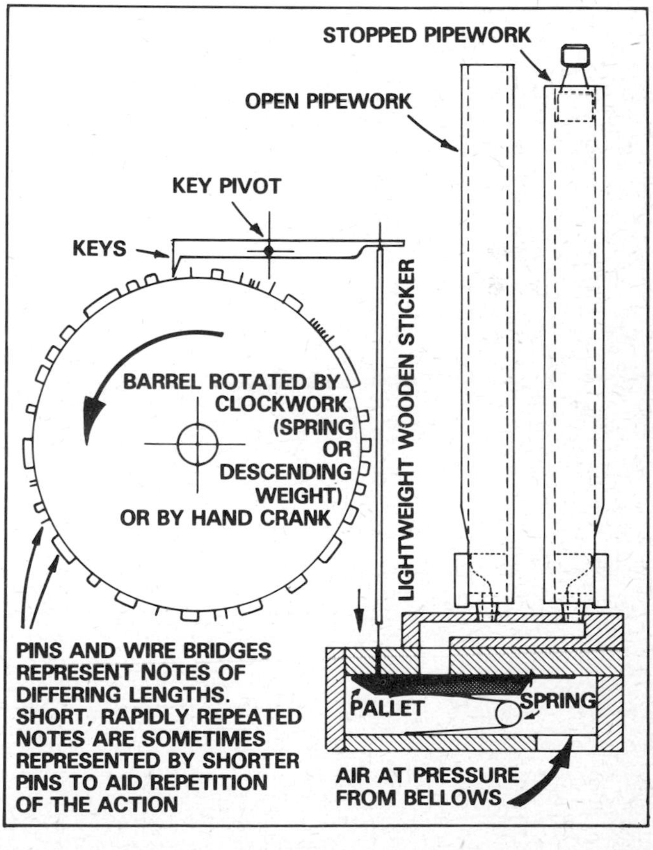

Fig. 3. The operating principles of the ordinary mechanical organ which plays music from a pinned wooden cylinder. There were many variants of the principle, the most imaginative coming from Augsburg in the seventeenth century, yet all employed the same components or their derivatives. For example, the barrel was sometimes replaced by a wheel with just a few rows of pins on its periphery to play a few pipes, or the wheel would be in the form of a disc with concentric rows of projections actually on its face. Pipework could be wood or metal, open or stopped, flue or reed. Power to set the machine in motion might come from a manually-turned handle, from the energy stored in a descending weight and line to a winch, or by clockwork motor.

the baryton, violin or trumpet, it was incumbent upon the composers of such special compositions to bear in mind the capabilities of the particular mechanical organ for which they were writing. Since some organs were very small and had but a limited number of notes, it was essential to tailor the music to such a scale. With much larger instruments like the giant orchestrions or mechanical orchestras which were to become so popular around the closing decades of the eighteenth century, it was perfectly feasible to play quite complex music with interplay between registers of soft and loud pipes, woodwind and reeds as well as percussion effects, while the full chromatic canvas allowed modulation and harmony without restriction. Composers who availed themselves of the opportunities afforded by these mechanical organs of differing sizes included Handel (who produced some interesting pieces for the organ clocks of Charles Clay[9]), Mozart who, in spite of protesting that the instrument was too shrill and sounded childish, composed three delightful pieces for mechanical organ[10] for the musical cabinet of the Count Deym,[11] and Cherubini, who produced a sonata for barrel organ as well as several pieces for Mälzel's Panharmonicon. There were others, of course, such as Hassler and Erbach (whose lives spanned the sixteenth and seventeenth centuries), Johann Caspar Kerll, Dandrieu, Frantisek (Franz) Benda, Kirnberger, Wolfgang Amadeus Mozart, Carl Philipp Emanuel Bach, Eberlin and Leopold Mozart.[12] The organ makers themselves were often highly-skilled in music and several contributed their own musical offerings.

Mechanical organs both with and without timepieces became cherished gifts between rulers, princes, kings and the nobility. Perhaps one of the most famous of such gifts was the instrument made by Charles Dallam and presented by Queen Elizabeth I to the Sultan of Turkey in 1599.[13] Frederick II, King of Prussia and known as Frederick the Great, gave his brother-in-law Ferdinand, Duke of Brunswick, a 'clock with organ' which came from the art gallery of the royal castle in Berlin.[14] At the end of the Seven Years War in 1763, Frederick the Great, who was something of a patron of the instrument and certainly a great lover of it, brought together a number of experienced clockmakers from Geneva and Neuchâtel in Switzerland. They set up an industry in Berlin under the guidance of Abram-Louis Huguenin.[15] With the active support of the King, the manufacture of mechanical organs prospered in that city around the 1760s and rapidly attained pre-eminence in Europe, thus stealing a lead on the later important centres of organ-clock making, Dresden and Vienna in Austria. Indeed, the

[9] Ord-Hume, *op. cit.*, p. 546.

[10] K. 598, K. 608, K. 616. It is also possible that a further work, an Adagio in C major for glass armonica, K. 356, was also intended originally for use on an automatic instrument. Significantly, when Alfred Einstein made his own revision of Köchel's catalogue in 1937, he gave this one the number '617a'. It was written in Vienna during the first half of 1791.

[11] O.E. Deutsch, 'Count Deym and his Mechanical Organs', published in *Music and Letters*, vol. 29 (1948), reproduced in facsimile in *The Music Box*, vol. 3, pp. 204–209 (1967).

[12] For a detailed conspectus of the works of these and other composers who wrote for mechanical musical instrument, see Ernst Simon, *Mechanische Musikinstrumente.*

[13] An account of the commissioning, building and subsequent delivery of this instrument is contained in Stanley Mayes, *An Organ for the Sultan.* The original drawing for this organ has been lost since it was copied by *The Illustrated London News* in 1860.

[14] Ernst Simon, 'Friedrich der Grosse und die Mechanische Musikinstrumente', in *Zeitschrift für Instrumentenbau*, Berlin, vol. XXXII, p. 744 (1912–13).

[15] A. Chapuis, *Le Grande Frédérick et ses Horlogers*, Lausanne, 1938; Rachel: *Das Berliner Wirtschaftsleben des Frühkapitalismus*, Berlin, 1931, p. 198.

manufacture of mechanical organs and timepieces flourished in Berlin right through to the last century.[16] Many of the products of this fruitful enterprise adorned the rooms of the Potsdam Palace and to this day there stands an organ clock constructed by the court official J.L. Bauer who was in the employ of the Prince of Prussia, nephew of Frederick the Great and, later, King Frederick William II. This piece dates from 1763 and was subsequent to an earlier one which was commissioned by the prince's father, William I, as a present to Peter the Great. This is preserved in the Hermitage Museum, Leningrad. In 1784, Bauer the chancellor provided a fine instrument to the Czarina Catherine the Great for 3,000 roubles.[17]

Frederick the Great collected about him the best of the German makers of mechanical organs and he owned an instrument made for him by his court clockmaker, Christian Ernst Kleemeyer who was, with Möllinger, arguably the most important builder of these pieces in the closing years of the eighteenth century.[18] This particular instrument, which has pipework made by the Berlin instrument maker J. Kalix, was intended as a gift to the Duke of Moldavia but unfortunately the Duke died before it could be presented. As a result, Frederick the Great chose to keep the piece for himself. Other examples of the work of Kleemeyer are to be found in the Museum of Musical Instruments at the Karl Marx University in Leipzig[19] and in the Marble Hall of Potsdam Castle.[20]

There were two other notable makers of the period — David Röntgen (1743–1807) and Peter Kintzing (1746–1816). Both had their workshops in Neuwied, a town on the Rhine between Koblenz and Bonn. As Heinrich Weiss-Stauffacher relates in his book *Mechanische Musikinstrumente und Musikautomaten* (Seewen, Switzerland, 1973), their exceptional skill and inventive genius gave them a reputation which spread, primarily among the aristocracy, far beyond the bounds of their own country. Kintzing became court clockmaker to Frederick the Great, presumably on the death of Kleemeyer, while Röntgen held the title of 'secret Councillor of Commerce'. Kintzing not only made clocks but was also something of an inspiration to the cabinetmaker Röntgen. In his story *Neue Melusin*, the poet Goethe says of the magic castle that 'anyone who has seen an artificial writing-table by Röntgen in which one pull sets in motion many springs and mechanisms, desk and writing materials as well as letter and money compartments opening up simultaneously or in swift succession, will have some conception of how that palace unfolded and emerged'. This gives us a notion that Röntgen must have been an expert at crafting pieces with concealed compartments. Today

[16] F. Nicolai, *Beschreibung der Königlichen Residenzstädte Berlin und Potsdam*, Berlin, 1786, vol. II, 3rd ed. p. 579.

[17] P. Seidel, 'Potsdamer und Berliner Standuhren in den Kgl. Schlössern', in *Hohenzollern-Jahrbuch*. 1908, p. 252.

[18] S. Jacobsson, *Technologisches Wörterbuch*, Berlin, 1782. See entry under 'Kleinuhrmacher'.

[19] This organ was bought by Frederick William III in 1825 (relates Buchner). The instrument plays only at sunrise and sunset. See also E. Simon, *op. cit.*, p. 744.

[20] These pieces come from the collection of the Musikhistorisches Museum of Wilhelm Heyer in Cologne. See P. Rubbardt, *Führer durch das Musikinstrumenten-Museum der Karl-Marx-Universität Leipzig*. Leipzig, 1955, p. 69.

the visitor to Leningrad can still admire a magnificent Empire
table representing a 'carillon engainé', an invisible piano inside a
table, the table serving as its case. This last item was made to a
commission by Catherine the Great of Russia. Röntgen, who
always delivered his creations in person and must have been a sort
of Fabergé of his time, made the journey to St. Petersburg no
fewer than seven times. Even the selling price of some of his
pieces is known to us today. Among other things he supplied was a
'mechanical cabinet' to the French Court which cost 3,300 louis-
d'or, for which he also received the title of *ébeniste mécanicien du
Roi et la Reine de France.* And a long-case clock which Catherine
the Great bought from the two craftsmen pleased her so much
that she at once offered more than the price agreed upon.

Alexandr Buchner, who has studied the Berlin makers closely,
listed other notable Berlin makers including Conrad Ehrbar,
Johann Elffroth,[21] and F. Pohlmann. Cylinders for these makers
were all pinned by a musician named Kummer who was himself
to become a well-known maker of barrel organs.

If Frederick the Great had been a great enthusiast for the
mechanical organ then his nephew, Frederick William II, was
even more of one thanks to the influence of Bauer his chancellor.
The chief maker of his period was indeed Christian Möllinger
who became a master clockmaker in Berlin after he had produced
an astronomical clock complete with mechanical organ in 1786.
Möllinger made a similar instrument for Frederick William II
which was placed in the rooms of the Berlin Castle. Alexandr
Buchner relates that many of Möllinger's pieces and the work of
other makers were kept in the Hohenzollern Palace in Berlin.[22] A
later master was Johann Friederich Lieder who began making
mechanical organs at the beginning of the last century. One of his
organs played the overture to Gluck's *Iphigenia in Aulis.* This
particular organ was kept in the Märkisches Museum in Berlin
where it was destroyed in the Second World War.

While the Berlin and Viennese makers concentrated on the
production of instruments as musical interpreters of the highest
order, the burgeoning musical clock industry in the Black Forest
concentrated on making comparitively low-cost organ-playing
clocks. These were the so-called flute clocks or flute-playing
clocks which were always built around a wooden-framed weight-
powered timepiece. The Black Forest organ-clocks ranged from
small instruments which played popular music and dances in an
essentially simple mode right up to the extremely complex barrel
orchestrion which, although still clockwork-driven, was in no way
part of a timepiece and was a musical instrument in its own right.
The Black Forest produced very many instruments. While the

[21] An outstanding Elffroth mechanical
organ and timepiece is kept in the
Märkisches Museum in Berlin.

**Plate 2. Outstanding musical
clock by Möllinger of Berlin. The
time band on the globe moves
round and on the hour the organ
mechanism plays.**

[22] Buchner relates that one of them played
the overture to Grétry's opera *La
Cavaranne du Caire* of 1784, the libretto
for which was written by Louis XVIII.
See: 'Illustriert Führer durch das
Hohenzollern-Museum' in *Schlosse
Monbijou,* Berlin, 1907, p. 47.

smaller organ-clocks were often of indifferent quality, and were thus nowhere in the same category as the instruments we have been discussing (they were also manufactured at a later and hence less musically interesting date), the larger instruments were impressive and in some musical cases important.

The manufacture of barrel organs was not solely the prerogative of the artisans of Central Europe and one specific variety was almost exclusively a British product. This was the church and chamber barrel organ which gained favour in the mid-eighteenth century and was to become the musical mainstay of many a village church and chapel right through to the end of the last century.

As we shall see further on, many Viennese organs were pinned with music by Haydn which was abstracted or adapted from his symphonic works. One very popular work which received such treatment on numerous occasions was the so-called 'military movement' from his Symphony No. 100, the one which bore the title of the 'Military' Symphony. This piece has a somewhat

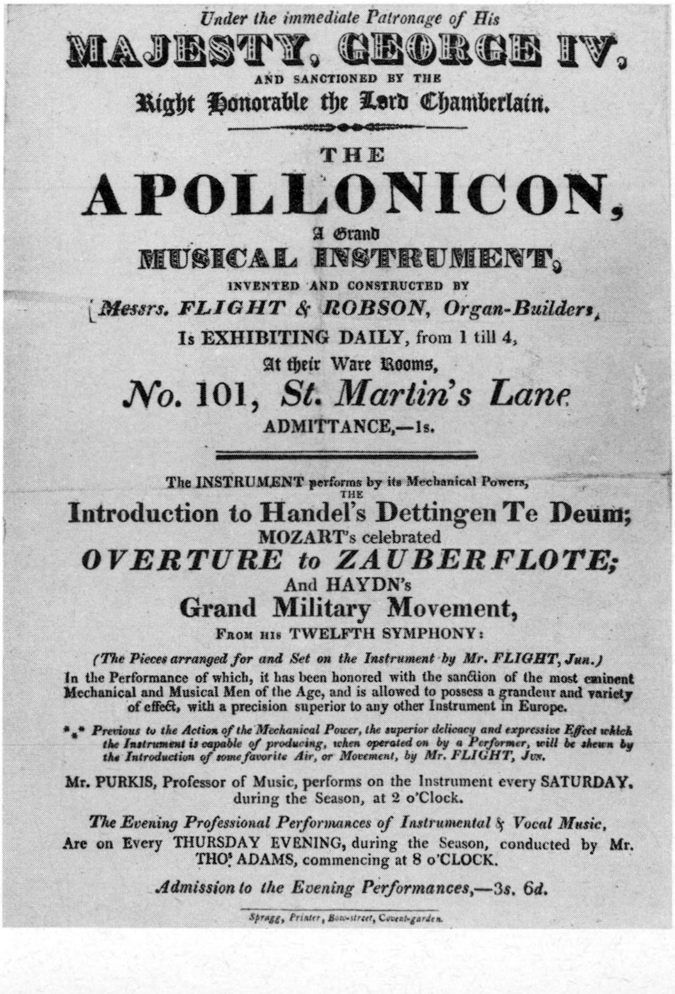

Fig. 4. For more than a quarter of a century, Flight & Robson's enormous Apollonicon was London's only recital organ. Besides being capable of being played by no fewer than five organists at once, this could also be played automatically by sets of pinned wooden barrels, three being used for each piece of music. This early 1820 bill shows Haydn's 'Grand Military Movement' from his Twelfth Symphony, presumably the twelfth London symphony, number 104 in D major dating from 1795.

Under the immediate Patronage of His
MAJESTY, GEORGE IV.
AND SANCTIONED BY THE
Right Honorable the Lord Chamberlain.

THE
APOLLONICON,
A Grand
MUSICAL INSTRUMENT,
INVENTED AND CONSTRUCTED BY
Messrs. FLIGHT & ROBSON, Organ-Builders,
Is EXHIBITING DAILY, from 1 till 4,
At their Ware Rooms,
No. 101, St. Martin's Lane.
ADMITTANCE,—1s.

The INSTRUMENT performs by its Mechanical Powers,
THE
Introduction to Handel's Dettingen Te Deum;
MOZART's celebrated
OVERTURE to ZAUBERFLOTE;
And HAYDN's
Grand Military Movement,
FROM HIS TWELFTH SYMPHONY:
(The Pieces arranged for and Set on the Instrument by Mr. FLIGHT, Jun.)
In the Performance of which, it has been honored with the sanction of the most eminent Mechanical and Musical Men of the Age, and is allowed to possess a grandeur and variety of effect, with a precision superior to any other Instrument in Europe.

⁎ Previous to the Action of the Mechanical Power, the superior delicacy and expressive Effect which the Instrument is capable of producing, when operated on by a Performer, will be shewn by the Introduction of some favorite Air, or Movement, by Mr. FLIGHT, Jun.

Mr. PURKIS, Professor of Music, performs on the Instrument every SATURDAY, during the Season, at 2 o'Clock.

The Evening Professional Performances of Instrumental & Vocal Music, Are on Every THURSDAY EVENING, during the Season, conducted by Mr. THO⁵ ADAMS, commencing at 8 o'CLOCK.

Admission to the Evening Performances,—3s. 6d.

Spragg, Printer, Bow-street, Covent-garden.

unusual history as far as mechanical organs are concerned. This was probably because it enjoyed a high degree of popularity with the builders of the instruments. As a result of this, it came to be treated as a sort of folk-tune and travelled across Europe to appear on many British-made barrel organs under the guise of the title 'Lord Cathcart'. In a letter from Mr Fritz Spiegl, quoted by Robbins Landon,[23] he relates that he found the melody pinned on the barrels of three instruments. I have an organ in my possession which plays this under the title 'Lord Cathcart's Reel' and it has also been found with the title 'Lord Cathcart's Welcome to Scotland', while another contemporary manuscript dated 1807 calls it 'Lord Cathcart's Wee'. The Lord Cathcart here is presumably Sir William Shaw, tenth Baron Cathcart and First Viscount and Earl Cathcart (1755–1843) who, after a distinguished military career, was created Viscount Cathcart in 1807 and appointed Commander in Charge, Scotland, presumably in the same year.[24]

There seems no doubt that the melody which is called 'Lord Cathcart' is derived from Haydn rather than vice versa. Mr Fritz Spiegl copied the notation from one of his instruments and, with grateful acknowledgement, I reproduce it here. It agrees almost exactly with the notation on the organ which I own. Robbins Landon, however, compounds the mechanical organ confusion by referring to this as a piece for 'musical clock', which it is not.

Fig. 5. Types of mechanical organ. (1) Central European shallow case style, fusee-wound spring driven. (2) Black Forest type also made in Holland and Scotland, weight-driven and with the longest, bass pipes arranged horizontally and mitred. (3) Augsburg, 1617. Three rows of horizontal pipes played from a broad-rimmed wheel. (4) Dutch single-wheel weight-driven. Very large air-brake. (5) Stockholm, late eighteenth century with characteristic arrangement of pipework above and below the organ table. (6) The compactness of the Niemecz mechanical organs.

[23] *Haydn in England*, p. 564.

[24] English Folk Dance and Song Society, quoted by Robbins Landon, *op, cit.*

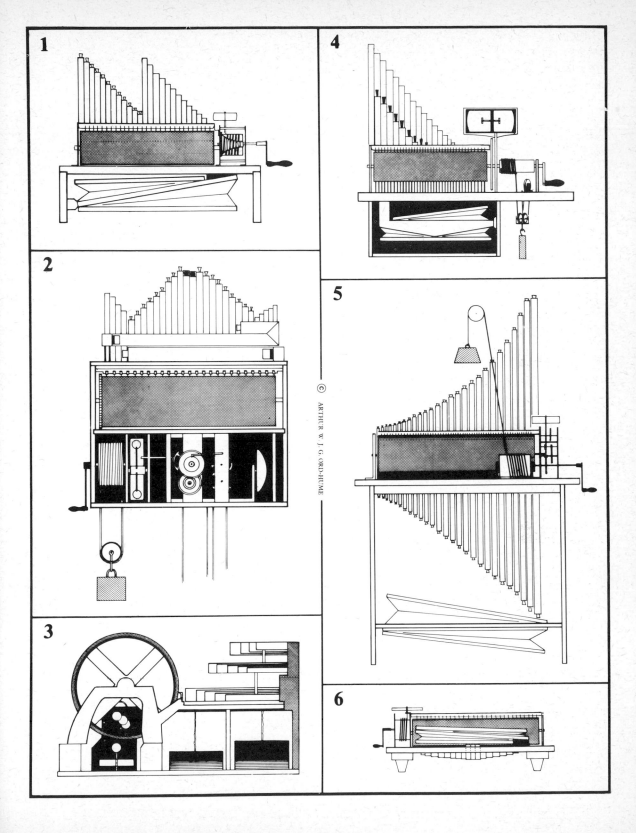

The clockwork organ, whether driven by a coiled spring or powered by a heavy weight which had to be wound up to the top of the organ case after every few tunes, always comprised the same basic components. These were the windchest, the pipework, the bellows and the pinned tune barrel. However, these four components could be arranged in a number of different ways and there was no definite pattern of layout. Several differing types of layout for clockwork organs are illustrated in the accompanying drawings. These layouts also depict an organ in conjunction with a timepiece in the form of a musical clock. It is understood, one hopes, that the clockwork organ does not necessarily have to incorporate a timepiece and that if it does, the two normally have not just different spring-driven wheel trains, but quite separate clockwork motors. And nor is the instrument in any way a 'toy organ' although it might be classed as a toy of the idle rich.

While the illustrations depict the operational principles of the mechanical organ as manufactured at the time of the events which concern the characters of this book, it ought to be remembered that the three instruments which Niemecz was involved in manufacturing to perform Haydn's music were of a substantially different layout and construction to the style and layout which was widely used and which might therefore be described as 'normal'. This format, characteristic of the organs known to have been

Plate 3 (lower left). 16-key 8-tune London-made organ clock by George Lindsay. Two stops of wooden pipes selected manually. Date c.1760.

Plate 4 (below). 19-key organ clock by George Hewitt of Marlborough, c.1750. Four stops of wood and metal pipes are manually selected.

Plate 5 (facing page, left). The face of an impressive organ clock made in 1760 by George Pyke in London.

Plate 6 (right). Detail of the 10-tune 2-stop organ mechanism. The clock also has complex automaton scenes on the face.

made under the Esterházy influence, is described in full in Chapter 3 although, as related in Chapter 5, components of these instruments may have been made by Viennese organ builders to the specification of Niemecz. The particular form of constructional layout which might almost be considered as a 'trade-mark' of the Niemecz pieces is no more than a most unusual yet distinctive method of arranging the component parts of the organ mechanism in order to produce a very compact and symmetrical organ. Idiosyncratic layout was nothing uncommon at this time and as one further example of individualistic construction, I would cite the mechanical organs built in Scandinavia by Petter Strand.[25]

The accompanying illustrations show the basic components and styles of mechanical organs. For further details of mechanical organs and flute-playing clocks, the reader is referred to the book *Barrel Organ* which is a more specific work on this instrument.[26]

One should not lose sight of the fact that the mechanical organ was no more than a machine for playing music automatically. It was a device for playing pre-programmed music at will and without the need for the intervention of skilled performers. In this respect, the instrument afforded the enterprising composer and the person who had the job of arranging the music for the organ barrel certain attractive opportunities due to the unique features

[25] *The Music Box*, vol. 9, p. 277 (1980).
[26] A.W.J.G. Ord-Hume, *Barrel Organ*.

Plate 7. Clockwork table organ made in France about 1820 by Davrainville. There are 32 keys and the pipework is all open-foot voiced.

Plate 8. Brass-cased organwork from a French-style bracket clock with 8-tune mechanism in the base. Dating from about 1760, there are fourteen stopped metal pipes.

Plate 9 (left). Outstanding three-stop London-made organ clock by George Pyke c.1750–70. Compare with Plates 5 and 6 on page 29. The barrel has ten tunes and the case is reputed to have been painted by Zoffany.

Plate 10 (above). 33-key Swedish organ clock by Petter Strand plays the second movement of Haydn's Symphony No. 100 on one of twelve barrels.

of the instrument. Perhaps the most important among these features was the ability to perform a sequence of music precisely the way the composer wished his piece to be heard. There was, for example, no confusion over notational symbols which might detract from the effect he desired. Nor was there any doubt concerning the virtuosity of the players. The mechanical organ had an established level of virtuosity which was set into the barrel by the person who hammered in the wire pins and bridges and consequently was incapable of varying from day to day as might the performance of an orchestra and its soloists. These features

Plate 11. Outstanding French-made automaton clock with mechanical organ in the base. Presented by the City of Lyon to Napoleon I on his accession as Emperor of France on 18 May 1804.

Plate 12. Louis XVI mechanical organ with clock. made by Jean Andre Lepaute between 1740 and 1774 in Carrera marble mounted in finely-chiselled ormolu. Reputed to have been made for Marie Antoinette. The organ plays four times a day or at will and stands 3ft 7in high. The original sunburst pendulum to the clock is missing.

are the very ones which make the early mechanical music instrument of such great interest and value to the musicologist today.

But perhaps the prime characteristic of the instrument was its ability to play in a manner which was quite different from that possible by human players. There was the great speed of articulation and the ability to produce music at any speed desired by the composer with precision, particularly in rhythm and tempi. The skilled composer and the musically knowledgeable engineer who had the responsibility for setting the music on the barrel could — and not infrequently did — produce between them some extraordinarily brilliant results. There is no doubt, judging from the three surviving organs, that the combination of Niemecz and Haydn fulfilled these conditions to the extreme.

Plate 13 (right). Formerly in the Heyer Museum and now in Leipzig is this impressive mechanical organ which plays an abbreviated version of the Mozart Fantasia K. 616.

Plate 14 (below) shows the small mechanical organ made in Amsterdam by Winkel which plays variations on a Tyrolean melody written by Mozart and existing only on this barrel. The organ has two fully-chromatic ranks, Stop selection being automatic from the barrel pinning. The mechanism features only one wheel, hence the enormous air brake.

CHAPTER 2

Haydn, Niemecz and the Princes Esterházy

In the same way that virtually every type of musical instrument and, indeed, even the piece of music which they performed or which was otherwise associated with them, has played some important part in both reflecting and shaping the social and cultural form of its age, mechanical music and self-playing instruments also performed a vital function in their contemporary times. While thorough historical investigations of the more common instruments have documented this influence, the particular circumstances surrounding the mechanical organ have received only passing attention from both historian and musicologist alike. This is all the more surprising when one realises that this was the only instrument of any consequence which encouraged master composers to have their music preserved within its self-playing or re-performing capabilities. The reproducing piano of the early twentieth century was too late to be granted such an opportunity, concentrating as it did more on performer interpretations.

As we have seen from the preceding chapter, the beginnings of the mechanical organ are shrouded in the mists of a long-past age when man believed in the probability of alchemy and sought to achieve perpetual motion by mechanical means. Life and folklore were equally steeped in magic. And the underlying goal was the age-old one — that of creating an artificial or automaton humanoid figure. Advances in mechanics seemed only to bring that possibility closer within the grasp of man and culminated in the many attempts, some more successful than others, at manufacturing artificial life forms by mechanical means. The androids of myth amd magic took on the mantle of reality in the shape of Vaucanson's duck and flute-player, and Kaufmann's realistic military trumpeter. For these and other endeavours, it was believed that the mechanical technician had finally usurped the realms of the magician and the alchemist, both of whom has laboured for so long and produced nothing. Others eschewed that such work was the work of the Devil himself since only God should create. One of the masterpieces of Jaquet-Droz was smashed to smithereens by the Spanish authorities who viewed it and attributed its lifelike performance to evil![1]

From the sixteenth century onward, there were many who attempted to create robots and mechanical animals, including the Nürnberg craftsmen Werner and Bullmann.[2] Phenomenal strides were made by the Swiss clockmakers and craftsmen of the Jaquet-Droz workshop, as well as Vaucanson and, much later, Maskelyne.[3] What would such visionaries make of today's science of robotics which began largely in myth and now forms the very backbone of industrial assembly lines, genetic research, nuclear technology, and the ability to transmit pictures of the planets from man-directed spacecraft roving through the cosmos?

It was from such early beginnings and from the world of make-believe androids that the seeds of successful mechanical music were spawned. Perhaps then it is not all that surprising that, because of its extreme antiquity, the self-playing flute should emerge as the direct ancestor of all the mechanical instruments that followed and that the mechanical organ attained an early status in the world of self-playing musical instruments.

The mechanical organ must indeed have appeared to be a work of magic to those who first heard it. It must have seemed a direct challenge to the real world by contradicting the hitherto accepted principles that such sounds can only be produced by the direct action of man. And this machine did it by itself! This is the fundamental reason why such instruments have always held a fascination for man. Perhaps this was never more so than during the seventeeth and eighteenth centuries. Like the charm of Haydn's own puppet plays, it is a mixture of make-believe and reality where the dividing line between the two is never really clear.

There is nothing particularly unusual about the construction of the small mechanical organ and as already seen it is basically little different from the ordinary hand-played organ save that it is much smaller and that it is driven by, in the case of the Haydn instruments, a clockwork motor.

As far as one can tell, although the mechanical organ is of great antiquity and was well established in the first millenium, the history of the instrument in Germany dates back at least as far as the time of the renaissance. In contrast to the record-player of today which is confined in its capabilities to the faithful reproduction of living music produced by a live performer or group of performers, the mechanical organ has its own voice which can be induced to produce a fresh performance every time it is played. But more particularly, throughout its centuries the instrument has amassed its own priceless and unique repertoire of music contributed by the greatest masters of music including

[1] This was 'The Grotto', probably the most complex and intricate of all the works of the Jaquet-Droz automata created by Pierre and Henri Louis Jaquet-Droz. It featured fountains, singing birds and animals which went about their occupations on a model hillside behind which the sun rose and set. Taken to Spain for exhibition, it was believed to be the demonstration of witchcraft and was destroyed. For detailed description see Charles Perregaux and Fr. Louis Perrot, *Les Jaquet-Droz et Leschot*, A. Hinger Freres, Neuchatel, 1916. English translation and illustration published in *The Music Box*, vol. 2, p. 140 *et seq.* (1965); illustrated in A.W.J.G. Ord-Hume, *Collecting Musical Boxes & How to Repair Them.*

[2] Johann Heinrich Moritz von Poppe, *Geschichte aller Erfindungen und Entdekkungen . . .*, Stuttgart, 1837, pp. 227 *et seq.* See also Klaus Maurice, and Otto Mayr, *Die Welt als Uhr*, München, 1980.

[3] Alfred Chapuis and Edouard Gelis, *Le Monde des Automates*, Paris, 1928, vols. 1 and 2.

Mozart, Beethoven and Haydn.

Hans Leo Hassler was moved to write about 'the organ that will play a series of melodies all by itself without any manual operation' and directed that the music should be pinned on the barrel in the same way as it was done on the organ he had had built for himself at Augsburg in 1601 by the celebrated fustian-weaver-cum-organ-builder, Georg Heinlein.[4] Augsburg was one of the first towns in Germany to encourage the building of barrel organs.

The mechanical organ gained in significance, particularly in the closing years of the eighteenth century when the shift to less-rigid doctrines combined with the more joyous spirit of the rococo to herald the colourful and more ebullient times of the entrepreneur. The music exhibition — the so-called 'cabinet' — and the travelling attraction became part of the life of the well-to-do.

It is thus understandable that we should find that some of the finest and greatest names of this era should have been inspired by this strange little musical instrument to such an extent that they enriched its repertoire with their own works. We know already that Handel wrote music for mechanical organ in his closing years.[5] But there was something extremely fortuitous about the choice of European centres for the manufacture of the instrument. Berlin and Vienna were the two great cities where music reigned supreme and in their environs there lived, worked or just visited for extended periods the greatest of the European composers. This formed a most rewarding conjunction with the skill of the clockwork organ builder on the one hand and the presence of the composer on the other. Evidence abounds that this situation resulted in these composers leaving their marks on the literature of the mechanical organ. With the staunch advocacy of Frederick the Great for the instrument and in particular his influence both in the narrow region of direct contact with the builders and the composers as well as in the wider circles of reputation, the instrument flourished on all counts. Through his aegis, many were encouraged to write music for it and soon the repertoire was enriched with works by the talented flautist Johann Joachim Quantz (born Oberscheden, nr. Göttingen, 30 January 1697; died Potsdam, 12 July 1773), the kapellmeister of Frederick the Great, Carl Heinrich Graun,[6] as well as the musical theoretician and composer Johann Philipp Kirnberger,[7] not to mention Carl Philipp Emanuel Bach[8] and Wilhelm Friedemann Bach.[9] These men contributed numerous works for the mechanical organ, supported and inspired by the flourishing instrument makers of Berlin. In the centre of Germany, the

[4] See Friedrich Roth, 'Der grosse Spieluhrprozess Hans Leo Hassler von 1603–11' ('The enormous musical clock development of Hans Leo Hassler from 1603 to 1611') in *Sammelbände der Internationalen Musikgesellschaft*, vol. XIV, p. 34 *et seq.* Hassler was an early, major figure in musicwork. Concurrent with this, Achilles Langenbucher in Ausburg built 'ein grosses Instrument in eine Kirche, welches eine ganze Vesper von 2000 Takten von sich selbst schlug' ('a big instrument in a church which played a whole vespers of 2000 bars by itself'). This was an astonishingly large instrument for its time. See Paul von Stetten, *Kunst-, Gewerb- und Handwerksgeschichte de Reichsstadt Augsburg,* 1799, vol. 1, p. 190. Additionally Paul de Wit, 'Über die Musik mechanischer Musikwerke . . . ' in *Zeitschrift für instrumentenbau,* vol, VII, Leipzig, 1887, p. 122, and Adolf Sandberger. in *Denkmäler der Tonkunst in Bayern,* vol. V part 1, page LXXIII. The name, one should note, is Langenbucher not 'Landenbucher' as erroneously printed there.

[5] Handel was inspired by the English musical clock or mechanical organ-making industry which was, even at that comparatively early time, well developed. See Ernst Simon, *Mechanische Musikinstrumente früherer Zeiten und ihre Musik,* Wiesbaden, 1960, p. 44 *et seq.*'

[6] See Ernst Simon, 'Friedrich der Grosse und die mechanischen Musikinstrumente' in *Zeitschrift für Instrumentenbau,* vol. XXXII, Leipzig, 1912, p. 744.

[7] One of his works titled 'Allegro für die Singuhr', was published in vol. 4 of the *Musikalisches Allerley von verschiedenen Tonkunstlern,* Berlin, 1761, p. 93 *et seq.*

[8] See Alfred Wotquenne, *Thematisches Verzeichnis der Werke von C. Ph. E. Bach,* Leipzig, 1905, number 193. Contrary to the belief of Simon (*vide supra,* p. 745 *et seq.*) all the pieces have been preserved and have subsequently been documented.

[9] See Martin Falck, *Wilhelm Friedemann Bach,* Leipzig, 1913, p. 42. Much discussion has followed the reference in this book regarding a musical clock in Dessau playing music by Johann Sebastian Bach. This has never been corroborated and is thought likely to be in error.

contribution of the Court musical director of Dessau, Friedrich Wilhelm Rust, should not be overlooked.[10] Born in Wörlitz, Dessau, 6 July 1739, he learned composition from W.F. and C.P.E. Bach and later came to write music for the instrument. He died in Dessau on 28 February 1796. Builders of organs in Dresden at this time included Johann Gottfried Kaufmann[11] and Edouard Bohn, both of whom enjoyed a high reputation.

But it was in Vienna, Austria, that the industry was destined to flourish in the extreme during the classical period for both the repertoire and the construction of the mechanical organ. Here were to be found makers of high standing such as the remarkable brothers Johann Nepomuk and Leonard Mälzel who were both friends of Beethoven, as well as the group of mechanical organ and musical clock builders comprising Johann Georg Strasser, Joseph Hain, Johann Adolf Hoyer and many others who together provided the eminent Viennese composers of the time with on-going inspiration and encouragement — and more often than not actual demands — for the composition of mechanical music.

It was due to both the proclivity and the geographical density of builders such as these that much fine music was written for this medium, among them the works composed by W.A. Mozart for the renowned 'art cabinet' or mausoleum created by Joseph Müller, the Count Deym, in Vienna, and by Beethoven.[12] Additionally, Anton Eberl and Maria Luigi Carlo Cherubini wrote extensively for the musical automata of the Viennese makers and for the works of the brothers Mälzel in particular.[13]

Only in recent times, however, was it discovered that amongst the greatest of the Viennese masters, Franz Joseph Haydn was by far the most intimately involved with the whole craft of mechanical music, indeed the whole process of designing and making instruments through to their ultimate musical performance must clearly have been within his expertise. This revelation is of relatively recent origin and even C.F. Pohl's biography of the composer makes no reference to this aspect of his work. Indeed, it was not apparent until 1922 when the work of Alfred Schnerich[14] pointed out for the first time that, based on the suggestion of writers Julius Schlosser and Robert Lack, he had discovered that Haydn had indeed composed original pieces for the mechanical organ. In 1926, Schnerich published a detailed description of the instrument and its history.[15] By examining the information provided by Schnerich, it showed that not only several old organs survived which played original works of Haydn, but also a quantity of manuscripts, partly written in his own hand and partly in the hand of somebody else, was still extant.

In all, no fewer than thirty-two works for the mechanical organ

[10] See Wilhelm Hosaeus, *Fr. W. Rust und des Dessauer Musikleben 1766–96*, Dessau, 1882, p. 71 (footnote).

[11] See A.W.J.G. Ord-Hume, *Barrel Organ*, London, 1979, p. 168 *et seq.*

[12] Three pieces for mechanical organ by Beethoven are preserved in an edition published by A. Kopfermann (*Die Musik*, March, 1902 p. 1059 *et seq.)* and G. Becking, 'Studien zu Beethovens Personalstil' in *Das Scherzothema*, Leipzig, p. 165 *et seq.*). Within this is also presented the original version of his 1813 composition for Mälzel's Pan-harmonicon entitled 'Auf Wellington's Sieg bei Vittoria' — the so-called 'Battle' Symphony or 'Wellington's Victory'. An arrangement of the three pieces as a suite edited by Ludwig Altman is published by Hinrichsen (No. 1438).

[13] See *Vaterländische Blätter für den österreichischen Kaiserstaat*, Vienna, 1808, p. 112 *et seq.*, and also the *Allgemeine Musikalische Zeitung*, Leipzig, 1801, p. 736 *et seq.*

[14] Alfred Schnerich, *Joseph Haydn und seine Sendung*, Zurich/Leipzig/Vienna, 1922, pp. 76 *et seq.* and 204, with some additions in the second edition of the title in 1926 (pp. 64 *et seq.*, 188 and 263).

[15] Alfred Schnerich, 'Haydn's Orgelwerk' in *Alt-Wiener Kalender*, 1926, p. 139 *et seq.*

have been found which have now been published in at least two editions in a transcription for piano taken from the original musical notation.[16] Some of the pieces, namely those from the two later surviving instruments, have been issued on gramophone records.[17] Several of the pieces have also been transcribed (in 1979) for the classical guitar.[18]

Joseph Haydn was acutely interested in the musical instruments of the time. Besides the music for the clockwork organ, he wrote an extensive work for an instrument which was extremely fashionable during the rococo period. This was the so-called *lyra organizzata* or hurdy-gurdy.[19] Additionally, he had a strong interest in the art of the mechanical theatre of the time. Whether this was a personal interest or whether he was obliged to become involved with it because of his position in the Esterházy Court is another matter. Suffice to say that he wrote several short operas for the German marionette theatre of Prince Esterházy which so pleased the Empress Maria Theresia that she summoned the whole small opera theatre to her palace at Schönbrunn.[20]

Haydn was encouraged by many different people to write music for self-acting instruments. Besides Mälzel, the clockmaker Strasser played an important part in acquainting Haydn with the potential of the mechanical organ. Strasser was born in Baden near Vienna and was responsible for setting Haydn's music on the barrels. Together with his son and the organ-pipemaker Gabrahan in Petersburg, Strasser built a giant mechanical orchestra which had a repertoire of fifteen barrels each of which played for more than ten minutes. The musical programme included Mozart (no less than the complete piano concertos in F major and B flat, and the String Quintet in B flat), and pieces by Eberl and Haydn.[21] This great instrument apparently cost 10,000 roubles. On the tenth of the fifteen barrels was set Haydn's Military Symphony (No. 100 in G major), a piece which was obviously a favourite with Mälzel because he frequently used it on his own barrels. The fifteenth barrel comprised 'eine grosse Pièce von Haydn von diesem grossen Mann für dieses Werk komponiert' ('a grand piece composed by Haydn for this instrument'). Johann Nepomuk Mälzel frequently received original compositions for his mechanical instruments from Haydn. A contemporary writer, reporting on one of these pieces of musical engineering, said: 'I heard several compositions by Haydn, one overture by Mozart and one aria by Crescentini played with the greatest precision'.[22] Another writes about this gifted mechanician: 'He has friendly relations with Haydn, Salieri and Cherubini, who have written many musical pieces for

[16] Joseph Haydn, *Werke für des Laufwerk (Flötenuhr) für Klavier zu zwei Händen* arranged and edited by Ernst Fritz Schmid, Nagel, Hannover, 1931. A second edition, 1956, includes a supplement showing the alternative bars Haydn sketched out for numbers 1 and 30. The first English-language edition includes this supplement and was published in 1965 by R.D. Row Music Co. Inc., New York.

[17] The first recording was published by Carl Lindström A.-G, Berlin, on Parlophon B37040 and Odeon 0 4495. A fresh recording dating from 1974 appeared on Candide CE 31093 and a new and markedly better edition from the same original master tapes was published on Turnabout in 1977 as TV 37085S (stereo).

[18] Arranged by Alan Lawrence and published in London by Breitkopf & Härtel 1979 under the name *Time Pieces* along with arrangements of some of the Handel pieces for Charles Clay's organ-clock. The Haydn pieces, in the order in which Lawrence uses them are: *Allegro* (piece number 10, transposed from C into D; *Andante* (number 2) originally 2/4 in C, transposed 2/2 in E; *Minuet* (number 6) transposed from C to E; *Minuet* (number 17) transposed from F into E; *March* (number 25) originally 2/4 in D, interpreted 2/2; *Allegro* (number 23) transposed from C into D.

[19] This was one of eight *Notturni* for two hurdy-gurdys, two clarinets, two horns, two violins, two violincellos and bass composed in 1790. There were also five concerti for one and two hurdy-gurdys with orchestra, &c, all written for King Ferdinand IV of Naples and the Imperial and Royal legation secretary, Norbert Hadrava in Naples. See also C.F. Pohl: *Joseph Haydn II*, Leipzig, 1882, p. 287. All of the nocturnes mentioned have been published in an edition in which the hurdy-gurdys are replaced by flute and oboe. The publisher of two of these was the Karlsbad firm of H. Hohler. All have now appeared under Diletto Musicale nos. 301–8. See also Ernst Fritz Schmid, 'Joseph Haydns Werke für die Drehleier' in *Münchner Neueste Nach.* for 22 November 1931, p. 8.

[20] Unfortunately the music for Haydn's puppet opera is missing with the exception of just a few small fragments.

[21] *Allgemeine Musikalische Zeitung*, July, 1801, p. 736 *et seq.* The actual report, which states that 'eleven of the barrels may be heard already', lists the programme as follows:
(1) *Ouverture de l'Opéra: la Flûte magique de Mozart*
(2) *Concerto pour le Fortepiano in F de Mozart* [K. 459].
(3) *Allegretto assai du même Concert de Mozart*

his mechanical works of art'.[23] An announcement by the Viennese art dealer and publisher Karl Mechetti dated 7 November 1801, may also refer to one of Mälzel's instruments. This read: 'Karl Mechetti, Imperial and Royal private art and alabaster dealer of Burgerspitalplatze, opposite the princely Lobkowitz Palace, has the honour to announce to the high nobility and venerable audience that he is in the possession of a new large harmonical instrument. In this instrument are set on 12 barrels 19 of the most selected pieces by the most famous masters, e.g. Haydn, Mozart, Cimarosa, Paesiello, Weigl, Wranitzky, Sussmayer, &c.'[24]

A large panharmonicon which was built by Mälzel for the Empress of France performed works by Mozart, Cherubini, Rigel, Steibelt and the builder himself as well as the 'finale of a symphony by Haydn' and 'the military symphony with Turkish music by Haydn'.[25] Haydn's 'Military' Symphony dated from 1794 and it seems to have captured the imagination of the public and so Mälzel was quick to identify its popularity for he frequently made use of it, no doubt also because it provided an opportunity to show off the capabilities of his instruments which, from published specifications, seem to have been well provided with brass, reed stops and percussion effects. One panharmonicon which was exhibited in Vienna in 1813 played, besides the works of Cherubini and Handel ('the overture and the dramatic chorus from Handel's *Timotheus*') this self-same 'Military' Symphony[26] while yet another of his mechanical organs played the *andante* of this work.[27] It was around this time that the London organ builders Flight & Robson issued the prospectus which announced their planned construction of what was to be the world's biggest barrel organ, the famed Apollonicon which could be played upon by five human organists at once or played mechanically from sets comprising three barrels per work. One of the first sets of barrels to be completed and played at 101 St. Martin's Lane in the summer of 1817 was described as the 'Grand Military Movement from (Haydn's) 12th Symphony'.[28] Exactly what this was is uncertain as it was likely to have been from the 'Military' Symphony (which was the *eighth* of the so-called 'London' symphonies) rather than from the twelfth 'London' symphony which was No. 104 and named 'The London'. Haydn's actual Symphony No. 12, dating from 1763, is unlikely to have been the piece which was played, particularly as it was probably almost unknown in London at that time.

We have seen how Haydn was exposed to mechanical music as a normal part of his musical life but the question which so far has not been posed is from whence did he obtain the stimulus and the inspiration for composing the thirty-two little pieces for

(4) *Allegro assai du même Concert de Mozart*
(5) *Ouverture, Marche et Chorus de l'Opera: La Clemenza di Tito, de Mozart*
(6) *Concerto pour le Fortepiano in B de Mozart* [presumably in B flat major, K. 456]
(7) *Andante du même*
(8) *Allegro vivace du même*
(9) *Adagio, Allegro et Rondeau d'Eberl* (composed for this machine)
(10) *Sinfonie militaire de Haydn*
(11) *Fantasie à 4 mains de Mozart* [presumably K. 594]
   the following barrels are in preparation:
(12)
(13) *Quintetto in B de Mozart* [possibly in B flat major, K. 174]
(14)
(15) *A large Pièce by Haydn,* composed for this machine by this great man.

The *Allgemeine Musikalische Zeitung* comments that 'the barrels are prepared according to the scores of these pieces — without cuts. . . ' Robbins Landon (*Haydn: The Late Years*) suggest that the 'large Pièce' by Haydn was the authentic arrangement for mechanical organ of Symphony No. 99's Finale, the missing number 32 of the mechanical organ pieces. Sadly, Robbins Landon again refers to this as a 'musical clock' piece. There is no shred of evidence to suggest that it was ever penned for an organ with a timepiece: certainly Strasser's orchestrion had no timepiece.

[22] *Allgemeine Musikalische Zeitung,* Leipzig, 1800, p. 414.

[23] *Vaterländische Blätter, op. cit.,* Vienna, 1808, p. 113

[24] *Wiener Zeitung,* 1801, p. 3993.

[25] *Vaterländische Blätter, op. cit.,* Vienna, 1808, p. 113

[26] *Ibid,* 1813, vol. 1, p. 32

[27] *Berliner Musik Zeitung,* 1805, No. 40.

[28] A.W.J.G. Ord-Hume, *Barrel Organ,* p. 103.

mechanical organ which form the subject of this book? The affair of the 'Military' Symphony and the 'London' Symphonies in general is well documented. The question is what made him compose these delightful little cameos which are as far removed from the bombast of a Mälzel Panharmonicon as is a minuet from a fanfare. It is possible that he did not receive the stimulus from the instruments, nor did he find himself spurred on by the existence of the works of others for this medium, but from his association with a most unusual and gifted man in the closest environs of the palace of Prince Esterházy, namely the court librarian, Father Primitivus Niemecz.[29]

Joseph Niemecz was born on 9 February 1750, the year in which Johann Sebastian Bach and Tomasso Albinoni died, and two years before the birth of Muzio Clementi and six years before Wolfgang Amadeus Mozart. The son of Jakob Niemecz and his wife Maria Magdelena of Vlašim near Benešov in Bohemia (today Czechoslovakia, twenty-five miles south-east of Prague), he was christened on 10 February — the day following his birth — by Matthaeus Kalina, the high priest.[30] He was born at a time of great conflict. Bohemia had been secured to Austria by treaty in 1648, but the 1740s brought disquiet and the Austrians were defeated by the Prussians in a fierce battle at Prague. This was followed by the seven-year war between Austria and Prussia which began when Joseph Niemecz was just six years old. The young Joseph applied himself to the study of philosophy and at the age of 18 in 1768 he joined the convent of the Barmherzigen Bruder (Brothers of Mercy) in Prague[31] at the instigation and nomination of the Imperial Countess Maria Josepha of Auersperg, described by the documentation as 'the lady of Vlašim whose subject and servant he was'.

Upon completing his year of probation, he took his vows on 29 August 1769, under the prior Fr Caesaeus Rohlicek in the church of St. Simon and Juda as Father Primitivus.[32] In 1776 he was ordained as a priest in the Koniggratz on the twenty-sixth day of December in a manner which is described as 'contrary to the conventional habits of the Brothers of Mercy'.[33]

Meanwhile, the Royal Librarian of the palace of Prince Esterházy, Philip Georg Bader, died. It is important at this stage in the story to introduce into the picture the part which was played by Joseph Haydn in the House of Esterházy. Paul Anton Esterházy was a staunch patron of music. His home was at Eisenstadt, a small village dominated by the royal palace of Kismarton. The name Kismarton, however, was not preserved and the palace is always referred to as 'Eisenstadt'. Paul Anton Esterházy maintained an orchestra with choir and the finest solo

[29] C.F. Pohl (*Joseph Haydn, loc. cit.*, vol. II, p. 100) mistakenly bestowed upon him the title of 'Primitio of the Order of the Barmherzigen Bruder' Primitiv (Primitivus), however, was only his convent name. F.S. Gassner *(Universallexicon der Tonkunst,* Stuttgart, 1849, p. 656) describes him as 'Peter Primitivus Niemecz', mistakenly taking the title Pater for Peter.

[30] Extract from the parish register of the Dean's office in Vlašim, collated with the certificate of baptism in the archives of the Barmherzigen Bruder (Brothers of Mercy) in Prague dated 15 July 1768. Refer to Gottfried Johann Dlabacz's *Allgemeines historisches Künstler-Lexikon für Böhmen,* Prague, 1815, vol. II, p. 390, the birthplace is incorrectly given as Domazliče (Taus) and this error is repeated by Konstant von Wurzbach in his *Biographisches Lexikon des Kaisertums Österreich* published in Vienna (vol. 20, p. 347).

[31] See *Weglosbrief* by the Countess Auersperg dated 13 July 1768, in the archives of the Brothers of Mercy in Prague.

[32] According to the published records of vows dated 28/29 August, 1769, in the archives of the Brothers of Mercy in Prague.

[33] *Catalogus. . . R. Fratum. . . Ord. St. Joannis dei ab Anno 1683–1788* in the archives of the Brothers of Mercy in Vienna.

singers at this country seat. Their job was to provide the music for church services and to take part in the occasional operatic presentation for the enjoyment of the Prince. Kapellmeister or choir-master was a musician named Gregor Werner.

Prince Esterházy had heard of the fine work of the then young Haydn at the seat of the Bohemian Count Ferdinand Maximilian Morzin who employed him to lead his small orchestra at his country house at Lukavec near Pilsen. When Count Morzin fell upon hard times and had to dismiss his musicians, Haydn was not out of a job for long, for Paul Anton Esterházy took him on as assistant kapellmeister under the ageing Werner. Haydn took up this appointment on 1 May 1761, and took full charge upon Werner's death in 1766. However, Paul Anton Esterházy was not destined to see the ascendence of his protegy: he died four years earlier to be succeeded by his brother Nicolaus who came to be known by the soubriquet 'the Magnificent'. He was one of the greatest benefactors of the arts in the whole of the age of patronage. As early as 1721 work had begun on a magnificent new palace at Süttör beside the Neusiedlersee and the new Prince Esterházy lost no time in completing this. It was said to rival that of Versailles in its splendours. It was named Eszterháza and it was here that Haydn flourished. Enjoying an excellent relationship with his employer and patron, he received a commensurate salary and had charge of a fine orchestra for whom music was all that mattered. Eszterháza was a true musician's dream.

This idyllic existence continued until 28 September 1790, when Prince Nicolaus died leaving Haydn an annual pension of 1000 Florins so long as he remained in his job. The new prince, the second Anton, increased the benefits to Haydn by an extra 400 Florins but soon afterwards decided that the orchestra was an expensive luxury. Within two days of the death of his father, who was in his seventy-sixth year, Anton paid off the entire orchestra and choir. Haydn retained his official position but was free to accept other engagements. By this time, he appears to have been somewhat disillusioned with Eszterháza and its new ruler, for he quickly left for Vienna, leaving behind most of his possessions including musical scores. He took rooms overlooking what is now the Stadtpark and it was in these rooms, after his first visit to London at the behest of Salomon, that he took a young pupil called Beethoven in the years 1792–3.

During the Eszterháza period in his life, Haydn had been fairly free to travel although mostly only as far as close-by Vienna, and through these visits and also via his publisher, Artaria, he had made a number of valuable contacts throughout Europe. Indeed he had met many of the great composers and performers of the time. Haydn died on 31 May 1809, the year in which his pupil Beethoven's Piano Concerto No. 5, 'The Emperor', received its premiére, and the year in which Felix Mendelssohn was born.

To return to the circumstances which followed the death of the librarian Bader,[34] it will be appreciated that this was not just a turning point in the careers of Haydn and Niemecz, but that it created the atmosphere for the formation of an extraordinary partnership. Niemecz was appointed Bader's successor in the year 1780 at the Eszterháza Palace at a salary of 643 Gulden and 45 Kreuzer a year.[35] When Prince Anton closed down his orchestra and moved to Vienna, Niemecz travelled with him. The year was 1795 and there was the important library in the royal palace in Vienna for which he was to assume responsibility[36] besides which Haydn was there as well.

In the winter of that year, Niemecz was allowed the services of a library assistant, a man called Joseph Gurck who had formerly been the servant of the recently deceased Baron Guntherode.[37] Guntherode was one of the most adventurous personalities of his era. Gurck was, in the years to follow, to play an important part in the world of Viennese mechanical musical instruments and in many ways assumed the mantle of Niemecz's reputation, although never his style of organ building nor his mechanical ability.

In his position of librarian, Niemecz was also active in the literary world. In all probability he was the author of the work *Beschreibung des Schloss Esterház* published anonymously in Pressburg (now Bratislava) in 1784.[38] Besides his functions as librarian, he had the title of Court chaplain and according to the church records he practised frequently in Süttör.[39] But his favourite occupation was music, an art in which he was highly gifted. He played a number of instruments with a high degree of skill including the keyboard, harp, violin, viola da gamba and baryton, this last being the favourite instrument of Prince Nicolaus Esterházy.[40] The additional abilities gained him the extra appreciation of the prince who, when appointing his librarian, must have taken his many musical talents into consideration. Thus it is no wonder that Niemecz should have found himself welcomed into the orchestra of the opera in the royal theatre at Eszterháza. He must have been unusually noticeable amidst the other musicians with his monk's habit and shaven head. He played the cello seated, we are told, next to Haydn who provided the thorough-bass on the harpsichord.[41] This close proximity in every sense of the word was especially beneficial to Niemecz. He quickly became friends with the master who considered his abilities of such potential that he gave

[34] Philipp Georg Bader was also engaged at the same time with the princely theatre as technical director. Additionally, he made several translations into German of Italian libretti (C.F. Pohl, *Joseph Haydn II*, p. 8). He was born in 1745 and died on 2 January 1780, in Eszterháza, his death being registered at the vicarage in Süttör in Hungary.

[35] Simon Meller, *Az Esterházy képtár története*, 1915, p. 16. He received this salary until the end of his life; the *Personal und Salarial Stand des Hochfürstl. Esterházyschen Majorats vom 14ten Julii 1801* (handwritten manuscript formerly in the possession of Frl. Marianne Fajt in Eisenstadt) indicates that in addition to him there was also Jean von Marialla, described as 'librarian' with a salary of 1000 Gulden as well as the above-mentioned Joseph Gurck, described as 'librarian assistant' with a salary of 108 Gulden.

[36] Simon Meller, *op. cit.*, pp. XXXIII and XLII.

[37] Simon Meller, *op. cit.*, p. 13. Karl Freiherr von Guntherode (born in Fontefonto in 1740 and who died in Eisenstadt 16 October 1795) was a member of the Order of Servitenordens, within which he was supposed to wear a beard. However, he cut off his beard which he then proceeded to carry in his pocket. He made himself very unpopular with the clergy by his anonymous anti-clerical publications which were tinged with sarcasm, such as *Der Bart: Eine wahre Geschichte aus dem Reich der Legendigen* of about 1785; *Geschichte der Männer ohne Hosen. . . Ein Roman* of 1788; *Komische Merkwürdigkeiten aus alter theologischen Makulaturen, Rom, Madrid und Katzenellenbogen* of about 1790. Prince Esterházy somewhat surprisingly, bought great numbers of Guntherode's publications and copperplate prints and this close connection no doubt brought him into contact with Gurck and secured him the offer of a position on Guntherode's death.

[38] Simon Meller, *op. cit.*, p. XXXIII.

[39] Andreas Vályi, *Magyarországnak leiräsa*, vol. 1, Buda, 1796, p. 629.

[40] Gottfried Johann Dlabacz, *op. cit.* II, column 390.

[41] Alfred Schnerich published a picture of a painting said to represent this scene in *Joseph Haydn* II, p. 65. H.C. Robbins Landon also used this in *The Symphonies of Joseph Haydn* (London, 1955) but has since determined that the attribution of the scene is incorrect and is nothing to do with Haydn or Niemecz.

him thorough lessons in composition and harmony. Besides this instruction, and no doubt in some way forming part of it, Niemecz composed a great number of sonatas, duets and concertos for the various instruments which 'due to their original nature of composition met with the approval of all musical experts'.[42] Unfortunately, all these appear to have been lost and nothing of Niemecz's musical output has so far been identified.

[42] Dlabacz, *op, cit.* II, column 391.

However, what was probably the most notable talent of Niemecz lay in a quite different field. He possessed an extraordinary knowledge and practical ability in the field of mechanics which, together with his musical abilities, combined to make him an outstanding master in the field of mechanical music. Just from whence this interest and ability came is unknown. He may have been inspired from his Bohemian homeland where clockmaking had already achieved a very high standard (see Chapter 5), but whatever the inspiration, his work stands today as outstanding in an age characterised by outstanding craftsmen. One of his contemporaries wrote of him: 'Moreover he also made very interesting and successful experiments with various organ and clock mechanisms and equipped them with figures, and recorded upon their music barrels sonatas and short concertos (arranged) in the way one builds table organs'.[43] And so it was that in the princely castles of the Esterházys the works of Niemecz were to be found in the shape of highly artistic and elaborate musical automata. As early as 1786, the encyclopaedist Korabinszky made detailed reference to musical automata by Niemecz in his entries concerning Eisenstadt and Eszterháza. He refers to a musical spinning-wheel, a musical chair, a musical pocket-watch, musical chessboard and many other instruments of this kind. The most grotesque mechanical display appears to have been a tableau of the naked figures of Adam and Eve combined with fountains and other waterworks in the large room of the castle of Eisenstadt.[44]

[43] *Ibid,* column 391.

[44] Matthias Korabinsky, *Geographisch-historisches und Produkten Lexikon von Ungarn,* Pressburg, 1786 (see under headings 'Eisenstadt' and 'Eszterháza'). Also see André Csátkai, 'Kis képek az Esterházyak kismartoni udvarából', in the *Zeitung Sopronvármegye* for 4 November 1923, and also Otto Aull, *Eisenstadt, Ein Führer durch seine Geschichte und Kunst,* Eisenstadt, 1931, p. 85 *et seq.* In the possession of the Eszterháza museum there is a very sumptiously decorated virginal fitted with a self-playing barrel mechanism. Originally in the possession of Countess Maria Anna Louise Esterházy (who died in 1782), this is a clockwork-driven instrument of the type made in Augsburg by the Bidermann family. Haydn, who is reputed to have made music with the countess on numerous occasions, would certainly have known this early instrument. The actual maker is unknown but automatic spinets were in existence as early as the seventeenth century (see Ord-Hume, *Player Piano,* London, 1970). See also the *Fachkatalog der Musikhistorischen Abteilung von Deutschland und Österreich-Ungarn zur Internationalen Ausstellung für Musik- und Theaterwesen,* Vienna, 1892, p. 272 (number 10).

Niemecz's reputation as an artist in this field rapidly spread far and wide so that by 1795 Andreas Valyi was writing: 'a brilliant and great master is the highly-esteemed Primitivus Niemecz, the librarian of his princely grace, who is an outstanding and great master at making remarkable musical clocks which even the most famous masters of Vienna admire and cannot match in perfection. Even abroad he is highly esteemed for his abilities'.[45] The mechanical organs which survive, as we shall see further on, fully justify the enthusiastic approbation of this respected Hungarian lexicographer.

[45] Andreas Vályi, *op. cit.*

In 1798, Niemecz achieved his greatest success with the construction of a large mechanical organ which he had built to his plans by the Viennese organ-builder Anton Walter.[46] The *Wiener Zeitung* reports on the first public showing of this piece: 'Last Friday afternoon, 30 March, the famed mechanician Father Primitivus Niemecz of the Order of the Brothers of Mercy and librarian of the Prince Nicolaus Esterházy, presented to the audience in the local university a self-playing organ which is intended for England. The extreme precision and delicate technique demonstrated in the playing of the specially selected pieces was received by the connoisseurs of music once more with the greatest approbation.[47] The charge for admission was donated to a poor family in a typically noble gesture.[48] The length and width of the machine was 78 centimetres and it was bought by a merchant of London'. Ernst Ludwig Gerber, who considered Niemecz to be among the most famous mechanicians of the era ('berühmten Mechanikern unseres Zeitalters'),[49] describes the organ as comprising 112 pipes in two unison eight-foot stops with a scale extending from C to g'''. It played the overture to Mozart's *Die Zauberflöte* 'like a great orchestra', as well as three other pieces of Mozart and two of Haydn.[50] Count Zinzendorf, the Austrian statesman (1739–1813), who visited the exhibition, wrote: 'apres midi je fus a l'Universite au premier etage entendre l'orgue sans clavessin execute par Walter d'apres les principes du P. Primitivus Niemecz de l'ordre des freres de la misericorde. Elle est vendue en Angleterre. On la fait aller moyennant une manivelle qui ne change jamais de vitesse et produit cependent toutes les variations....' (in the afternoon I went to the university where on the first floor I heard the organ which plays without a keyboard that was built by Walter after the principles of Brother Primitivus Niemecz of the Order of the Brothers of Mercy. It is sold to England. The organ is played by means of a winding handle which never changes its speed yet nevertheless creates all possible variations....).[51] It is a great pity that so far we do not know anything about the final destination of this organ or its whereabouts today, if it still survives. This is all the more unfortunate as there is just the chance that, being a large instrument, the two pieces of Haydn which appear to exist in manuscript only could be on the barrel and perhaps even the Mozart pieces might just turn out to have been original compositions. The thought is tantalising.

What, one might well ask, was the librarian of the royal palace doing exhibiting an instrument in a public place? Or did Niemecz lose his position the same way as Haydn had when Prince Anton succeeded Nicolaus? There is some evidence to suggest that Anton did indeed dispense with Niemecz's services at this time. For this and some indication of Niemecz's closing years, we turn

[46] Anton Walter, Court and civil organ-builder and piano manufacturer, was born about 1751 and died in Vienna on 11 April 1826. Mozart preferred his pianos but Haydn was not all that keen on them. He wrote to Frau von Genzinger in 1790 about Walter's pianos: 'I certainly receive a lot of politeness from my friend Mr. Walter who is very well-known but between you and me I have to admit honestly that sometimes among 10 pianos there is only one which is worth considering as very good; besides, he is extremely expensive' (see C.F. Pohl, *Joseph Haydn II*, p. 157). Even so, Walter did a great deal of work on the Esterházy instruments and according to an invoice of his dated 3 March 1781, he spent 12 days at the Esterházy court (see Horst Walter, 'Haydns Klavier' in *Haydn-Studien*, vol. 2, no. 4, Köln, 1970, pp. 256–88).

[47] The admission fee was about 40 Kreuzer (see the *Zeitschrift Magyar Hirmondó* for the year 1798, p. 26, quoted by Csátkai [*op. cit.*] and Schmid [*op. cit.*]).

[48] *Wiener Zeitung*, Wednesday, 4 April 1798, p. 963.

[49] See *Magyar Hirmondó, loc. cit.*

[50] Ernst Ludwig Gerber, *Neues historisch-biographisches Lexikon der Tonkünstler*, Leipzig, 1813, vol. III, p. 589 *et seq.* Gerber's account is based on the above-mentioned passage in the *Wiener Zeitung* and on the *Allgemeinen Literarischen Anzeiger*, Leipzig, for 24 May 1798, p. 840.

[51] Handwritten (manuscript) diary of Prince Zinzendorf dated 30 March 1798 onwards, preserved in Haus-Hof und Staatsarchiv, Vienna.

to an extraordinary new source of information which only came to light in the 1950s. This is the diary of a nobleman called Beda Plank which has survived in manuscript form in the archives of Kremsmünster Abbey and was first published in P. Altmann Kellner's *Musikgeschichte des Stiftes Kremsmünster* (Kassel, 1957). The date is 1801 and Plank writes:

> On March 20, a friend took me to the suburb of Spitelfeld to the building of the Hungarian Noble Guards in which now lives Father Primitiv. He is from the Order of the Brothers of Mercy and is famous because of his clockwork instruments. He showed us several of his creations which, when he winds them up, play whole pieces by Mozart and Haydn in the finest organ tones and with such a degree of precision that not the smallest appogiatura or trill or other like ornament is missed out. Even the echo effect comes over excellently. I would wish only that the bass were a little stronger, and the *forte* and *piano* to be more clearly distinguishable. He works out the position of the notes in a piece (of music) before he even starts and does this with such care that you cannot detect the slightest sign of a misplaced pin in the cylinder. This priest is very happy in his work. The late Prince Esterházy took him to Esterház (sic) and left him a good pension which he enjoys (still) under the present Prince who has provided him with a place to stay. For the present Prince (Anton) he will soon complete a new mechanical organ which will surpass the others in value and pleasantness of sound.

The experience obviously left an impression on Plank for less than two weeks later he was once again off to visit Niemecz.

> On March 31, I persuaded the two Abbots (of Lambach and Kremsmünster) to walk to the handsome building of the Hungarian Noble Guards to see and hear the mechanical organs which so delighted my ear on the 20th inst. This most pleasant priest showed us today, besides other organs, a large musical machine which he had not quite finished. This machine, on pressing a button on the spring, plays the most excellent pieces all by itself. After each piece, another cylinder is inserted: there are six of them entirely finished on which he has chosen to pin two (pieces) by Mozart, three by Haydn and one by Beethoven. One of the most difficult pieces from the newest quartets by Joseph Haydn, which the best violin players in Vienna could not master, was produced by this machine with such precision that neither the least appoggiatura nor even the smallest note is missed.'

This pair of most illuminating references tells us that Niemecz indeed gave up most of his other interests to concentrate on making mechanical organs. It also shows that while the three organs forming the thesis of this book each had only one barrel, Niemecz did indeed progress to making instruments with a much wider repertoire through the medium of interchangeable barrels. And as for that difficult piece from one of Haydn's 'newest quartets', this was most likely to have been the Finale of the 'Lark' Quartet, Opus 64, No. 5, which is also to be found on the 1793 Haydn/Niemecz mechanical organ, i.e. Number 30 in the conspectus.

Niemecz seems to have spent the rest of his life happily

engaged in his task of mechanical organ making. It seems inconceivable that the total output of this man's genius over the years subsequent to his departure from the close involvement with Haydn and the Esterházys should have disappeared. One instrument at least he apparently gave to Prince Anton as mentioned above. What happened to this? If it went into the Vienna palace, then it must still exist, no doubt unidentified within its cabinetwork. If it went to Eszterháza, then it must have been destroyed during the Soviet occupation in the years following the war. But what about the other pieces? They must exist somewhere in private collections, in noble homes — somewhere. If Niemecz was as unwilling to mark his organs of this period as he had been in the days of Eisenstadt, then they may be hard to identify.

The long periods spent at the palace of Eszterháza with its damp atmosphere had, however, taken their toll. Niemecz was a sick man and he battled for some years against tuberculosis. According to the death register, this was the cause of his ultimate demise. He died on 9 January 1806, in 'the Russian House, No. 60 St. Ullrich in the Langensucht'.[52] He was fifty-one years of age.

On 17 January at the instigation of Brother Paschalis Fiala, prior of the Brothers of Mercy, a Court Order was secured to protect Niemecz's property as there was a real danger that his house and belongings would be dispersed.[53]

A few months later we learn from a Viennese newspaper something more about the effects which Niemecz left. This also tells us that Niemecz's assistant must either have received powers of attorney or indeed his master bequeathed his estate to him, for we read that Joseph Gurck was selling off his master's property and, surprisingly, taking orders for fresh work.[54] The publication says: 'Joseph Gurck has the honour to announce to the highly-esteemed public that in his house at the Glacis in the Royal Hungarian Noble Guard House on the first floor they can buy for the very lowest prices several musical clocks and machines that can be seen daily from 9 to 12. They are from the recently-deceased Father Primitivus Niemecz, the erstwhile librarian to the Palace who was extremely well known in his art. Also at the above-mentioned apartment there can be accepted orders for such musical machines to be made'. Gurck goes on to infer that in his position as apprentice to so great a man as Niemecz, he could produce pieces of an equally high quality.

And so it came to be that the effects of the talented Brother were finally scattered to the four winds. However, thanks to a series of strokes of luck, three of his magnificent mechanical

[52] Death register for the City of Vienna, 1806, in Vienna State Archives.

[53] Vienna State Archives, *Schottenabhandlungen 1806*, 2nd series, 316 *Sperrs-Relation*. We gather from this document several extremely interesting facts in the revelation that Gurck owned the formerly-attested last will and testament of the Primitivus Niemecz whose closest relatives were two unmarried maid-servants at that time living in Vienna. These were Marianne and Anna Niemecz and the inference is that they were his sisters.

[54] *Wiener Zeitung*, 1806, p. 2586 (28 May 1806).

organs have been preserved for our study. Each is unique and important because it forms a unit in the trio of organs that play exclusively original compositions of Haydn. Schmid writes that Niemecz received the compositions for his instruments immediately (directly) from the hand of his music teacher and friend and qualifies these as being treasures of the finest art. As we shall see further on, the existence of the first of these mechanical organs and its date has long presented some confusion for the historian which may now be settled.

Meanwhile, Haydn's health was deteriorating and he was becoming less and less mobile. His early biographer, Albert Christoph Dies (born Hanover, 1755; died Vienna, 1822), describes how on 18 June 1806, he had visited Haydn's house and discovered that the previous day, in the company of some friends, who had invited him to go along with him, Haydn had paid a visit to 'a famous instrument maker':

> there to inspect a new musical instrument with organ pipes worked mechanically. Haydn was easily persuaded even though the artist's quarters were far from Gumpendorf. When the carriage stopped, the young men leaped out and eased Haydn's descent, then carried him up the few flights to the artist's apartment, The (mechanical organ) also played a Haydn composition. Haydn listened with pleasure, and this pleasure imparted new strength to his spirit.

This description tallies well with the testimony of Joseph Gurck regarding his instrument which he showed to Haydn and requested Haydn to name. Did Dies actually visit Haydn the day Haydn sent the 'German note' with the suggestion that Gurck should call his instrument the Panharmonicon? Perhaps Dies himself delivered the note![55] The unanswered question here is whether Gurck and Niemecz shared the same workshop. After the death of Niemecz, Gurck appears to have taken it over for his own use. At all events, Dies' reference, quoted above, may mark the last occasion when Haydn was given the opportunity to see a mechanical organ. Less than two months later, Michael Haydn died and this contributed to the steady decline of Joseph Haydn.

[55] See p. 133, column 1.

Plate 15. Towards the end of his life, Haydn had this visiting card printed with which he acknowledged invitations. The text, from the works of the poet Gellert, reads: 'Gone for ever is my strength: Old and weak am I' and he had used them in a vocal quartet in 1799 from which the first four bars are taken.

CHAPTER 3

The Three Organs

The three surviving organs upon which Haydn and Niemecz collaborated all share certain common features. There is a clear family style extending from the first organ (the one reputed to have been built in 1772) through to the third, dated 1793. Previous historians have never questioned the date of 1772 for the earliest of the three. Apart from the fact that it is unsigned whereas the barrels of the others are clearly inscribed and dated, it is said to have originated some twenty years before the second organ, itself separated from the third by only one year. Now, though, there is no doubt that the attribution of the instrument to 1772 is not just incorrect or improbable but definitely impossible. Although we are told on reliable authority that Niemecz built mechanical organs prior to this one, they were all much later than 1772 and far from being a slow worker, Niemecz must have been able to turn out instruments quite rapidly. The evidence for this revision in dating is outlined in the next chapter and expanded upon in the summing-up in Chapter 5. For the time being, then, I will treat the '1772' instrument as did Ernst Simon in his survey of composers of mechanical music[1] and show its date of construction in inverted commas.

For the purpose of this book, I have been able to examine most thoroughly the two most important instruments — the first and the third.[2] The well-documented Urban instrument, sold after the Second World War and the present location of which is unknown, has the advantage of being the central one of the three, a sort of pivot point in the stylistic development of the detail construction of these singular organs. The general description of this one, then, fits neatly into the comparison of the earliest and latest instruments.

Each organ has a rectangular base made of oak which stands on four short, squat feet so that it can be stood upon a surface without damage to the pipework beneath. The base forms the mounting board for all the organ components. These comprise the wind department consisting of two single-acting, alternately pumping feeders and the reservoir, the tune barrel, the fusee-wound spring-driven clockwork motor, and the pipework. It is the

[1] Ernst Simon, *Mechanische Musik-instrumente früherer Zeiten und ihr Musik*, p. 61 *et seq.*

[2] An examination of the organs show that the mechanical construction of the three instruments, '1772', 1792 and 1793, corresponds in all essential details. Schmid, in his 1932 treatise, said he detected what he called a logical development in the execution of the construction of the three. The implication was that the builder was getting better at his craft with each instrument. If Niemecz were to have been responsible for the entire organ building process, then this would follow automatically, but this may not entirely have been the case. This improvement, related Schmid, is noticeable in the keyframe area, the keys, stickers and so on from which he concluded that the earliest organ, whatever its actual date, was indeed the first (or among the first) to have been built by or under the influence of Niemecz. This does not take into consideration the reports that the Esterházy palaces were apparently already well-appointed with other and obviously earlier Niemecz instruments which must therefore have been even more primitive in construction. One fact becomes obvious here and that is that although Schmid published a description of the three organs in 1932, either he did not examine them in detail or he had an extremely limited experience of the *Flötenuhr* and Viennese clockwork in general, and thereby he failed to be able to make constructive observation on the standard of workmanship and to detect various singular details and features in their construction.

positioning of the pipework which is most characteristic, for it lies horizontally under the baseboard. This will be detailed in a moment.[3]

The instruments differ in size and each has a markedly different tonal compass. Although each could well have been made to take advantage of the tonal colouring possible through extended pipework, there is only one rank of pipes so the number of pipes equals the number of keys on the organ keyframe. These are as follows:

Organ No. 1 — '1772' — 25 pipes c¹ to d³ (playing 16 pieces)
Organ No. 2 — 1792 — 17 pipes c¹ to c³ (playing 12 pieces)
Organ No. 3 — 1793 — 29 pipes g to d³ (playing 12 pieces)

In all three instruments, the pipework comprises one four-foot stopped rank of flutes (see illustrations). It will be seen that the smallest organ was the second, and the largest the third, while the one with the most extensive repertoire was the first.

The pipework is arranged in a more or less symmetrical triangle and the pipes are push-fitted straight into the inner side of the pallet chest. The pipes have short narrow-bored feet

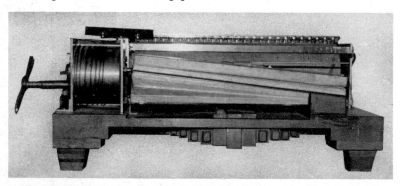

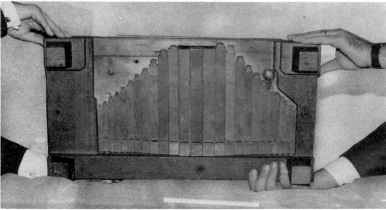

Plate 16 (above). View on the front of the first organ showing the pipework.

Plate 17 (below). Looking on the underside of the organ, the arrangement of the pipework can be seen with the longest pipes — the lowest notes — in the centre. In the foreground is a 15cm rule.

[3] The design concept of using horizontal pipework in an organ has already been linked to the organ-building book of Dom Bedos. There was, however, at least one instrument built prior to the publication of this book in the year 1778. The inventor of the so-called Viennese or German pianoforte action was the organ-builder Johann Andreas Stein, born in Heidelsheim, Baden, in 1728. He was a pupil of Silbermann in Strasbourg, built an organ in Augsburg, worked in Paris, and finally settled in Augsburg where, besides making harpsichords and the new pianofortes, he experimented with a number of unusual instruments including mutant piano/harpsichords, harpsichord/organs and so on. In 1772, he completed his *Melodika*, the outcome of fifteen years of work. This was a small manually-played pipe organ made to sit on top of a piano or harpsichord for melody playing. It had a compass from g to c⁴, was housed in a spinet-like wing-shaped case 3½ ft long, and had a touch volume control (no doubt a venetian or horizontal swell). The interesting feature of this is that the pipes were arranged horizontally so as to keep the instrument as small as possible. Stein had two children, a daughter who married Streicher, the Viennese piano-maker, and a son, Matthais Andreas Stein, who was also a piano-maker in Vienna. It was this Stein who built Mozart's piano (there is a reference, [see page 82] to the existence of a copy of a tuning fork which Stein used to tune Mozart's piano). Mozart was a close friend of Haydn and both men had access to the Viennese musical instrument makers. J.A. Stein died in 1792 and the fate of the *Melodika* is unknown. Later, the infamous Mälzel took rooms in the piano-factory of his son, M.A. Stein. For a detailed description of the *Melodika* see Stein's work, *Beschreibung meiner Melodika, eines neuerfundenen Clavierinstruments*, published in Augsburg in 1772 and probably available in Prince Esterházy's library at the time Niemecz joined his staff in 1780.

Fig. 6. The earliest of the three Haydn/Niemecz organs, originally attributed to 1772 but now believed to have been made in 1789.

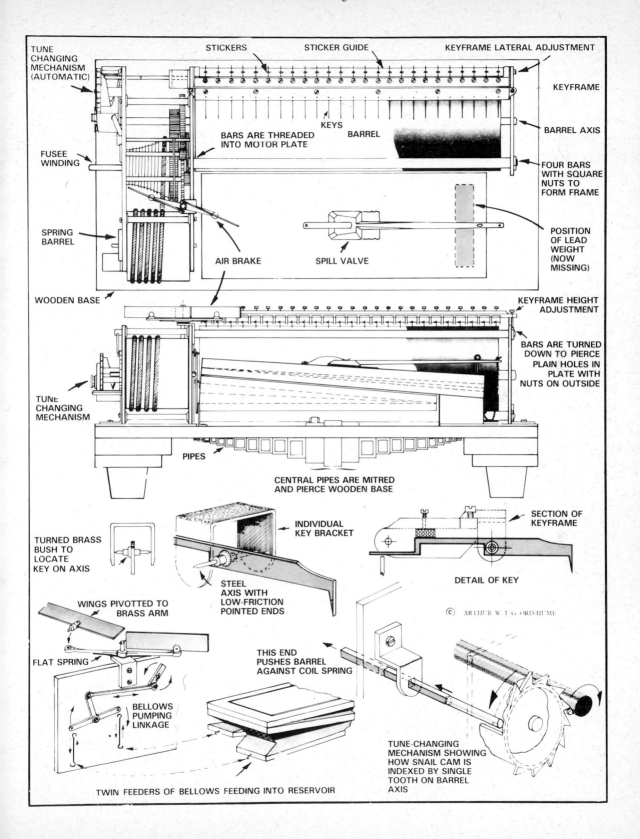

TUNE CHANGING MECHANISM (AUTOMATIC)

STICKERS

STICKER GUIDE

KEYFRAME LATERAL ADJUSTMENT

KEYFRAME

BARS ARE THREADED INTO MOTOR PLATE

KEYS

BARREL

BARREL AXIS

FUSEE WINDING

FOUR BARS WITH SQUARE NUTS TO FORM FRAME

SPRING BARREL

AIR BRAKE

SPILL VALVE

POSITION OF LEAD WEIGHT (NOW MISSING)

WOODEN BASE

KEYFRAME HEIGHT ADJUSTMENT

TUNE CHANGING MECHANISM

BARS ARE TURNED DOWN TO PIERCE PLAIN HOLES IN PLATE WITH NUTS ON OUTSIDE

PIPES

CENTRAL PIPES ARE MITRED AND PIERCE WOODEN BASE

TURNED BRASS BUSH TO LOCATE KEY ON AXIS

INDIVIDUAL KEY BRACKET

SECTION OF KEYFRAME

STEEL AXIS WITH LOW-FRICTION POINTED ENDS

DETAIL OF KEY

WINGS PIVOTTED TO BRASS ARM

© ARTHUR W J G ORD-HUME

FLAT SPRING

THIS END PUSHES BARREL AGAINST COIL SPRING

BELLOWS PUMPING LINKAGE

TUNE-CHANGING MECHANISM SHOWING HOW SNAIL CAM IS INDEXED BY SINGLE TOOTH ON BARREL AXIS

TWIN FEEDERS OF BELLOWS FEEDING INTO RESERVOIR

without wind-regulating plugs in the bore.[4] They speak clearly from the underside of the organ, the propagation of the sound being aided by the stand-off feet. In each instrument, the longest pipes are mitred, the lowest notes (meaning the longest pipes of all) being double mitred so that they lie back along themselves. The lowest notes are in the middle with the treble notes (i.e. the shortest pipes) extending to each side. The oak baseboard is pierced to let the mitred pipes penetrate into the open space beneath the bellows. This arrangement of pipes, each being sounded direct from the windchest pallet above it and without the interjection of rollers or levers, means that the barrel pinning process called for care and attention in pricking since the sequential notes of the scale do not appear to be sequentially arranged on the surface of the barrel.

The pipework has been manufactured using several different woods. The front faces, together with the upper lip, are cut from single pieces of pearwood. In both the '1772' and 1792 organs, the other three sides of each pipe are made of spruce while in the last instrument of 1793, they are of maple. In all three, the languid of each pipe is formed in two pieces.

Tonally, the loudest or most powerful instrument is that of 1793, yet all three possess a quite distinctive sound reminiscent of

[4] An organ pipe is normally 'planted' upright, wind entering it through the foot. However, since the purpose of the exercise is purely to inject a measured puff of wind into the pipe, this can be achieved through a hole in the bottom of the pipe, or one in the back. Back-blown footless wooden pipework is almost a universal feature of the portable street organ whose wooden diapason pipework is usually packed horizontally beneath the organ table. Niemecz fitted his organs with 'normal' pipework planted horizontally (see below).

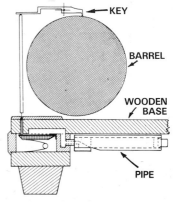

Plate 18. Detail of the clockwork drive motor.

the soft and somewhat stringy tone of a stopped labial pipe rank in a South German church organ of the period. This sound has a character which differs from that of the contemporary Viennese *Flötenuhr*. It has not proved possible to measure the wind pressure of the pipework but, judging from the area of the bellows and the weights or springs used to produce pressure, the speaking pressure must be extremely low — something in the order of little more than one-inch water-gauge pressure or rather less than a quality Black Forest orchestrion organ of the mid-nineteenth century.

The scale of each organ is related directly to the special pieces of music which each plays. This means that the instruments are not fully chromatic and the lower notes are diatonic. One is inclined to wonder whether organs were designed first and Haydn created the music to suit or *vice versa*. Some of the musical annotations which Haydn made (see next chapter) suggest that he offered a choice of compass in some of the music, leaving Niemecz the choice of which arrangement to use for the instrument in hand.

Each of the Haydn/Niemecz organs has just one barrel,[5] this being hollow and formed from more than thirty pieces of wood. The outer shell or casing is of lime and the whole surface

[5] This is in striking contrast to the greater majority of organs of this size and quality wherein a number of interchangeable barrels would be made so as to offer the owner a wider choice of music. As many as fifty tunes could be provided by the simple expedient of removing one barrel and replacing it with another belonging to the organ's repertoire. While many Black Forest musical clocks of the organ-playing variety were made with only one barrel of up to ten melodies, the more expensive and important the organ, the greater the incentive which the builder had to provide it with a wide repertoire. One famous mechanical organ — that built in or about the year 1762 for the Earl of Bute in England — had no fewer than sixty-four barrels while the average chamber barrel organ was often provided with up to half a dozen barrels. It is important to point out here that while such organs were provided with mechanisms to enable them to take extra barrels (such as a detachable end bearing, lifting key-frame, adjustable barrel-locating gear and so on) and, usually, storage space for the spare barrels, there is no question that the Niemecz organs under examination were at any time intended to have more than the one barrel each. Not only is there no barrel storage space, but the barrel drive mechanism does not include the mechanical features which would make it possible to remove and replace the barrel with ease. These organs were thus a very extravagant series of machines dedicated to playing just a few tunes.

Plate 19. Keyframe detail showing the unusual shape of the individual keys and their separate mounting in needle bearings.

wrapped in paper. The dimensions of the barrel vary in each case according to the number of bars and lengths of the tunes which they play. Each tune represents one revolution of the barrel.

The barrel shifts laterally in the normal manner in order to change the tune. While the keyframe has the usual vertical and horizontal adjustments, there is no mechanism for lifting the keys or the keyframe during tune-changing, the quite wide space between the beginning and the ends of the tunes allowing the keyframe keys clearance from the pins on the barrel while the barrel shifts sideways along its axis. A further characteristic of these interesting organs emerges in the system used for changing the tunes. This change mechanism operates using a snail and a ratchet wheel which has sixteen teeth (in the case of the '1772' organ) or twelve (with the later two). The pins and bridges which form the musical notation on the surface of the barrel are made of brass wire.

To a student of organ-building and of the *Flötenuhr* in particular, the keyframe of the '1772' instrument is a most remarkable and complex piece of engineering. One's first reaction is to wonder how Niemecz (or his organ-parts builder) could have produced such a cumbersome yet beautifully over-engineered piece of mechanism when the ruling technology was practising such apparently better and certainly simpler keyframe technology. Indeed, at first sight the shape of the keys in the keyframe appears eccentric in the extreme when viewed in comparison with the majority of contemporary and later instruments. However, the shape has obviously been created for a purpose and arrived at as the result of experiment in order to improve repetition of the shortest musical notes in the barrel pinning. By throwing all the weight forward of the key pivot, a long tail is possible so that a very small amount of lift at the tip of the key, i.e. by a very small brass pin representing an extremely short note, will be translated into a larger amount of movement at the key tail, so depressing the sticker and opening the pallet in the windchest an ample amount. These keys, then, are most delicately balanced and, furthermore, by the clockmaking style of individually mounting them in separate axes with needle bearings, friction is reduced to the very minimum. What at first looks like a piece of needless over engineering suddenly emerges as a most carefully designed device totally suited to the playing of these involved and highly-ornamented pieces of Haydn.

It is worth pointing out at this stage that the pinning in the barrels of a mechanical organ or stringed instrument can vary in height above the barrel surface, short and particularly repeated notes being represented by pins which protrude noticeably less

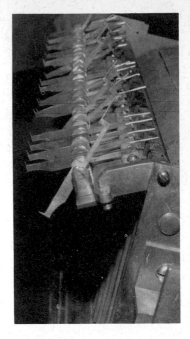

Plate 20. With the keyframe carefully reversed just for this picture, the full shape of the keys is clearly revealed. Note how all the weight is kept forward of the key pivot line.

Plate 21. This view, right, shows the method of changing the tunes. The large snail cam at the right impels a rod which is of circular cross-section at the outer plate, changes to square section as it passes through a guide bracket at the inner plate, and terminates in a wheel which runs around the inside edge of the barrel end on a prepared and faced track. At the end of each tune, the cam is indexed one step, the push-rod wheel re-aligning the barrel so that the pins of the next melody come under the keys.

Plate 22. The speed-regulating air brake and its method of driving (right). The stop-start detent can be seen engaged with a projection at the top of the worm gear while a peg on the lever has dropped into a recess on a 'quick-start' cam attached to the face of the worm drive wheel. Note the angle of the teeth in this wheel.

than those of a longer note. This is to ensure the staccato operation of the organ's mechanical tracker-type action and were these pins to be at the same height as those of longer notes, musical blurring would result as the notes failed to articulate

Plate 23. Relationship of the bellows to the clockwork and the barrel in its four-bar cage. The end of one of the narrow lead strips which assist in opening the feeders can just be seen near the end of the one visible feeder. The stranded steel wire on the motor barrel is not original.

Plate 24. The strong influence of clock-making is clearly seen in the method of mounting the keys, the keyframe and the adjustments. The very first key has sprung from its pivot point yet, because of the needle bearing, still works. The fine pinning of the barrel can also be seen.

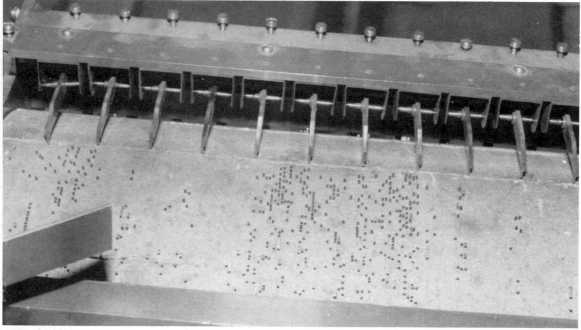

individually. This characteristic is employed extensively by Niemecz and these balanced extended-leverage keys aid musical perfection.

The illustration shows details of the '1772' keyframe and

Plate 25. The connecting link for pumping the bellows feeders is driven from an eccentric attached to the extended shaft of the wheel which turns the air brake shaft.

clearly indicates the individual mounting of the keys as well as their most extraordinary shape which should be compared with the shape of conventional barrel organ keys in Fig. 4. The keys of this instrument are made of what looks like steel but could be a refined clockmaker's iron. The tails have no adjustment to the stickers, the correct operation and delicacy of response being achieved by bending the thin, circular-sectioned rear ends of the keys up or down to suit the individual sticker. This must have proved a little too delicate for setting up and running adjustment for, by the 1793 organ, we find the keyframe of a more conventional construction with a common key axis and a guiding 'comb' made of brass for the front ends of the keys. The tails now have neat adjustments so that each can be regulated to its sticker

Plate 26. Back view of the organ showing the stickers which operate the pallets in the wind chest. The plug or access board to the chest can also be seen. Removal of this allows adjustment to the pallet springs when required.

without risk of breaking the keys or bending them too far. The stickers themselves are of very light and thin strips of lime.

It is worth commenting that the system of bushing a lever to a pivot shaft is a practice followed quite widely in the field of clockmaking in the eighteenth century. From this I am almost inclined to the conclusion that the keyframe, if nothing else, was the work of an organ novice who was a skilled clockmaker. The same type of bushing is to be found in the pumping linkage to the bellows

The windchest is built integrally with the baseboard beneath the barrel and has the type of plug access board which was to be a feature of Black Forest orchestrions and Viennese organ clocks. This makes any maintenance and pallet adjustment simple and does away with the need for screws in the chest.

The wind supply in each organ is provided in the conventional way by two windfeeders and a reservoir bellows. The flexible sides and hinges of these follow normal organ-building practice and construction in that they are covered with thin white leather stiffened with card — the leather of the first instrument appears to have been replaced at some time and is in part unstiffened which means that the leather tends to bulge out and interfere with the correct pumping action. The top and bottom boards of the bellows are, in the case of the '1772' instrument, inlaid with a simple stringing of dark wood, a feature which records show exists on the 1792 instrument as well.

The bellows board measures 144×392mm and has only one pressure spring mounted on the one side between bellows and barrel. There is, however, evidence to show that at some time at least two lead weights have been glued to the top surface of the board. The relief pallet is made of wood with the later addition of a leaf spring. Each feeder carries a compensating weight in the form of a lead bar recessed across its end. This allows the feeders to open quickly after each stroke.

By comparison, the 1793 instrument has its bellows upper board, which measures 182×530mm, cased in brass which covers the top surface and the sides. This also mounts the relief valve, nicely formed in brass. The weight of this brass sheathing no doubt helps both to stiffen the upper board and to provide weight to the reservoir. Two iron wire springs, one each side, also aid the wind pressure.

The wind feeders are connected by linkages to the clockwork which also serves to rotate the wooden barrel upon which the music is pinned. However, the means of doing this differ between the three instruments. The first and second organs are each powered by a single fusee-wound clockwork or spring motor and

Fig. 7. The third and last-known Haydn/Niemecz mechanical organ, seen here, bears the signature of Niemecz and the date 1793. All of the instruments known are built on the same basic principle with the single barrel for the musical programme being contained in a four-bar framework formed as an extension of the inner motor plate, which is secured to the plate at the opposite end by threaded brass nuts. These nuts, in the case of the first instrument, are square in shape while in the 1793 instrument they are octagonal.

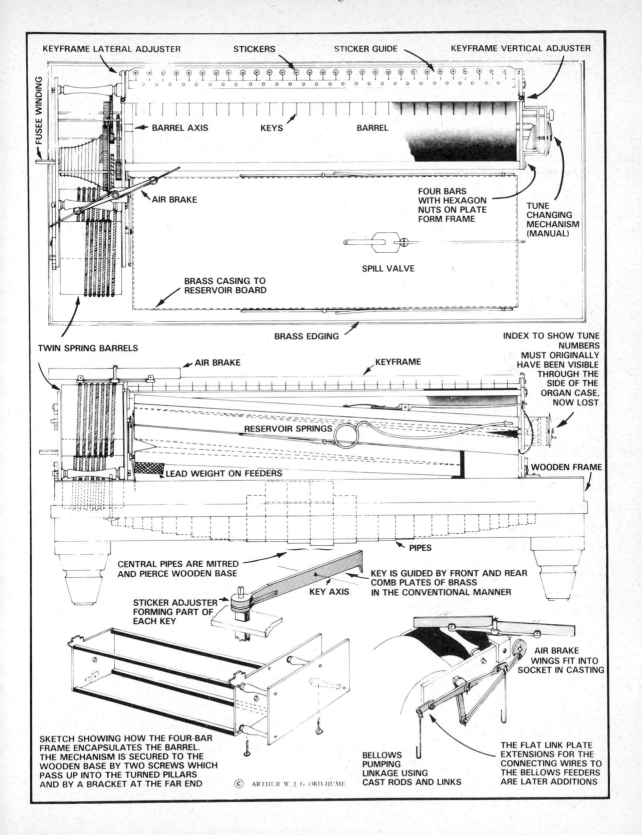

KEYFRAME LATERAL ADJUSTER   STICKERS   STICKER GUIDE   KEYFRAME VERTICAL ADJUSTER

FUSEE WINDING

BARREL AXIS   KEYS   BARREL

AIR BRAKE

FOUR BARS
WITH HEXAGON
NUTS ON PLATE
FORM FRAME

TUNE
CHANGING
MECHANISM
(MANUAL)

SPILL VALVE

BRASS CASING TO
RESERVOIR BOARD

BRASS EDGING

TWIN SPRING BARRELS

AIR BRAKE   KEYFRAME

INDEX TO SHOW TUNE
NUMBERS
MUST ORIGINALLY
HAVE BEEN VISIBLE
THROUGH THE
SIDE OF THE
ORGAN CASE,
NOW LOST

RESERVOIR SPRINGS

LEAD WEIGHT ON FEEDERS

WOODEN FRAME

PIPES

CENTRAL PIPES ARE MITRED
AND PIERCE WOODEN BASE

KEY IS GUIDED BY FRONT AND REAR
COMB PLATES OF BRASS
IN THE CONVENTIONAL MANNER

STICKER ADJUSTER
FORMING PART OF
EACH KEY

KEY AXIS

AIR BRAKE
WINGS FIT INTO
SOCKET IN CASTING

SKETCH SHOWING HOW THE FOUR-BAR
FRAME ENCAPSULATES THE BARREL.
THE MECHANISM IS SECURED TO THE
WOODEN BASE BY TWO SCREWS WHICH
PASS UP INTO THE TURNED PILLARS
AND BY A BRACKET AT THE FAR END

© ARTHUR W. J. G. ORD-HUME

BELLOWS
PUMPING
LINKAGE USING
CAST RODS AND LINKS

THE FLAT LINK PLATE
EXTENSIONS FOR THE
CONNECTING WIRES TO
THE BELLOWS FEEDERS
ARE LATER ADDITIONS

Plate 27. The third surviving organ of 1793 showing details of the clockwork and the linkage for pumping the bellows feeders.

Plate 28. Only four pictures are known of the second Haydn/Niemecz organ of 1792. These are two virtually similar views of the instrument from the front and again a pair of similar views on the open back. Plate 39 on page 67 shows one of these front views while above is a look inside this now-lost instrument. Note how the feet of the instrument serve merely to block up the bottom of the organ so that the pipework is not subjected to possible damage. The third organ, however, has proper feet which are more presentable. Clearly visible here is the lever on the backplate of the timepiece from which runs a line down through the floor of the clock compartment to an arm pivotted above the bellows reservoir of the organ and sited so as to be able to free the cranked stop/start detent of the organ clockwork. In this view the pendulum of the timepiece is removed and the object lying on the floor of the clock compartment over the slot for fitting the pendulum is a French-style clock winding key. The organwork has its own winding handle just visible at the extreme left.

the reciprocating drive to the feeders is achieved by an inverted T-shaped lever mounted below the drive spring arbor and with its upright cranked so as to clear the protruding end of the arbor. The top end of this lever is linked to an eccentric arm on the end of the shaft which carries the special angled-tooth wheel which itself drives the endless screw. This linkage is by means of a connecting rod.

In the last organ, whose larger number of pipes and greater demands on wind suggested to Niemecz the use of two connected spring barrels wound from one fusee, the bellows drive is again achieved using a T-shaped lever, this time mounted the right way up, the lower end of the vertical stem being joined to an eccentric as before using a nicely-journalled connecting rod. Significantly, the air brakes of these two organs turn in opposite directions as can be seen from the shape of the angled teeth of the worm drive wheel and also by the lie of the airbrake wings. The speed of rotation and thereby the speed of the music may be adjusted within certain limits by closing up the adjustable wings of these fans; at present both organs play with their fans in the widest open

Plate 29. General view of the organ of 1793 with its brass covered bellows reservoir and refinements of construction. The small white dial at the right is the tune indicator on the changing mechanism.

Plate 30. The twin spring barrels and fusee winding can be seen here together with the stop/start mechanism which is not original.

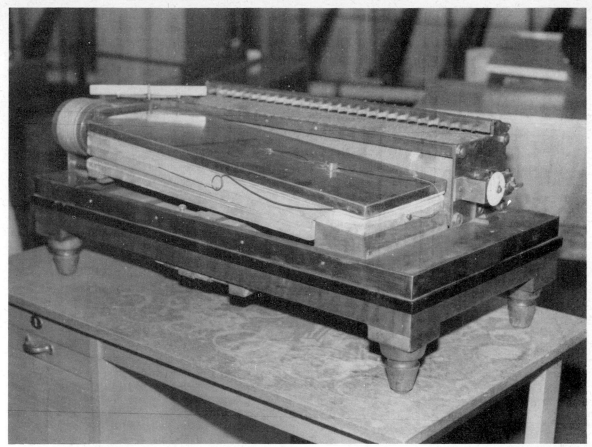

position so that they play as slowly as possible. In each case, winding was originally achieved using a strong gut line and a detachable crank handle to the fusee arbor, but in both the '1772' and the 1793 organs this gut has been replaced by flexible steel cable — a modification which, while undoubtedly accelerating the wear of the fusee and spring barrels, is preferable to the certain catastrophe brought about by the breaking of a gut line.

Plate 31. Compact proportions of this organ are evident from this view which also shows the feet — a considerable difference from the simple wood blocks of the 1792 organ, themselves cruder even than the feet of the first instrument.

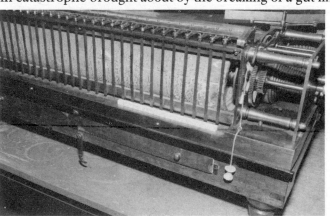

Plate 32. View on the back of the organ shows details of the key-frame and stickers against a 15cm rule. On this organ, the tune changing mechanism operates at the other end of the barrel hence the compression spring just visible on the barrel access. The wind chest now has a proper plug access board with a hook-and-eye catch to keep the centre air tight. Button catch at the end is a later addition.

The mechanism is set in motion using a simple detent or starting lever. With the first and second instruments, the organ plays right through its repertoire, one piece of music following another. However, the last organ was provided with a manual tune-selector lever so that the barrel could be shifted to play any piece of music on the barrel at choice. A dial pointer indicated which piece of music was being played and in this manner the

Plate 33. Museum technician Johannes Hornsteiner of the Münchner Stadtmuseum (left) and Jörg Lässig show the underside of the organ with its finely-crafted pipe-work.

Plate 34. The clockwork of the 1793 instrument should be compared with Plate 22 on page 52 showing the first organ. While the actual stop-start lever — the one which curves over the pillar at the left — is not as original, the detent itself is. The 'quick-start' cam shows that the instrument was playing when this shot was taken. Note the angle of the teeth in the worm drive wheel.

operation is similar to that used in both the carillon clock and the later musical box, both of which were provided at one stage in their development with a device for allowing the selection of a chosen tune as distinct from the inflexibility of strict sequential playing.

Each of the Haydn/Niemecz Esterházy organs was probably incorporated with a timepiece when it was built. On the evidence of the number of tunes played, the two which each perform twelve melodies (those of 1792 and 1793) were most likely crafted to be controlled by a timepiece so that one tune could be performed at each hour. Only one of the organs is known to survive with its original timepiece and case and that is the 1792 instrument.[6] It is still capable of playing a tune on the hour by means of a detent and a cord running from the timepiece clockwork to the clockwork motor which drives the organ.

There is some evidence to suggest that the organ of 1793 was also intended to have been controlled by a timepiece. Besides playing twelve tunes, the instrument displays several holes and other marks about its framework which could at one time have been associated with a discharge mechanism from the striking work of a timepiece mounted somewhere above. Furthermore, the starting detent as present today is the wrong shape and appears not to be original. It also seems to be upside down. At the moment, the organ plays by the rather clumsy process of pushing this lever down to form a geometric lock with the locking detent

[6] The case of this organ is indeed original which is contrary to the opinion of Schnerich (*Joseph Haydn*, 2nd ed., p. 263) who believed it to have been re-cased in 1870.

Plate 35. The paper-covered surface of the barrel is seen here and the 15cm rule is resting on the keyframe. Just visible above the right hand wing of the air brake is a tapped vertical hole in the forward bar of the barrel cage. In the present state of the instrument this appears no longer to have any purpose but it may have once been part of a timepiece detent mechanism of the type seen in Plate 28 on page 59.

Plate 36. End view of the instrument showing how the second spring barrel is housed in a recess in the woodwork in front of the chest. Certain details of this clockwork are strongly similar to the specifications shown in the illustrations in Dom Bedos reproduced in Appendix 2.

and so raise it to free the clockwork. This cannot in any way be as originally intended.

Whatever way the partnership actually worked, it is certain that the Haydn/Niemecz organs were better planned at the design stage than many other contemporary instruments as well as quite a few which were to follow. As an instance, there exists a most delightful classical barrel organ of the same period and similar compass to the Esterházy products in the Nationaal Museum van Speelklok tot Pierement in Utrecht. Made by the Dutch organ builder Diederich Nicolaus Winkel, this has fully-chromatic pipework — including the D sharp in the bass. Many of the salon barrel organs by the French builder Davrainville and some of the Black Forest products of Imhof & Mukle were similarly scaled, clearly because they were built to be able to play a wide variety of music on a selection of barrels, the choice of the music to be played seldom concerning the organ building but being the responsibility of a separate department of the organ-building process.[7]

Both of the later mechanical organs are signed on the barrel by the builder. The inscription, in ornate and careful lettering placed across the whole width (length) of the barrel in the space between the finish position of the tunes and the start, reads, in the case of the 1792 model: 'P. Primitivus Nemetz Ordinis S. Joan. de Deo Sacerdos fecit in Esterhas Anno 1792'.[8]

The inscription on the 1793 piece does not refer to the Order but simply says: 'Primitivus Niemecz C^{mi} Principis Esterhazy Bibliothecarius fecit in Esterhas. Anno 1793'.

The earliest of the three organs, '1772', corresponds in every

[7] This is because these instruments were made for interchangeable barrels — see note 5 above.

[8] St. Johannes de Deo is the patron saint of the Barmherzigen Bruder or Brothers of Mercy.

stylistic way with the latter two as already outlined. It can thus be said with little doubt that it, too, was built by the same hand and that, along with the two subsequent organs, it was connected with Niemecz[9] although it bears neither inscription nor date.[10]

Externally, the three appear quite similar in design and construction, but differ in regard to their constructional details. That of 1792 which is the only one to survive complete with its clock, has a very interesting and decorative case.[11]

[9] The survival of these instruments in working order is due to the efforts of various craftsmen over the years who have devoted their skills to maintaining them. The first organ — '1772' — was apparently attended to by a Viennese clockmaker named Graf in the year 1832. It is possible that this was Salomon Graf. The owner, Frau Paula Teubner-Reghem, worked on it in 1895 (see Chapter 5) although the extent of her work may not have extended beyond a cautious cleaning and lubrication. For the instrument of 1792, the clockmaker A. Schell (1862) and the organ-builder Franz Maretka of Olmütz (in 1894) were followed by the Viennese musical mechanician Philipp de Ponti in 1898. Franz Maretka was in business at Oberring 28 as late as 1909, described in directories as an organ and harmonium-builder. The 1793 organ received the careful attention of the clockmaker Jörg of Meran in the Austrian Tirol. In the years which preceded the Second World War, the two latter organs were under the care of Philipp de Ponti's son, Richard de Ponti.

[10] It is rather interesting that when a maker signs a barrel organ the most logical place to make his mark is on the key-frame where it can be clearly engraved. If a maker is disposed to mark his work, then this is the place where one would look. Niemecz marked the second and third instruments, but only on the paper covering of the barrel and only in ink. In view of the conclusions in Chapter 5, there is a strong possibility that although these instruments appear to represent style and design which is singularly characteristic, and although their scaling and repertoire is singular, they may have been manufactured by somebody else to the design and specifications of Niemecz and that his sole involvement may have been no more than the highly skilled task of noting and pinning the wooden barrels with the music. This seems a likely explanation of his otherwise strange failure to mark other than the barrels of the instruments with his name. It should be said, however, that many builders did not mark their instruments and some later makers placed their trade labels on the barrels.

[11] A front view of this organ is to be found in the 1932 edition of the Haydn music for mechanical organ as published by Nagel of Hannover. This seems to be the earliest traceable published illustration of the piece.

Plate 37 (top). Part of the inscription by Niemecz on the paper covering of the 1793 barrel.
Plate 38 (left). From the first organ the bellows reservoir shows the stain where a lead pressure weight was at one time glued.

The first of the three is said originally to have been connected with a timepiece of the Josephenic style which was decorated with a Blackamoor head and which set off the music by the fall of a ball. This undoubtedly artistic piece, both highly decorative as well as functional, was bequeathed by Franz Reghem[12] to a one-time parson in Vienna, a man named Michael Blümml. Unfortunately, the timepiece component and the rest of the original cabinet have since disappeared.

The mechanical organ component, however, remained in the possession of the Reghem family. One would imagine that the separation of the organ and the original clock took place around the middle of the last century, for at this time the clock was built into the upper portion of a desk or bureau in the style known in Germany as Laxenburger gothic.[13] It is concealed behind a dummy drawer with a somewhat coarsely fretted tracery forming a screen in front of the mechanism. The height of the organ is 26cm, the width 61cm and the depth 31cm (see page 49). An affidavit by Klara Brandeisky née Minetti[14] and dated 18 December 1905 gives some details as to the originality of the instrument as follows: 'When I was nine years old in 1834, I was witness to the occasion when Anna Fux (née Gassmann) played the 16 tunes to a man who visited her and pointed out their origin and authenticity'.

Family tradition states that Joseph Haydn had given the instrument to Barbara Gassmann (née Damm) who was the wife of his friend the composer and court conductor, Florian Leopold Gassmann, on the occasion of the birth of her daughter, Anna Maria. Anna Maria Gassmann, who was the sister of the then-popular operatic singer Maria Therese Rosenbaum-Gassmann, herself a close friend of Haydn, took up singing and finally married the Viennese Court conductor, Peter Fux.

This apparent dating of the instrument by association with events is interesting. Florian L. Gassmann was born in 1723 and met his end suddenly on 21 January 1774, having been thrown from his carriage. The last year in which, presumably, his wife could have produced his child is thus 1774. Anna Maria, though, was indeed two at the death of her father. In Chapter 5 I will show that this family tradition based on the recollection of circumstances surrounding the gift of the organ cannot be accurate.

Anna Maria later took the name Fux-Gassmann by marriage and looked after the organ throughout her life until finally, in her old age, she lived with her husband's niece, Josephine Reghem-Minetti, who was her sole heir.[15] Through this connection, the organ passed into the care of the Reghem family.

[12] This is the great-grandfather of the present owner.

[13] This cupboard or bureau may have been manufactured about the same time as the organ is said to have been made, i.e. 1772, although Schnerich (op. cit.) believed it to date from around 1810. Several illustrations of the instrument are known from this period. Wolfgang Teubner has told the author that he thinks the cabinet, while certainly not original, is a contemporary piece.

[14] Schmid in his history of the piece says: 'Klara Brandeisky, née Reghem . . . &c'. However, a manuscript note in the hand of Frau Paula Teubner-Reghem on her own copy of Schmid's article corrects this to Minetti. This document is preserved in the Teubner documentation with the instrument.

[15] She died on 27 August 1852 and not 1856 as suggested by Schnerich (op. cit.) on page 140.

Only a few months after the death of Anna Fux-Gassmann, the instrument was offered for sale by Frau Reghem-Minetti but luckily did not attract a buyer. The *Österreichische Volksbote* for 1 January 1853[16] carried the following notice: 'It is said that in Mariahilf, Siebensterngasse No. 91 on the first floor there are still some unknown compositions by Haydn to be heard. The musical clock (*spieluhr*) can be obtained there where the seller maintains that it plays 16 pieces by means of one single barrel. All the pieces for that musical clock were composed by Joseph Haydn and have never appeared in manuscript.[Well, it's possible but improbable!]' (sic).

The instrument stayed in the family and in the closing years of the last century it became the property of Frau Paula Teubner-Reghem of Vienna, a grandchild of Josephine Reghem-Minetti. It was she who, as related further on, carried out simple repairs to the instrument which is now in the possession of Wolfgang Teubner, Dipl. -Ing. in Vienna.[17]

The second organ is hidden in the base of a mantle clock in the Louis XVI style.[18] The timepiece indicates days, hours and

[16] This was No. 1 of the fifth year of publication under the editorship of Bäuerle. Konstant von Wurzbach quoted this same passage in his *Biographischen Lexikon . . .* of 1862 (see entry under 'Haydn').

[17] This instrument is carefully preserved with its documentation and, wisely, no attempt has been made to carry out more than conservative maintenance. The future of the instrument has also been secured.

[18] This resumé of the history of the instruments is based on Alfred Schnerich (*op. cit.*), Ernst Fritz Schmid (*op. cit.*), and the subsequent researches of William Malloch and the author. The width of this base is 51cm and the depth 35cm.

Plate 39. The middle organ of the three — the 1792 'Urban' instrument. In this front view can be seen the two carved figures seated on lions which flank the timepiece, the central circular window through which the pendulum might be seen, and the oval medallion on the front of the base containing a reversed image of the Watteau scene *Leçon d'Amour*. Although the instrument is for the present lost, its repertoire has been recorded.

minutes and sets off the music automatically every hour when one tune is played. The dial of the clock itself is ornamented with a delicate picture in black and white enamel which shows a commissioned officer with tricorn hat and sword mounted on horseback in a meadow. In the background there stands a fortress with battlements and turrets. There is a possibility that this picture represents something to do with the original owner of the clock and could indicate that he was a soldier or warrior. Indeed, the scene depicted so delicately may represent an actual place and an actual scene or event as yet unidentified.

Beneath the clockface there is a circular window through which one can see the finely-shaped brass pendulum bob. The base of the cabinet is considerably wider than that of the timepiece itself and it is in here that the musicwork is contained. On top of this base and seated either side of the upper casework which contains the timepiece is a pair of carved and painted wooden figures representing two bearded old men in colourful and old-fashioned robes. Each wears upon his head a golden laurel wreath and holds an open book. Both are seated facing sideways on golden lions which sit with their front paws crossed. The image appears to be that of two aged philosophers or might indeed be some symbolic representation of Niemecz the librarian.

Sited centrally on the front of the base is an oval medallion in a gilded surround which contains an oil painting on wood. This is a copy of the well-known miniature by Antoine Watteau (1684–1721) which features a group of musicians and was originally entitled *Leçon d'Amour*. However, the image is here reversed left to right which implies that this copy was made from an engraving of Watteau's painting.[19]

This very beautiful instrument and its timepiece was sold by an antique dealer in Vienna's Karnbresstrasse to the editor of a Viennese journal, a Dr. Karl Urban,[20] who bought it in 1898 as a Christmas present for his wife.[21] The piece had originally been the property of the noble family of Liechtenstein[22] in Mähren and this is corroborated by the discovery of a repairer's label fixed to the bellows which shows the name of an organ-builder called Maretka of Olmütz.[23] Indeed, the wife of Prince Nicolaus II, Maria Josepha Hermenegild, née Princess Liechtenstein, was also Haydn's special patroness and he was inspired to write several of his later great masses for her name-day and in addition dedicated some piano sonatas to her.[24]

It has been suggested that Haydn gave the organ to a member of the Liechtenstein family as a present. This seems rather unlikely since the instrument was most probably built and

[19] The first person to make this suggestion was André Csatkai of Eisenstadt.

[20] The instrument subsequently passed to the son of Dr Karl Urban, Hans Urban, who some years after the Second World War disposed of the piece to an unknown private source. So far all efforts to trace the instrument have failed.

[21] This information was provided to Schmid by Richard de Ponti whose father was responsible for repairing the instrument at that time.

[22] This statement is based on information which Dr Karl Urban is said to have given Schmid before he died. It is known that the Liechtensteins were interested in this type of instrument. Among the orders for musical clocks, musical beds and smaller musical secretaires manufactured by J.N. Mälzel, for instance, the reigning Prince of Liechtenstein is also mentioned. See *Vaterländische Blätter* (Österreich Kaiserstaat 1) Vienna, 1808, p. 113. Haydn's relationship with the Liechtenstein family was long and respectably intimate. His diary, for example, contains entries such as the one for 16 July 1777, in which he records: 'On Monday (a visit to the) porcelain factory . . . lunch at Prince Franz von Lichtenstein's (sic) . . .' (see H.C. Robbins Landon: *Haydn in England*, p. 406). Ten years later, on 10 June, he wrote to his publishers Artaria & Co. in Vienna from 'Estoras' (sic) saying: 'Most highly respected sir! I have revised and corrected the *Seven Words*, not only for full band but also for quartet and piano score; but I cannot send it today with the Hussars because the parcel is too large, and so I shall send you everything, together with the fourth and fifth quartet (opus 50) on Sunday at the latest, with the widowed Princess von Liechtenstein . . .' This was Leopoldine, Princess von Liechtenstein (née Countess Sternfield), the mother of Princess Maria Hermenegild (Robbins Landon, *Haydn at Eszterháza.*, p. 694). Twelve years later, when the subscription list for *The Creation* was being formed, the names appear of the Princess Liechtenstein and 'Liechtenstein Fürst Louis'.

[23] See note 9 above.

[24] The Princess was born in 1768 and died in 1845. In 1783, she was married to Prince Nicolaus who acceded to the throne in 1794. From Haydn came musical tributes in the form of two masses for her name-day. Her picture is reproduced in Alfred Schnerich: *Joseph Haydn*, 2nd edition, 1926, p. 140.

financed under the jurisdiction of the Prince Esterházy and thus it is more likely that, had it been given by anybody, it would have been the Prince who made the presentation or instigated its gift.

The third and last of these three organs has also lost its case and with it its controlling timepiece — that is assuming, for the reasons already given, that it did originally have one. This organ has a height of 30cm, a width of 74cm, and a depth of 36cm, and is the largest of the preserved ones both in dimensions and tonal range.[25]

It would appear that in 1790, when Prince Anton Esterházy dissolved his orchestra,[26] Haydn presented the twelve pieces of music to his pupil Niemecz with the instruction that he was to pin these on to the barrel of the organ. If this is so, then Niemecz must have worked on this organ for three years since it is dated 1793 in which case the construction of this one must have been undertaken concurrently with that of 1792. Upon its completion he dedicated it, by the inscription, to Prince Anton Esterházy whose successor, Nicolaus II, came to the throne in 1794.

The successor to Nicolaus II was the second Paul Anton Esterházy and he became the Austrian ambassador in London until 1842 following the sequestration of the Esterházy estates. Paul Anton, as was his father before him, was a great art collector and through this interest, he came to know a London architect and fellow art collector by the name of Peter Hubert Desvignes. As a result of this, when some alterations were required to the royal palaces, Prince Paul summoned Desvignes to Hungary. While he was in Central Europe, Desvignes also worked on the palace of the princes of Liechtenstein in Vienna and enjoyed a close relationship with both Esterházys and Liechtensteins as a result of which he was able to exchange paintings within his and the palaces' collections. At the completion of his work on the buildings in 1840, he returned to London where he lived in Hither Green, Lewisham. Among the mementos given to him when he finished his contract was a painting by Velasquez. Prince Anton also gave him the mechanical organ which suggests either that the prince did not value it very highly or that he held the London architect in exceptional esteem. Desvignes may well have seen and admired the organ and been particularly enthusiastic over it. Both men loved paintings and works of art, but Desvignes more than likely appreciated music more than his benefactor. Besides these gifts, Desvignes was given a plaque containing a letter of thanks from the prince.

After the death of Peter Desvignes, the organ passed into the care of his son, P.H. Desvignes, Jr. When this son died, the instrument was passed on to his sister, P.S. An der Lan von

[25] Early illustrations of this instrument appeared in Ernst Fritz Schmid: *Joseph Haydn und die Mechanische Musik* (Goethe-Haydn-Almanach, *Deutscher Sängerkalender*, Vienna, 1932, p. 61, *et seq.*, and p. 48); and by the same author: *Joseph Haydn und die Orden der Barmherzigen Bruder* in the work 'Die Barmherzigen Bruder . . .', Vienna, 1931, p. 195, *et seq.*

[26] See H.C. Robbins Landon: *Haydn at Eszterháza*, p. 748.

Hochbrunn, née Desvignes. Baron Otto An der Lan von Hochbrunn, the son-in-law of Peter Desvignes, lived in Meran and he lost no time in having the Haydn/Niemecz organ transported there. Shortly after this, the Heyer Museum in Cologne tried to purchase the organ but for various reasons (see note in Biography), the transaction did not take place and, after many an odyssey it ended up in the care of the daughter of Baron An der Lan von Hochbrunn, Frau Baron von Veyder-Malberg in whose family it remains to this day. The instrument rests in the Stadtmuseum in München where it is on indefinite loan.

Plate 40. Detail view of the tune-changing system on the first organ. One revolution of the music barrel results in a single tooth on its axis indexing the 16-step cam through one position via the 16-point star-wheel. It is this cam which is responsible for aligning the barrel pins so that successive tunes on the barrel may be played.

Plate 41. Unlike the tune-change mechanism of the first organ, above, the 1793 instrument changes its tunes manually from a mechanism which is at the other end of the barrel and which indicates with a dial and pointer which melody is being performed. This view also shows well the termination of the barrel cage, the four sturdy brass square-sectioned bars being secured to the end plate by octagonal nuts — an early use of this form of nut and a refinement in detail over the square ones used in the same position on the first organ.

CHAPTER 4

The Music Played

It is important to remember that at the time Schnerich and Schmid made their analyses of the music on these three instruments, neither had any reason to doubt that the date of the first instrument was anything other than 1772. Indeed, Schmid used this date quite extensively in his examination of the music and, because he did not question this for one moment, he was drawn into making a number of false assumptions and conclusions. And this was in the face of a number of arguments that pointed to the unavoidable probability that 1772 was far too early to make much sense. When Ernst Simon looked at the music twenty-eight years later, he expressed some nagging doubt about this, but went on to repeat Schmid's work.

When, in the Haydn jubilee year of 1959, Schmid came to commenting on his latest finds regarding the music (described further on), he cast some doubts himself on the authenticity of the date of the 1772 organ, but still harboured the belief that perhaps the music existed earlier than its written-down form. His findings, published posthumously in Volume 2 of *Haydn-Studien*, December 1970, concluded with a hope that further researches would succeed in solving the problem. However, although we must now re-date this first surviving organ (see the next chapter), the analysis of the music which Schmid made, but not all his deductions, generally holds good for us today.

The three mechanical organs together play a total of forty melodies by Haydn, ten of which are duplicated (see the conspectus of page 107). The organ of 1792 plays four[1] and that of 1793 six of the pieces which already appear on the barrel of the first, the '1772' organ.

These pieces have been published by Nagel of Hannover in an edition originally prepared by Ernst Fritz Schmid as an arrangement for two hands for piano. Although strictly speaking the pieces are presented in the wrong order, Schmid's scheme of numbering them (starting with the twelve on the 1792[2] organ, following with the six non-duplicated pieces from the '1772' organ[3] and then concluding with the twelve tunes on the 1793 organ,[4] all presented in the sequence as pinned on the barrels of

[1] Not three as was originally supposed in Schnerich's book, *Joseph Haydn*, 2nd edition.

[2] This is the second of the three known instruments.

[3] This is the first of the three known instruments but it actually dates from 1789 as explained further on.

[4] This is the third of the three known instruments.

the individual organs) is retained. This differs from the numbering system adopted by Anthony van Hoboken when he catalogued the pieces but it is justified as it happens to be the accepted form of numbering in the published edition by Nagel. Schmid, as we shall see, located the manuscripts for two more pieces which so far have not been found on any mechanical organ although there is no doubt that they were definitely written for this medium and there exists a mechanical organ scale to suit them. These two pieces Schmid added to the thirty known ones as numbers 31 and 32.[5] Hoboken lists the entire group in the catalogue as XIX: 32.

In addition to these three mechanical organs, there exists a collection of manuscripts for pieces of music for *Flötenuhr*. Fortunately, all this material survived the Second World War. First there is an extensive autograph which is in the possession of the Preussischen Staatsbibliothek in Berlin. This was formerly in the care of the Westdeutschen Bibliothek in Marburg. Originally this manuscript, which comprises eight sheets with thirteen sides covered with notation, was in the possession of Haydn's publishers in Vienna, Artaria. This publishing business had the foresight to preserve many original manuscripts from contemporary composers, Haydn being one of them. There is a note on this manuscript reading: 'Vienna, 16th October 1838' and dedicating the manuscript as a present from August Artaria to the privy councillor of Falkenstein in Dresden.

However, in the catalogue of the musical autographs held by Artaria in 1893 (which is entitled 'Verzeichnis von Musikalischen Autographen . . . im Besitze von August Artaria in Wien, 1893'[6]), this manuscript was still listed as in the collection which could imply that it was never presented. Schmid makes the somewhat unlikely suggestion that perhaps it was presented but that it was then given back.

The manuscript[7] is written in a clear, bold hand and contains the pieces Schmid catalogued as numbers 2, 3, 30, 27, 1, 32, 29 and 11 plus a page of crossed-out sketches.[8]

Additionally, two pieces for mechanical organ were found in the archives of the Gesellschaft der Musikfreunde in Vienna.[9] One of these autographs comprises just number 19 and bears the title written by August Artaria: 'Eigenhändige Handschrift von Joseph Haydn. Herrn Alfred Edl. von Frank von August Artaria'. The music is bound up with an engraving of Haydn and a printed title-page ('Handschrift des Joseph Haydn') in a binding with gilt embossed covers. This was also originally in the possession of the house of Artaria as the inscription tells us. From there it passed into the hands of a man named von Frank and finally it appeared

[5] This unknown pair of tunes are arranged for a mechanical organ of thirty-two notes the scale of which is shown in Fig. 8e.

[6] *Nr. 42. Mehrere Stücke für eine Spieluhr. Autograph. 8 B11* (Several pieces for a musical clock).

[7] Indicated throughout the following as the Berlin Collection (of manuscripts).

[8] The sketches comprise studies for a minuet with variations which was obviously intended originally for two violins and bass (cello). It is shown on two treble and one bass clef and is obviously nothing to do with music for a mechanical organ.

[9] Indicated throughout the following as the Vienna Collection (of manuscripts).

in the catalogue of a Berlin manuscript dealer, Paul Gottschalk, in November 1909.[10] Here it was described together with a facsimile of the end of the piece of music and also Haydn's signature.

According to a note on the flyleaf of this manuscript, it was purchased from Gottschalk by Helene von Schmitt of Aicha in Bohemia, and she then presented it to the archives of the Gesellschaft der Musikfreunde. Pasted into this volume is another autograph which shows number 28.[11] This takes up the inside pages of a single folded music folio on the first face of which is once again to be found the methodical written certificate of authenticity provided by August Artaria. This reads: 'Autographe de Jos. Haydn. — Nous en constatons l'authenticité. — Vienne, ce 11 Mai 1839. Artaria & Co.'

The Gesellschaft der Musikfreunde has another manuscript in Haydn's own hand. This is part of the bequest of C.F. Pohl and it shows a number of scales for mechanical organ. These scales are reproduced her as Fig. 8.

[10] Nr. 61. Haydn, Joseph. Manuscr. a. s. O. O. u. D. 2 S. Quer-Folio. Hübscher Leinwandband der Zeit. Verkauft. Kostbarkeit ersten Ranges. Ungedruckte ganz vollständige Composition Haydns für Spieluhr (Flötenuhr) . . . (Manuscript . . . attractive linen binding of the period. Extremely precious . . . Unprinted complete composition by Haydn for the mechanical organ). There is also a note in the catalogue which says that some twenty-four pieces by Haydn are to be found in the possession of the Preussischen Staatsbibliothek in Berlin but it was established by Schmid (Joseph Haydn und die Flötenuhr, p. 205) that this was an error.

[11] This second autograph comes from an album of works collected by Prince Wimpfen (volume 1, page 8). This album was started by Fraulein von Eskeles, a girl-friend of Beethoven who subsequently married the prince.

Fig. 8.

In addition to these autographs, contemporary copies of three sets of Flötenuhr music are also preserved in the Gesellschaft der Musikfreunde. These, too, originated from the Pohl bequest.[12] The first part comprises six pages and contains the music for numbers 24, 1, 12, 32 and 25. The watermark on the paper —

[12] The reference for these is VII 41 093 and in the following text this is referred to as the Contemporary Copies Collection (of manuscripts).

three half moons — is the same as that found on the autograph of number 19. The watermark on the paper upon which number 25 has been written differs, though. The title which precedes number 24 reads: 'Acht Laufwerck Sonaten Komponiert von Herrn Kapellmeister Joseph Haydn, und in die Walze gesetzt von Primitiv Niemecz Bibliothekar zu Esterhas 1789 in December'. It seems the eight sonatas promised in the title are not all present.

The second part also has the watermark of the three half moons. This comprises six pages with the pieces numbered 26, 28, 27, 30 and 29. The title of number 26, penned in a beautiful ornate italic script, reads: 'Laufwerck Sonaten componirt von Herrn Capellmeister Joseph Haydn; in die Waltze gesteckt von Primitiv Niemetz, Bibliothecar bei St Durchlaucht des regierended Herrn Fürsten Anton Esterhazy'. This part of the manuscript copy must have originated between 1790 and 1794 as 'Fürst Anton' only reigned between these years.

The third part comprises just four pages of manuscript and contains the pieces numbered 19, 20, 21, 22, 23 and 31. This collection bears no specific title.

Even though parts of the first set are very much faded, there is no doubt that all three of these collected manuscripts are in the same copyist's hand. Schmid concluded that the most likely copyist was none other than Niemecz himself, but since there is no certified example of Niemecz's handwriting available for comparison, this cannot be substantiated.[13] What is definite, however, is that this copyist had access to the same source of manuscript paper as Haydn himself.[14] Whilst Haydn's regular copyist would scarcely have needed to make these replicas, copies would certainly have been of use to Niemecz.

One other manuscript source should be mentioned. In 1958, Schmid was examining the music archives of the former Archbishop of Olmütz at the castle of Kromeriz (Kremsier) when he came across a score in Haydn's name which proved to be an expanded version of the piece numbered nine and which he had copied down from the 1792 organ 26 years earlier. The manuscript for number 24 was found in the Neuhaus castle, Jindřichův Hradec in Southern Bohemia.

From the foregoing it becomes apparent that some of the music does not exist in original manuscript or even in copy. The pieces numbered 4, 5, 6, 7, 8, 10 and 13, 14, 15, 16, 17 and 18 do not appear in any of these collections but only survive on the barrels of the organs. The first question to be asked here is whether one can be certain that this music is indeed by Haydn. Of these pieces, it is possible to trace the derivations of the following pieces — 4, 5, 6, 13, 15, 16 and 18. Number 10 was originally thought to be based

[13] The inscription upon the barrels of organs numbers two and three are the only certain examples of Niemecz's hand but these are not musical notation.

[14] Haydn used manuscript paper from a number of sources with several watermarks. One test not as yet carried out is a check on the watermark on the paper covering the circumference of the organ barrels (p. 51).

on a theme by Dittersdorf and the derivations of the others are unknown. Admittedly one of the pieces — number 16 — is overtly based on a work by another composer (in this case Wranitsky), but it appears unlikely that the Haydn/Niemecz/ Esterházy relationship would create instruments with music other than by the kapellmeister himself. Additionally, what we know of Haydn suggests that he was an extremely fair and honest man and it is not likely that he would assume the works of another composer. I therefore believe there can be no question that all the music upon the three instruments is from the pen of Haydn. Stylistically, it is impossible to gainsay its authorship (see page 120).

The non-existence of manuscript notation for these pieces has, however, necessitated the writing-down of the music from the barrel pinning.[15] The thought of transcribing music from the positions of the pins and bridges of wire on the surface of the barrel may at first appear both a superhuman task as well as one of dubious accuracy. Nothing could be further from the truth for the process is nothing more than the reverse of the original method of barrel notation which takes a musical score in familiar staff layout and translates it into the mechanical means for operating the organ in the correct note sequence and note duration.[16] In this process, the position of each barrel pin is carefully plotted and translated back into staff notation (from which it undoubtedly originated). This method is by far the most reliable method of transcribing the music for it is possible to recreate without any error not just the proper musical notes, but the precise articulation of the organ which, by the nature of its special capabilities, may differ slightly from the original staff notation for the music. Mordents, trills and other embellishments were seldom written out in full and only appear in detail in the mechanical version.[17] The alternative method, of course, is to listen to the music very carefully and copy it down by ear. For some music, this is perfectly adequate and while such a practice is solely the province of the musically-minded person (the other can even be followed by the non-musical technician!), there are many who would prefer it. The pieces of music listed here for which no manuscript has yet been traced have been copied down, some by ear and some by what one might term 'caliper'.[18]

In evaluating this music, the pieces which offer us probably the greatest opportunity to learn from are those for which Haydn's original manuscript (or contemporary copy) survives. Furthermore, those pieces for which Haydn has given several versions from which to select give us an insight into the composer's methods of working and illustrate his appreciation of

[15] This task was undertaken by Schmid with the assistance of Frau Paula Teubner-Reghem and the clockmaker Richard de Ponti in Vienna.

[16] The most comprehensive document-ation extant on arranging music for organ barrel is contained in Dom Bedos, *L'Art du Facteur d'Orgues* published in 1778. It provides exhaustive instruct-ions and copious practical illustrations, some salient ones being reproduced in this present volume. It is thought likely that Niemecz used this book in his experiments in organ-building.

[17] Again this information is to be found in Dom Bedos *(vide supra)* where the musical examples are shown first in normal, unembroidered staff notation, then in written-out embellishment, and finally drawn as an arrangement of brass pins and staples on the barrel surface.

[18] The source of the pieces of music is as follows:
No. 1 Berlin Collection; No. 2
No. 2 Berlin Collection; No. 1; No. 2
No. 3 Berlin Collection; No. 2
No. 4 No. 2
No. 5 No. 2
No. 6 No. 1; No. 2
No. 7 No. 2
No. 8 No. 1; No. 2
No. 9 Kremsier castle MS; No. 2.
No. 10 No. 2
No. 11 Berlin Collection; No. 1; No. 2
No. 12 Contemporary Copies Collection; No. 2
No. 13 No. 1

the mechanical organ and its specific limitations and musical benefits. The limitations one can describe as the restricted range of notes available, and the benefits or advantages of the ability to employ the use of more notes at once (which, thankfully, he did not take advantage of unlike Stravinsky 130 years later with some of his piano rolls) to make greater tonal 'leaps' than the human performer can make with precision, and to contrive embellishment with rapidity and dexterity which would tax the manual performer.

As an example, look at the very first piece — number 1. The autograph (Artaria) is the first attempt at writing this piece it would seem, and gives every appearance of having been written down in a great haste. The later corrections and variations, however, demonstrate a clear and more painstaking writing. Bars 10 and 11, for instance, were first written in a simple form as shown in Fig. 9.

This gives the manuscript sources, where extant, as well as the number of the organ which plays the pieces.

Fig. 9.

However, this was crossed out and replaced by a richer version of the same shape of phrase — Fig. 10.

Fig. 10.

In bar 23 and onwards, a quite different conclusion is presented which reverts to the original form by bar 27 (I have doubts that this was actually written by Haydn: see caption to Plate 45 on page 83). Figure 11 refers.

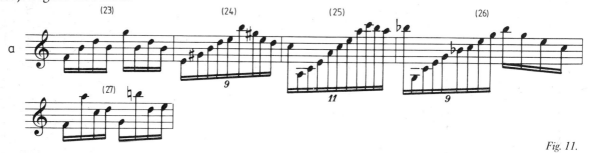

Fig. 11.

instead of

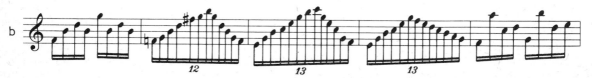

The same applies to the bars following number 27 where he also added a series of variations as shown in Fig. 12.

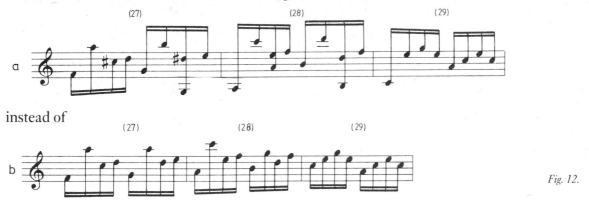

instead of

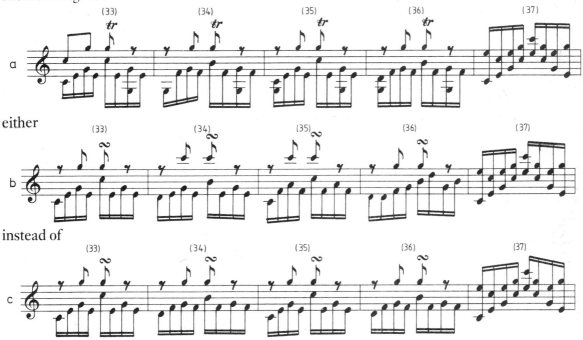

Fig. 12.

For bars 33 onwards, two alternative variations are offered as shown in Fig. 13.

either

instead of

Fig. 13.

The examples shown as Figs. 11a, 12a and 13a have clearly been written to suit a larger instrument possessing a wider tonal range than that of the 1792 organ for which these were impractical since they included notes which were beyond both the upper and lower limits of the seventeen-note organ. These versions appear in the manuscript Contemporary Copies Collection. They are, however, suitable for both the '1772' and 1793 instruments. The notes g, a, g sharp', b', c sharp', d sharp', g

sharp", b" and d" were not available on the 1792 instrument and so the variations shown in Figs. 11b, 12b and 13c were created.

As these examples show, the extended scale of the other instruments permitted Haydn to use both fundamental movements in the bass accompaniments as well as allowing the music to modulate in F major and E major (A minor). This was a facility which had not been possible earlier and one can imagine that Haydn turned to his illustrious organ-builder priest and asked him to extend the scale of his organs so that the music might be more venturesome. In connection with this, there is also a passage near the end of tune number 30 as published for which Haydn presented no fewer than three different variations besides the one shown in the printed edition. Here Haydn obviously left the final decision as to which version to use on the organ barrel to the arranger responsible for noting the barrel — in this case Niemecz. This piece, presented on the 1793 organ, uses the original version as presented in Contemporary Copies Collection and shown in Fig. 14.

Plate 42. The Berlin Collection manuscript for piece number 2 *Andante,* and number 3 *Presto.* In the second piece it will be seen that the first eight bars are indicated as being repeated, although the 1792 mechanical organ did not have this repetition. Observe also the Da Capo ending to this. Of particular interest here are the calculations towards the end of this second piece which shows clearly provisional estimates for the spacing of the barrel pins — the space to be allotted to each measure of music. Here Niemecz has established a value of 9×38, allowing him 384 turns (possibly of one of the clockwork's wheels) and providing a space of 42 at the end for tune changing.

Fig. 14.

There are numerous other examples in the manuscripts which indicate a very close relationship — perhaps even an exchange of ideas — between Haydn and Father Niemecz. One can almost imagine Niemecz extolling the potential of the mechanical organ to his master and suggesting more and more imaginative uses.

Haydn has maintained careful note of the exact numbers of bars possible in order to make the best use of the scope of the barrel with its finite time of revolution. Frequently he also provides suggestions as to small abridgements which we can match more or less precisely to the way in which the barrel is pinned. Examples of this can be found in piece number 27 bars 21–24, piece number 28 bars 34–41, piece number 29 bar 16 and bars 26–27, 42–55, 68 and 78–79. Of particular interest within the Berlin autographs are the inclusion of additional notes and calculations in numbers which most certainly refer to the mechanics of setting the music on the barrel and are thus almost definitely in the hand of Niemecz. There are similar figure calculations to be found in some of the other manuscripts, namely in Contemporary Copies Collection and particularly that at the end of piece number 25 (on the 1793 mechanical organ) where there is a remark written at the end which reads: 'Den zweiten Theil repetiret das Werk nicht wegen der Länge' (The work does not repeat the second part because of its length). At the end, the writer of this note lists the tonal ranges or scales of the instruments for which the music was intended. After the first tune, we find the scale of a mechanical organ with twenty-three pipes (Fig. 8b). After number 23 there is written out the scale of the preserved instrument of 1793 with twenty-nine notes (Fig. 8d).

There is in addition a mechanical organ scale written in Haydn's own hand (in the Vienna Collection) to which he comments: 'Mit 32 Tön. Der Haupt Ton dieser Scala ist F. es können aber auch zur abwechslung Stücke aus C, G, und D minor gemacht werden' (With 32 notes. The tonic note of this scale is F but for variation also pieces written in the keys of C, G and D minor could be used). This scale appears as Fig. 8e. It is a source of unfailing astonishment that Haydn managed to get the very most out of the often very small and drastically abbreviated sequences of notes available to him on these instruments. This is

Plate 43. This is the first of two folios which together form the original manuscript of piece number 24 *Fuga* which was discovered in the archives of the Schloss Neuhaus in Southern Bohemia in October 1958. This is discussed on page 120. Haydn's signature at the end (see Plate 44 facing page) with his characteristic 'laus Deo' and style of writing the year 1789 along with hook-like quavers prove that although at first sight the appearance of the writing is different from other authenticated examples of Haydn's manuscripts, the calligraphic variations are due purely to the type of pen used.

demonstrated most clearly by the mechanical organ of 1792 (Fig. 8a) whose fine repertoire of music (pieces numbered 1 to 12 inclusive) is among the most artistic and elaborate he ever created — an achievement heightened due to the taxing task confronting him due to the limited tonal resources.

As for the tuning of the instruments, it should be pointed out that at today's pitch, the instruments all sound approximately E flat. However, Haydn noted on his autographs that pieces numbered 1, 2, 3 and 11 were in the key of C. Schmid comes up with the rather improbable explanation that the pitch has changed over the years through the practice of the wooden stoppers of the pipes which are used for tuning having been driven in too far, so raising the pitches of all the pipes. He fails to note that on the treble pipes only a minute adjustment of the stopper would raise the pitch of the sound appreciably while for the lower pipes, the stoppers must be moved a considerable amount for but a small change in pitch. The organs examined show no sign of such mistreatment and it is unlikely that there would have been any need for their pitch to be changed since they are purely solo instruments and would not have to be in tune with any

Plate 44. The second folio of *Fuga* in the hand of Haydn. The clear instruction to Niemecz says: 'Whenever the theme appears, the following half mordent must be placed on each minim, e.g. on the first note'. He writes this out in full and it appears sixteen times in the work. Of great interest are the two variations penned in the blank staves Haydn left, one marked (1" above his signature, and the other marked '(2" at the bottom. These, apparently in the hand of Niemecz, represent reworks of the portions indicated in the first folio (Plate 43) by the marks '(1" and '(2", yet the Haydn original text was pinned on the 1793 instrument.

accompanying instrument. What is more certain is that pitch has changed over the years. The current pitch of A is 440 cycles per second, the pitch in common use in Central Europe during the first half of this century was around 435 cps, Mozart's pitch was 422 cps, yet in Vienna in 1859, A was 456 cps. The interesting one here is the Mozart pitch because this is said to have been established from an authentic copy of a tuning fork that belonged to Stein, the clavichord maker of Vienna, and to which Mozart's pianoforte was tuned.[19] If the pipework of Niemecz's organs was Viennese in origin, then it may well have been made to correspond to current Viennese pitch although this would not have been essential. I believe that the tuning of the organs has remained largely untouched over the years and it is probably a safe assumption that the original tuning corresponded to what was then called C major. The printed edition of the music corresponds to this as well.

A number of these thirty-two pieces of music deserve individual comment. Number 6, for instance, has the nickname *Wachtelschlag* which literally means the Song of the Quail. The cognomen was coined for the tune by the Fux-Gassmann family. At the time this piece was written, the quail (and its larger-songed variant, the cuckoo) was a popular subject of literature and music. It was, for example, the inspiration behind Beethoven's song *Der Wachtelschlag* dating from about 1799, as well as featuring in his 'Pastoral' symphony, finished in about 1807. Additionally, it is found as a frequent motif in other works by Mozart as well as Haydn.[20]

Number 8 of the pieces is a particularly elegant little minuet which, we are told, was apparently the favourite tune of Anna Maria Fux-Gassmann (according to the recollection of the family). And in number 10 we find a concluding sequence which comprises a rhythm which seems to have been a favourite of Haydn's and which is vaguely reminiscent of the shape of the main theme of the finale of his Symphony No. 88 (which dates from about 1786), although the melodic line is somewhat different.

Number 9 is a portion of a series of variations for keyboard, the manuscript for which did not materialise until 1958. In contemporary copy form, this Viennese copy is under the name of Haydn. An extensive piece, it begins as an andante in C major with a somewhat elementary theme and accompaniment. This is followed by four simple technical variations, also in C major. A development passage with the title 'Minore' follows. This does not follow the established form and uses more involved harmonies and modulations. The second part of the Minore is in

[19] See *Grove's Dictionary of Music & Musicians*, 5th edition, vol. 6, p. 793, footnote.

[20] See also the minuet in Haydn's A flat major piano sonata (Complete Edition, No. 43).

Plate 45. Perhaps the most revealing manuscript is this, the piece number 1. Note the extensive revisions at the bottom although, contrary to what others have said, I have reservations that the last line is in Haydn's own hand: note the careful shape of the crochets: Haydn's were usually hook-shaped. The hand is altogether neater. At the end it says 'etc' for etcetera whereas Haydn usually used the German abbreviation 'u.s.w.', the convention for *und so weiter*. Notice the extensive marginal calculations by Niemecz in connection with the divisions of the barrel. The similarity of the figures '3' make me consider that the variations are in Niemecz's hand — but why 'etc' instead of 'u.s.w.'? The Latin form might have appealed more to the priest than the composer.

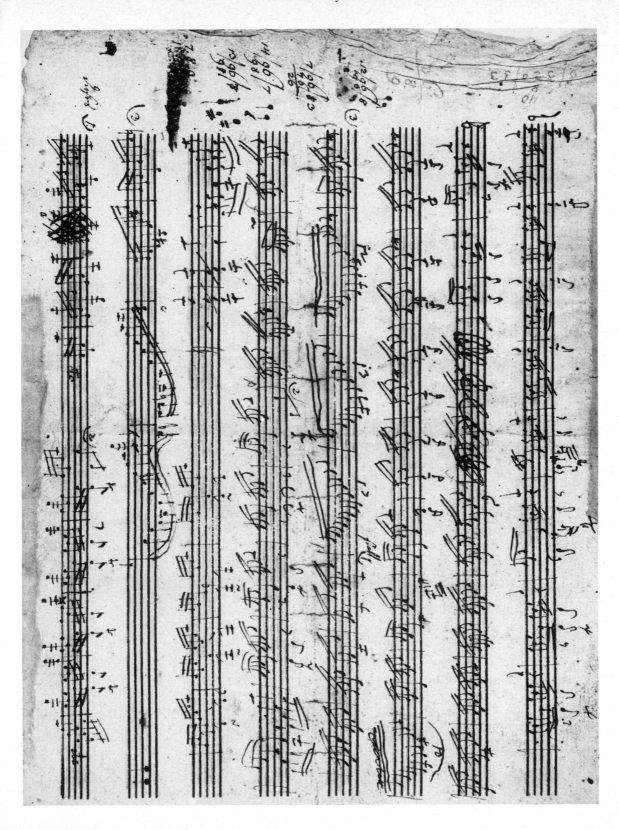

the key of C minor and develops into arpeggios which modulate after the style of C.P.E. Bach into a variation in A major. After an imaginative development, this reverts to three ornamented variations in the original tonality, the last of which employs 'crossed hands' playing. This is followed by an Adagio, also in C major and reminiscent of a theme in Mozart's *Don Giovanni*. An allegro variation once more in C major again dissolves into a rich harmonic modulation and development before entering a simple Allegretto which repeats the main theme with a somewhat more vivid accompaniment leading to a closing coda.

This final form proves to be virtually identical to the music on the 1792 *Flötenuhr* (Fig. 15).

Allegretto of Kremsier M.S.; closing bars

Mechanical Organ 1792 : opening bars as transcribed from barrel

Fig. 15.

The coincidence of the theme with the mechanical organ is unquestionable yet on the other hand, the structure of the whole piece is quite at variance with the style we come to associate with Haydn. This piece is, by comparison, somewhat elementary and lacks inventiveness, excelling only in its demands towards virtuosity in performance. One is inclined to suggest that this might have been a series of variations on a simple yet much-loved theme of personal meaning to Haydn or even to Niemecz, if not Prince Nicolaus Esterházy himself. In this connection, Haydn would not be acting out of character; he was later to arrange very many simple English and Scottish songs — and Mozart composed a series of variations on a popular Tyrolean melody (see Biography).

Number 11, which is to be found on the organ dated '1772', reads as a preliminary study for the minuet of the second Tost string quartet Opus 54 No. 2 which dates from about 1789.[21]

[21] Johann Tost was a violinist in the Eszterháza orchestra under Haydn. He appears to have been a somewhat unusual if talented man for whom Haydn had great admiration, hence his dedication to him of two of his finest sets of string quartets — the Opus. 54/55 and 64. However, Tost conceived the notion that he could make pirate copies of all the manuscripts belonging to Prince Nicolaus Esterházy and sell them outside the royal circle. After leaving the orchestra (was he sacked? Records do not say), he became involved in running a cloth-making factory and finally married Prince Esterházy's house-keeper.

This date, 1789, is a very significant one as will be apparent later on when we come to attributing a realistic date to the '1772' instrument. The opening two bars are very similar. In the surviving manuscript for this mechanical organ piece (Berlin Collection), this originally bore the marking *Tempo di Menuet* but later on Haydn changed this to *Menuet* and added a tempo indication with the word *Allegretto*. He retained this description *Menuet Allegretto* in the minuet of the quartet which is also in the key of C major. The first half of the thematic development agrees in both pieces although the modulation of the second half in the quartet follows an entirely different course (Fig. 16).

Fig. 16.

The second part is completely different as is the variation on the theme in bar seventeen of the mechanical organ piece which is not to be found in the quartet.

Number 14 is worthy of our attention because it is a very beautiful F minor melody in the Hungarian style for which Haydn had a predilection and which is so eminently suited to the small mechanical organ.

The main theme in number 15 reminds one strongly of the structure of the *andante* of Symphony No. 53 in D minor 'The Imperial' which was written around 1777–9 with a revised version c.1781–2. While the opening bars are familiar and although the whole approach to the piece is similar, it is but a superficial similarity from thence on, the musical theme and development being quite different.

Once again one turns to the obviously extensive recollections of the Fux-Gassmann family for a title to number 16. They knew this piece as *Die Dudelsack* ('The Bagpipe') yet it is in no way like the familiar drone instrument of the reed family which its name suggests. It does, though, offer us something of a musical surprise for we find that it comprises the well-known melody which Beethoven used as the central theme of his twelve A major piano variations. These date from 1796–7 and the first published edition of April 1797[22] carries the title: 'XII Variations pour le Clavecin ou Piano-Forte sur la danse Russe dansée par Mlle. Cassentini dans le Ballet: das Waldmädchen Composées et dédiées a Madame La Comtesse de Browne née de Vietinghoff par Louis van Beethoven . . . A Vienne chez Artaria et Comp . . .' (12 variations for the harpsichord or piano-forte on the Russian dance as danced by Miss Cassentini in the ballet *The Forest Maiden* composed and dedicated to my lady the Countess Browne, born de Vietinghoff, by Louis van Beethoven). The ballet mentioned here was first performed in Vienna on 23 September 1796 and originated mainly from Paul Wranitsky. Although some of the pieces were by Joseph Kinsky,[23] the majority were by Wranitzky to whom authorship of the entire music was credited. However, the so-called Russian Dance in this work is the only piece which originated from neither Wranitzky nor Kinsky. This was actually written by the virtuoso violinist Giovanni Mane Giornovichi, known also by the non-Italian version Jarnowick or, as Haydn wrote it in his often imprecise spelling, 'Jarnowich'.[24]

Schmid, still assuming that the first organ was no later than the date given by the Fux-Gassmann family of 1772, suggested that about that year Haydn probably heard the Russian original which he considered may have been a folk tune and that upon hearing Giornovichi, who liked to finish his recitals with variations on a Russian theme, adapted it into the mechanical organ piece which we find today. Schmid is even able to produce evidence to support his claim.[25] In the 1770s Giornovichi had been 'konzertmeister' for the Prince Rohan-Guémené who was the French envoy in Vienna from 1772 to 1774[26] and was during this time a frequent guest of Prince Esterházy in Eisenstadt and at Eszterháza. On the occasion of great festivities or parties given in his honour by the Prince, he and his concert leader would have had the opportunity to meet Haydn.[27] It is worth repeating here that Primitivus Niemecz did not enter the employment of Esterházy until 1780. Twenty-five years later, Giornovichi himself used the piece of music in a revised form as an intermezzo to Wranitzky's ballet. The *Moskowitische Tanz* is one of the most popular pieces of this work. As for Beethoven he for his part used it as a theme for his variations and there is just the chance that his use of it was an unconscious gesture towards his teacher, Haydn. Beethoven was in Vienna in the year 1795 by which time Haydn was in residence in a flat overlooking the Stadtpark.

[22] First listed in G. Nottebohm, *Thematisches Verzeichnis der im Druck erschienenen Werke von Ludwig van Beethoven* (Leipzig, 1864, 2nd. edition 1913 and 1925), p. 156. The opus number is believed to be 182 and Artaria published these variations in April, 1797.

[23] Paul Wranitzky (see Biography) was a violinist in Haydn's orchestra until 1785 and was a very close friend of his. His brother Anton (1761–1820) was one of Haydn's pupils and it does not seem impossible that with such close involvement both Wranitzky brothers may have suggested the melody to Haydn.

[24] *Das Waldmädchen, Ein pantomimisches National Ballet. In Musik gesetzt von Herrn Paul Wranitzky und Joseph Kinsky. In Wien bey Tranquillo Mollo.* Herein on page 20 we find, *Russe par Jarnovich.* Giornovichi was born in Palermo in 1745 and died in Petersburg on 21 November 1804. He was the favourite student of Lolli and attained great popularity as a travelling violin virtuoso.

[25] See C.F. Pohl, *Joseph Haydn*, vol. II, p. 141.

[26] He describes himself in this way on the occasion of a small performance in Frankfurt a. M. given in 1779. See also Robert Eitner: *Biographisch-bibliographisches Quellen-Lexikon der Musiker und Musikgelehrten der christlichen Zeitrechnung bis zur Mitte des 19-Jahrhunderts* (better, and more thankfully known as the Quellen-Lexikon), see entry under 'Giornovichi'.

[27] The fact that Giornovichi performed in Haydn's London benefit concerts (see C.F. Pohl, *op. cit*, vol. II, p. 49 *et seq*.) illustrates the friendly relationship between the two men.

Plate 46. The original manuscript for piece number 30 to which has been added several later annotations, most probably by Niemecz.

It is interesting to note how the two composers treat the musical theme in such a different manner. The original — let's call it Giornovichi/Haydn — gently veils the structure of the opening five bars whereas in the Beethoven version it emerges as a much more overt tune, more alive and clear — see Fig. 17, the first bar and then bar 5.

Interestingly enough, the ties over the quavers in bars 3 and 8 are missing in the complete edition of the Beethoven variations and were also missing in the first edition.[28] Nevertheless, it emerges from the structure of the tenor theme in Variation 4 that this can only have been an oversight and that the ties indeed belong here.

Haydn for his part added a further twenty-two bars to the completed melody thereby expanding and decorating the tune in a quite delightful manner. This development — spinning-out, if

[28] *Beethoven-Gesamtausgabe*, vol. XVII, p. 101 (Breitkopf & Härtel, 1866–68).

you like — is again to be found in Giornovichi's 'Russian' tune (Fig. 18).

Fig. 17.

Giornovichi, however, decided to enlarge the tune somewhat extensively by the insertion of a forty-bar central section which is musically extremely unsatisfying and does nothing to develop the theme or to add worthwhile new material. The major difference to be detected between the version by Haydn and that of Giornovichi lies in the embellishment of the accompaniment which weaves with great skill and subtlety through the melody in Haydn's scoring. This serves to add considerably to the interest

Fig. 18.

and presentation of the main theme. Giornovichi appears to have been perfectly contented with a very elementary and childishly simple accompaniment comprising chords with the emphasis of a drum beat — a treatment which seems to have encouraged Beethoven to seek a revised accompaniment for the theme when he came to prepare his own variations.

According to the Fux–Gassmann family, number 18 carries the nickname *Kaffeeklatsch* (the 'Coffee Party') which seems rather appropriate in view of the jaunty little theme which appears in the second part.

The fugue in number 24 reveals a toccata-like quality of the prelude which is similar to that we have already seen in number 1 and shows again how Haydn had the facility to accentuate or emphasise an ancient style with great effect on the *Flötenuhr* whilst at the same time giving more than a passing hint of the more noble great organ from which the little mechanical organ derives. This piece of music appears on two instruments, the first and the third. Apart from that, the fugue has been written in such immaculate double counterpoint that the organ of 1793 can play several passages with a true interplay of two voices (see Fig. 19b).

Fig. 19.

The performance agrees with the version in the Contemporary Copies Collection and the original MS at Neuhaus.

Numbers 31 and 32 are the only pieces in this series for which only the manuscript scores survive, i.e. there do not appear to remain in existence the instruments for which these were originally intended. Manuscripts or copies exist in both the Berlin Collection and the Contemporary Copies Collection. It is absolutely certain that these two works were once pinned to the barrel of a mechanical organ and this is substantiated by the survival of the additional organ scales which remain (see Figs. 8b and 8e). These provide us with proof that the three surviving mechanical organs only represent part of the Haydn/Niemecz output.

Within this whole repertoire of music, a special group is formed which comprises those pieces of music which were taken by Haydn from his other works and arranged for the mechanical organ. These are the pieces numbered 4, 5, 25, 28, 29, 30 and 32 and while most are adaptations with varying degrees of freedom, they are each a special creation by Haydn himself and to that extent they genuinely represent fresh works.

Number 4 originally appeared as the song *Warnung an Mädchen* (Jeder meynt, der Gegenstand, den er sich erwählet) written for solo voice with keyboard accompaniment. In this form, the melody is in F major and is marked *andante*. It was first published in December of 1793.[29] The version for mechanical organ is largely unaltered with the exception of some ornamentation which is set out in Fig. 20.

Plate 47. The original manuscript for piece number 32.

[29] The first edition of this song was published as number 13 in the collection *XII Lieder für das Clavier Gewidmet Aus besonderer Hochachtung und Freundschaft der Freülen Francisca Liebe Edle v. Kreutznern von Joseph Haydn Fürst Esterhazischen Capell Meister. II ter Theil. Herausgegeben und zu haben bey Artaria Comp. in Wienn* (12 songs for the piano dedicated with the greatest respect and friendship to Miss Francisca Liebe Edle von Kreutznern from Joseph Haydn, conductor of Prince Esterházy. 2nd Part. Published and available from Artaria Company in Vienna). See Hugo Botstiber and Franz Artaria, *Jos. Haydn und das Verlaghaus Artaria*, Vienna, 1909.

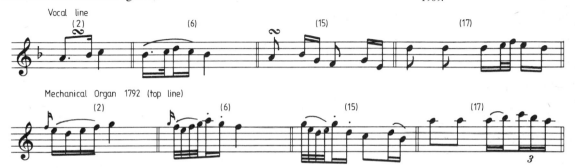

Fig. 20.

Number 5 is an arrangement of the *Trio des Menuetts* from the fourth of the six so-called 'Paris' symphonies — Symphony No.

85 'La Reine'[30] — which was composed in 1786. The theme differs somewhat in bars one and five and the version on the 1792 mechanical organ tends to concentrate the melody more on the triad. Aside from that, the exposition of the theme, which also returns in the reprise, is identical (Fig. 21).

[30] In Breitkopf & Härtel's complete edition is the first reference to this as the fourth 'Paris' Symphony.

Fig. 21.

Concerning this mechanical organ of 1792, the repetition of the first part which appears again in the reprise is in the form of a new variation which is very delicately worked out. The ornamented section comprises just two bars as follows (Fig. 22).

Fig. 22.

In each of these statements, Haydn manages successfully to inject new shades of meaning into the phrases. Reverting to the melodic line of the whole, the middle section of the piece differs almost entirely from that of the symphonic original. In the orchestral original, before the restatement there is a long organ point on the dominant upon which the concerted solo instruments are introduced so as to swell the music to the point where the full orchestra achieves the dominant septaccord.

In the 1792 mechanical organ, this same treatment is present. However, while it is compressed dramatically, somehow the effect is preserved successfully with the simplicity of but one voice. Of the full-score original, only the staccato crotchets remain and by the addition of several strong chords the dominant septaccord is finally and successfully reached (Fig. 23).

Fig. 23(a).

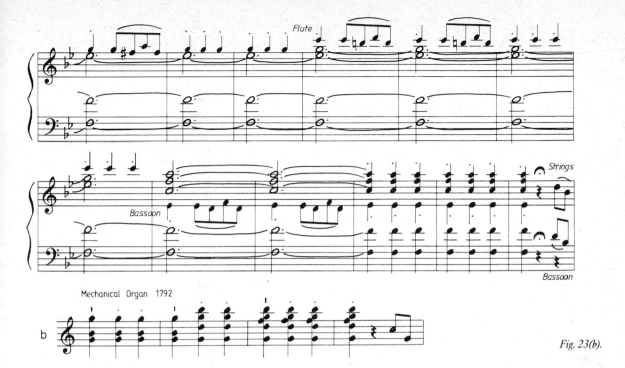

Fig. 23(b).

In the piece number 25, we make an interesting discovery for in the Contemporary Copies Collection manuscript, the piece is titled: 'Marche, von H. Kapellmeister Haydn'. Yet the same melody demonstrating only a few deviations and written in the key of F major, had been published in 1927 by Georg Kinsky as a 'musical clock' piece by Beethoven to which is added an interlude and a second march. The entire work was found on the seventh barrel of a mechanical organ formerly in the possession of the Heyer Museum in Cologne and now in Leipzig. This instrument was made in Vienna by the clockmaker Franz Egidius Arzt and the particular barrel bears the inscription: *Granadirs Marsch arranchirt von Herrn Ludwig v. Beethoven*. As Arzt died in 1812, the barrel most probably was made prior to that date although it could just as easily have been supplied to suit the instrument at a later date. Arzt was succeeded on his death by his son who was also a maker and vendor of musical clocks and at least three of the eight barrels were indeed manufactured after the death of the builder of the instrument (these are number 5, made in 1812; 6 made in 1818; and 8 which can be dated to 1819).[31]

While the second march on this organ barrel corresponds exactly with Beethoven's march in B flat major (written c. 1810 for two clarinets, two bassoons and two horns[32] the first march which, together with the second, is described as the *Grenadiermarsch* in F major by Beethoven, cannot have been the original work of Beethoven. This is established beyond all doubt

[31] Compare Georg Kinsky, 'Beethoven und die Flötenuhr' in the *Beethoven-Almanach der Deutschen Musikbücheri* for the year 1927 (Regensburg, 1927, p. 320 *et seq.*). The tune is published on page 330.

[32] Number 29 in the complete edition of Beethoven, Breitkopf & Härtel, vol. XXV.

by the examination of the Haydn scores and copies in the Contemporary Copies Collection and is further substantiated by the music on the 1793 mechanical organ. The Haydn original was written for two each of clarinets, horns and bassoons, and the autograph manuscript of this was formerly in the collection of Artaria in Vienna.[33] The note on the Beethoven organ barrel uses the word 'arranchirt' which appears to point to the fact that Beethoven produced an arrangement of his own march for the organ and then combined his own work with the one by his teacher, Haydn (which was written in the key of E flat major) through a suitable interlude (Fig. 24).

Here are the opening bars of the Beethoven published edition with the title *Grenadiermarsch*. Because this is a keyboard

[33] Compare Aloys Fuchs, *Handschriftlicher Thematischer Katalog* of Haydn's works in the possession of the Preussischen Staatsbibliothek in Berlin, p. 15, number 6.

Fig. 24(a).

transcription, there being no as-yet located manuscript of the Heyer/Leipzig organ barrel from the Arzt instrument, I compare this with the keyboard version prepared by Schmid from Haydn's number 25. This reveals clearly that we are indeed looking at the same piece of music with purely detail changes. Note also that in the Haydn score, even in the reworked music for two hands, the theme is crisper in realisation. The manuscript for this is in the Contemporary Copies Collection and the music appears on the barrel of the 1793 mechanical organ.

Haydn Mechanical Organ piece Nº 25 (1793 organ)

Fig. 24(b).

The title *Granadirs Marsch* on the barrel of the Arzt organ was no doubt inspired by the princely grenadiers in Eisenstadt and it seems likely that Haydn and perhaps his pupil Beethoven might have produced 'field music' for them. This would bear out the choice of instrumentation of the originals. The year 1792 is significant here for that was the date when Beethoven, just twenty-two years of age, first came to Haydn as a pupil.[34] The following year, Haydn took the younger man with him to Eisenstadt and here Beethoven would have had the chance to meet Niemecz and view the then-brand new 1793 organ.

Number 28 is a version of the finale of the string quartet Opus 71 No. 2 which was composed in London in 1793 and was dedicated to the Hungarian Count Apponyi.[35] The finale of that quartet is in D major and bears the marking *allegretto*, whereas the version on the 1793 mechanical organ is in C major and is marked *allegro*. Here Haydn replaces the dynamic effects in bars 10 and 11 by an ingenious increase in harmonic density (Fig. 25).

[34] Beethoven apparently attended a performance of the Mass in C major at Eisenstadt. It has been suggested by Schnerich (*op. cit.*, 2nd edition 1926, p. 149) that this Mass was written for the name-day of the Princess Maria Josepha Hermenegild Esterházy and this seems to have come from C.F. Pohl's attribution which he repeated in the first edition of *Grove's Dictionary*. The mass was composed at the request of an Austrian official for the Monastery of Mariazell.

[35] Haydn was particularly friendly with the Hungarian Chamberlain Anton Georg, Count von Apponyi from Pressburg and was an admirer of the Countess. However, he appears also to have enjoyed an infatuation with the Count's chambermaid, Nanette Peyer, to whom he ended one letter (see Robbins Landon, *Haydn at Eszterháza*, p. 679): 'Hoping to embrace you soon'. It was the Count who sponsored Haydn's admission to 'Zur wahren Eintracht' lodge when he became a Freemason.

Fig. 25.

In bars 16 onwards, the mechanical organ version achieves a thematic tension by the introduction of rests in the supporting voices which goes some way to making up for the absence of accents and *crescendi*, neither of which are possible in a 'non-enclosed' organ, i.e. one without a swell. The start of the *minore* very quickly demonstrates deviation from the quartet version. The conclusion, however, agrees with the former with a decrescendo and the *sempre piu piano* found in the quartet. This corresponds to the entry of *p* and *pp* in the mechanical organ score on the Vienna Collection manuscript.[36] While in the latter version

[36] This is the only instance in the entire mechanical organ manuscripts of Haydn where dynamic markings are shown. Indeed, such markings are beyond the ability of the Niemecz mechanical organs' single register to interpret. This form of expression was first achieved using automatically-selected unison stops to intensify the sound, and thence refined in later instruments by the combination of automatic register changing with different voices aided by swell shutters. This was one of the great advances possible with the orchestrion.

the tempo increasing *piu presto* starts right at the beginning of the *maggiore*, it occurs much later in the quartet finale, in fact in bar 75 where the marking is *allegro*. The repetition of the small fugue appears in the original as a variation whereas in the mechanical organ treatment it appears in unchanged arrangement. In bar 47 of the mechanical organ, the music shifts straight to the coda of the quartet finale (bar 107 forwards). The end of the piece again is quite different. Because the date of the composition is 1793 and the place London, it could be that the mechanical organ in fact represents the original or first approach to the piece, thus pre-dating the published work.

Number 29 is the minuet from the Symphony No. 101 in D major *Die Uhr* ('The Clock').[37] This was the ninth of the 'London' symphonies and was written in 1794. Once again this suggests that the mechanical organ version of 1793 was the first sketch of the work. The minuet of the symphony is in D major and bears the tempo indication *allegretto*. The main difference between the two versions concerns the ornamentation. In the symphonic version, this is entirely absent yet in the *Flötenuhr* it is highly developed. The theme itself is presented in a graceful form embellished with apoggiaturas and triplets.[38] The trills have been replaced in the symphony by *sforzandi*, a fine demonstration of the realisation of the same goal by two different means (Fig. 26).

[37] The nickname 'The Clock' refers to the slow second movement rhythm which is similar to the ticking of a clock although there could just be a subtle suggestion of the beginnings of the piece as a Niemecz mechanical organ work.

[38] Haydn makes use of this type of embellishment with great relish. See, for example, the minuet of the String Quartet Opus 50 No. 5, where he specifically demands this, according to the interpretation of the autograph by the musicologist Heinrich Schenker, by placing a dot over the first note.

Fig. 26.

It is interesting to see how Haydn was later to orchestrate this theme in a form which compensated for the inability of an orchestral version to re-create the rich decoration of the

mechanical organ. This is exemplified by the opening of the
second appearance of the theme (bars 29 of the mechanical organ
treatment onwards) — see Fig. 27

Fig. 27.

Significantly, it is the version for mechanical organ which
stands out here as displaying a much greater elegance and
delicacy in the sequence of the melodic line. In the further
developments again there are several minor deviations from the
1793 version.

In number 30 we find the rondo-finale of the Lark Quartet
Opus 64 No. 5, the eleventh of the so-called Tost quartets[39]
written in 1789. The subject of the piece is in the key of D major
whereas in the mechanical organ version it is transposed into G
major and the repetitions of the subject taken in variation mode.[40]
Besides this, there are many other detail deviations but above all,
the *Flötenuhr* is allowed the opportunity of substituting the *minore*
by a completely different couplet (bars 35–51) which does not
appear in the quartet at all.

[39] See note 21 above.

[40] For expansion on the subject of the
'variation repeat', see Ernst Fritz
Schmid, *C. Ph. E. Bach und seine
Kammermusik*, Kassel, 1931, p. 152 *et
seq.*

Number 32 is a revision of the finale of the tenth 'London' Symphony, No. 102. The *Flötenuhr* manuscript is in the Berlin Collection and dates from 1792. The key is F major and it is marked *allegro*. The symphonic version was written, according to Haydn himself, in 1794–5 and the particular movement is in the key of E flat major and is marked *vivace*. Of all the pieces for mechanical organ, this is by far the longest and, from its extended compass, and from the surviving suitable organ scale (see Fig. 8), we know it was for a fairly large instrument. Nevertheless when the music is compared with the orchestral version it becomes obvious that once more the abbreviations are considerable. For example, the delightful woodwind interlude of the symphony (bars 56–91) is missing as well as the extensive enlargement and development of the thematic repeat (bars 101–184). The coda appears similar in both treatments, but the mechanical organ piece does not achieve the delay in the musical climax by the process of tempo variation and *fermata* as in the symphony, but by the insertion of rests so that the passage is lengthened by one bar whilst at the same time the chromatic modulation is simplified (Fig. 28).

Fig. 28.

In reviewing all this, one must not forget that these mechanical organ works by Haydn provide us with valuable information regarding the style and ornamentation of those past times. It also tells us something of *tempi* and I will comment further on that aspect in a moment. What is apparent, though, is that above all else these pieces tell us something about Haydn himself thanks to the fortunate circumstances that have allowed both instruments and musical scores to come down to us.

The question of tempi, however, is still one area where we are left somewhat in the dark. It is not possible to draw absolutely positive conclusions from the instruments although we can gain some interesting relative comparisons. First, it is a characteristic of this type of mechanical musical instrument that the surface speed of the musical barrel and hence the speed of the music can be varied through quite broad limits. While there is the expected risk of speed variation occasioned by the variations in the tension of the driving spring in the clockwork motor between fully-wound and partially-wound, speed alteration can come about through wear and consequent increase of friction throughout the life of the instrument. And then there is the fact that every builder of these mechanical organs provided an adjustable regulator fan or air-brake. Mechanically, this served as a silent escapement to adjust the speed of the motor power. Without it, the full power of the driving clockwork would be exerted on the barrel with destructive force. By regulating this power by means of a worm gear or endless screw to which was attached a large fan, the speed could be controlled within usable limits. However, the wings of the fan were also made to be adjustable so as to offer more or less resistance to the air and so provide more or less braking to the power supply. The reasons for the provision of this adjustment was, we like to think today, to allow for the inevitable wear over the years (which would tend to make the instrument play slower for a given speed setting) and so provide a means of compensating for it. In actual fact, however, the owner of an instrument was allowed — indeed, encouraged — to vary the playing speed of his organ music at will, speeding it up for certain dances, or slowing it down as the whim took him. It is reported of the mechanical orchestra built by Johann Georg Strasser that its operating instructions included the message: 'Die Walzen... werden nach dem, einem jeden Stück angemessesen Tempo vorgetragen. Der Windfang ist innen im Werk angebracht und kann sehr genau nach dem gehörigen Tempo gestellt werden' (The cylinders... are played at a speed which should be suited to each piece. The wind brake has been located in the machine so that it can be adjusted very accurately to the appropriate speed of the piece).[41] Nevertheless, the surviving instruments allow one to draw relatively reliable conclusions as to the tempi, particularly in respect of the comparisons between one tune and another on the barrel of the same instrument. It emerges, for example, that the first mechanical organ plays the minuets number 6 and 8 at a considerable slower tempo (♩ — metronome 84) than for the minuets number 11 and 17 which turn out to be somewhat faster (♩ — metronome 100). The fugue, number 24, varies considerably in tempo between the two instruments upon which it is played — the first and the third. The first plays this at ♩ —

[41] See *Allgemeine Musikalische Zeitung*, Leipzig, 1801, p. 738.

metronome 88, while the later instrument plays it at ♩ —
metronome 126.

Regarding the *Flötenuhr* of 1793, in number 26, the crotchets
of the allegro demonstrate the same speed as the quavers in the
previous andante — a metronome mark of 138. All in all, the
tempi of the music on these mechanical instruments are very fast.
It should be remembered, in mitigation of this, that this
characteristic of speed and precision of execution was considered
to be one of the advantages of the mechanical instrument if not
one of its most endearing features. On the keyboard, it is
necessary to play the music much more slowly and this applies
both to the original compositions for the instruments as well as to
the versions of other instrumental works arranged for the
mechanical organ.

If tempi is a question which these instruments resolve into a
measure of confusion and conflicting data, then in the field of
ornamentation we are in more fruitful ground. It seems
inescapable that at the time of these pieces, the execution of
flourishes and other ornaments to the music was undertaken by
the performer more on whim and his understanding of the
current idiom rather than on the stereotyped manuscript. A clear
demonstration of this is to be found in the writings of Mozart, for
example, where embellishment and cadenza were considered the
ad libitum responsibilities of the performer whose talent would
dictate the type of musical embroidery he selected to drape over
the composer's melodic line.

From this it is abundantly clear that the musical decoration
formed an essential part of the inner composition and that taste
and the ability to extemporise were of paramount importance to
the human player.

There is within this framework, however, a certain formality of
the freedom which is so apparent. For example, the trills which
are performed almost in every case with a grace note, start with
the main note as in pieces number 2, 3, 6, 12, 19, 20 and 24.
Regarding this last-mentioned piece, Haydn added a postscript to
the manuscript saying: 'NB so oft als das Thema komt, mus bey
jedweder halben Notte folgender halber mordent'

(Whenever the theme appears, the following half mordent must
be placed on each minim). Intended as an instruction for
Niemecz, this theme appears 16 times throughout the piece. In
some of the other pieces, particularly in numbers 21, 22 and 26,
they all begin with the grace note. This is clearly to be seen in

number 26 with the added grace notes as scored in the manuscript in the Contemporary Copies Collection. In number 11, the trills begin with a short note above the main note and, on the long notes, on the main note itself. In number 27, they even begin with the lower subnote which is clearly indicated in the piece in manuscript in the Berlin Collection. Very often, the double beat appoggiatura above the note appears with its variations partly as an addition to the measure but in most cases it is subtracted from the note value. This latter is the case in all the appoggiatura in numbers 1, 20 and 21 which ornaments are partly written out and partly indicated as expected to be performed by the symbol (Fig. 29).

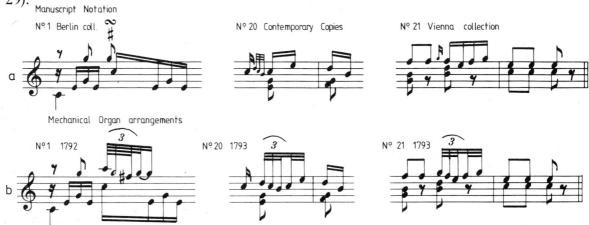

Fig. 29.

In number 19, the appoggiatura in bars 1 and 5 comprise additions to the note value whereas they are subtracted in bars 12 onwards, this being clear proof of the degree of elasticity (as Schmid so aptly termed it) with which these tunes were written with regard to the ornamentation of the period (Fig. 30).

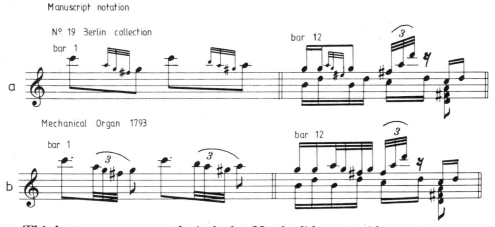

Fig. 30.

This last case proves conclusively that Haydn did not consider the treatment of appoggiatura on the note to be as inflexible as the manner in which Carl Philipp Emanuel Bach did. Indeed, he writes between the added or extended beat and the subtracted form. In number 9, for example, they are to be performed very short yet subtractionally. Another feature which becomes apparent is that whereas in the majority of his music Haydn generally avoided the use of arpeggio with acciaccatura, he makes use of this form of ornamentation in his works for mechanical organ. This is clearly due to the ability of the mechanical instrument to perform these with inflexible precision.

The use of ornamentation in music is the subject of a useful set of plates in the book of Dom Bedos which Niemecz and Haydn may together have used for inspiration. These plates are reproduced in Appendix 2.

There has been a great deal of interest in the past few years in the examination of mechanical organs from the point of view of detecting the presence of *notes inégales* or, in fundamental terms, the tell-tale signs of colloquial interpretation besides merely contemporary performance. Much of this has stemmed from the work of David Fuller in America who published a paper on this subject in the *Bulletin* of the Musical Box Society International in 1974 and subsequently carried out a partial analysis of two Handel organ concerti pinned on two barrels of a chamber barrel organ built by a maker named Henry Holland in the year 1809 and which is currently in the Colt Clavier Collection.[42]

The majority of people who collect and appreciate mechanical musical instruments are not necessarily musical and indeed few wholly appreciate the significance of items in their collections from the musicological standpoint. Unfortunately, the situation also prevails where the serious student of music who has little or no notion of mechanical organ building attempts to read into the instrument more than is actually there. It is a fact of life that no mechanical instrument of the period and type which we are discussing can be expected to perform with the nuance of a manual performer although it can undoubtedly exceed his abilities in areas of precision, accuracy and fluency of repeated performances.

The practice of *notes inégales*, nicely described by François Couperin in his *L'Art de Toucher le Clavecin* (1717), represented a sort of dichotomy between the written music and the interpreter. The French, as C.P.E. Bach commented in his *Versuch über die wahre Art des Clavier zu Spielen* (1753), 'write out their musical ornaments with a stubborn, fanatical accuracy'. And Couperin cited the difference between French and Italian music, saying that the Italians always wrote their music in strict tempo and note values whereas the French play a succession of quavers by

[42] *Mechanical Musical Instruments as a Source for the Study of Notes Inégales* by David Fuller in *Bulletin, The Musical Box Society International*, vol. XX, No. 5 (New Jersey, 1974). The two concerti by Handel (Opus 4, Nos. 2 and 5) are on a small chamber barrel organ built in around 1809 by Henry Holland and manufactured to a special order. The instrument is preserved in the Colt Clavier Collection at Bethesden, Kent. Fuller's analysis, made with the aid of a tape-recorder, is contained in *The Organ Yearbook*, vol. XI (1980), pp. 104–115, and the transcription of the right-hand only (the compiler did not think it worthwhile to transcribe the abbreviated accompaniment on the barrels) was published in 1980 by the Jerona Music Corporation, New Jersey.

lengthening 'the first of each pair and shortening the second'. Sadly many modern performers trying this end up producing a sort of lumbering incoherence which is far removed from the intended effect. A very good analysis of the subject of sixteenth, seventeenth and eighteenth century ornamentation is to be found in A. Geoffroy-Dechaume, *Les Secrets de la Musique Ancienne* (Fasquelle, Paris 1964) which contains much graphic explanation of the execution of phrases described mechanically by Engramelle.

Notes inégales in mechanical music may well be a misnomer in all but the instances where eighteenth century French music was set on the barrels of contemporary French mechanical organs. No doubt the great thirty-two cylindered organ built by de Castellet for the church of Saint Césaire in Arles around 1774 and destroyed only nineteen years later demonstrated the best of Couperin's *notes inégales* in its now-lost repertoire.[43]

However, the presence of *notes inégales* and even the Hungarian gipsy music's 'Scotch catch' on barrel-pinned interpretations of German and English serious music would indeed have been out of place, although possibly in keeping with certain styles of contemporary performance.

But it has been suggested by David Fuller that the irregularities which characterise this type of ornamentation and interpretation can be detected, and on the Handel-playing instrument to boot. The question thus remains did barrel pinners consciously make use of the practice of *notes inégales* or are we seeking to attribute a convenient and high-sounding musical definition to something else which has, in the mechano-musical history of the barrel organ, become forgotten?

The art, or whatever it was, was certainly lost by the time, in the past seventy years, when piano rolls were punched 'metrically', i.e. without having been recorded on a special piano.[44] With a metrically-cut roll, every note was of the correct length, every chord was cut absolutely straight and equal — and the result sounded depressingly mechanical. The so-called 'hand-played' rolls for pianos were generally punched from a real live performance, 'warts and all'. (This is not to be confused with the reproducing piano rolls which were authentic images of a live performance.) But with skill, a clever piano-roll arranger could create a 'hand-played' performance in a roll without the musical score ever even being near a keyboard.

Both Engramelle and Bedos on the one hand preached rigidity while on the other demonstrating decoration and dotting. In practice, the pinner of a barrel would learn, most probably through experience, that if he was pinning anything other than

[43] See Hamel: *L'Art de Construire les Orgues* (Manuels-Roret, Paris, 1849) vol. III, pp. 398–9. Also Ord-Hume, *Barrel Organ.* p. 437.

[44] The term 'metrical' applied to describing the style of rigid notation as a method of transferring music to an organ cylinder or a paper roll is my own and relates to the manner in which music was marked onto a barrel strictly by rule and caliper as distinct from melographically, i.e. from a live performance.

say, a hymn-tune or a chant, the very last thing that was needed was a 'metrical' performance. He learned to stagger the notes of a chord, to break up evenly-divided cadences into divisions which sounded more natural when played. In effect, he mastered the ability to encapsulate the hallmarks of a live-sounding, stimulating performance. The conventions were, in the final analysis, mechanical, even if their very existence were based on a thorough musical training.

Most of the London-made church and chamber barrel organs were built by craftsmen organ-builders who employed somebody else to prick the cylinders, quite often a wife or daughter possessing passable musical training and experience. John Flight of the organ-builders Flight & Robson was, however, a highly skilled musician and his pinning of the barrels for the great Apollonicon organ was acclaimed as little short of marvellous.

Occasionally, one finds an instrument with a particularly fine, 'hand-played' arrangement and this could imply that the pricking for the barrel pinning had been carried out by a master musician and mechanical expert.[45] For most barrel pinners, though, the teachings of Couperin were of little consequence. An analysis of the cylinders of German orchestrion organs made during the heyday of the Black Forest industry (1850–80) reveals just these characteristics of lyricism and whimsy blended with formality in an obviously highly competent, well-disciplined manner.

It is an unfortunate fact of life that what passes for inequality in some barrel organs is little more than poor regulation. This question is dealt with fully in *Barrel Organ*[46] but, expressed simply, it means that the keys must all be at the same height with all lost motion taken up in both keyframe and barrel pivots. The barrel pins have to be in good order, remembering that not all pins are intended to be at the same height, short repetitive notes generally being represented by single pins which were driven further into the cylinder than the wire staples or bridges of sustained notes. This effectively made the short notes shorter still by reducing the 'key-up, pallet open, key-down' cycle.

Inequality certainly exists deliberately: this is noticeable from the pinning of cylinders of such masters as Jaquet-Droz, Davrainville and Poirot, but it has to be remembered that these men were organ builders and the convention was quite interpretational and only to be expected.[47] But for the height of lyricism in interpretation — and what today we would eagerly grasp and enrich with the banner *'notes inégales'* — the organ barrels pinned by Petter Strand are well worthy of analysis.

What, then, can the Haydn/Niemecz *Flötenuhr* tell us about articulation, ornamentation and the *lourer* and *couler* of *notes*

[45] Examples of barrel organ notation are indeed rare. There exists in the British Library a handful of most interesting little books of manuscript music itemising the hymn tunes set on the barrels of three church barrel organs made by Flight & Robson. As already suggested, hymn tunes did not lend themselves to use as an exercise in over-embellishment but these are nevertheless interesting (see Ord-Hume, *Barrel Organ*, p. 547).

[46] See pp. 366, 386.

[47] The Jaquet-Droz, father and son makers of outstanding automata, were also accomplished musicians of a high order. Even so, the widely-held belief that Henri-Louis Jaquet-Droz composed all the music on the cylinder of the automaton lady clavecin-player 'La Musicienne' was finally dispelled in 1980 when, after restoration, the present author identified one of the pieces of music as *Fischer's Minuet* (see *The Music Box*, vol. 9, p. 171, 1980, also Biography, p. 172).

inégales? As we have seen from the earlier comments on the music, the answer is a reasonable amount. Where the matter becomes more interesting is in those instances where Haydn manuscripts can be compared with Niemecz pinning. Niemecz was clearly aware of the opportunities to break from metrical interpretation and it cannot be discounted that, as an avid student and librarian of a great library which claimed to contain a copy of every book so far printed, as well as having access to Engramelle and Dom Bedos, he would presumably have had this very lucid document of Couperin on hand.

It is thus worth observing that Niemecz did not make extensive use of such conventions which were, after all, not exactly in keeping with the Court of Esterházy, even if the French influence in music was on the increase. Listening closely to the organs and examining the barrels shows that a degree of intentional inconsistency is present in places which is not to be detected in the manuscripts. Examples exist in numbers 2, 6, 8, 15, 16, 19, 22, 25, 27 and 29. Number 26 shows examples of the *lourer* and the triplets with their incipit trills serve to offer their own form of unequal value in the little *Presto,* number 3, particularly noticeable in the reprise.

The works which Haydn created for the little organs made by Niemecz add an extra dimension to our appreciation of both the composer's talent and his music which is nowhere else available. If he was master of intellectual whimsy and humour, then it is readily to be appreciated in the thirty-two pieces, thirty of which are interpretationally locked into three time capsules[48] which form the hearts of the Niemecz mechanical organs.

The capabilities of the mechanical organ also appear to have rubbed off on Haydn's music as a whole and some of the keyboard works which he produced around the time appear to delight in emulating, within manual performance constraints, the effects and potential of the *Flötenuhr.* Pieces which I believe to bear clear signs of this influence are to be found included within the *forte-piano* compositions catalogued by Hoboken as XVII, particularly number four (the C major Fantasia of 1789) and the *Andante con*

[48] The present lack of availability of the second mechanical organ, the Urban specimen, is a great pity but, thanks to earlier detailed examination and the availability of several good published recordings, it is less of a limitation to this thesis. A paramount saving is the fact that the Urban organ is the middle one of the three.

* The 1789 organ number 1 is the correctly-dated instrument hitherto described as the '1772' instrument.
† No manuscript exists for these and they were noted by ear.
Note: In listing the music which Haydn composed for the Niemecz clocks, it has hitherto been customary to place the pieces in the order as defined by the clock of 1792 as playing 'the first 12 pieces', that of 1789 (1772) playing 'pieces 13–18', and the organ of 1793 as playing 'pieces 19–30'. This assumes that the yardstick for collating these pieces is the second of the three known mechanical organs which is somewhat illogical. It would be better to start with the earliest organ but since this numerical sequence has already been established and appears as the order in which the pieces are presented in the several published versions, any alteration to the numbering at this stage can only cause further confusion. However, the table here takes a more logical approach to the presentation in that it shows the three organs and their repertoires in chronological order of manufacture. The numbers adjacent to the tunes played by each instrument indicate their relative positions on the actual organ barrel, the sequences of the second and third organs assuming their natural positions. All keys shown are major (i.e. F signifies F major).

Conspectus of music composed or arranged by Joseph Haydn for the mechanical organs of Father Primitivus Niemecz

Hoboken Werkgruppe XIX: 1–32

Piece number Schmid	Hoboken	Time, key signature as arranged, title and derivation		Organ 1 1789*	Organ 2 1792	Organ 3 1793
1	17	2/4	C Allegro moderato		X1	
2	10	2/4	C Andante (Allegretto)	X1	X2	
3	18	3/8	C Presto (Allegro moderato)		X3	
4†	19	2/4	C Andante *Warning to a Girl (Warnung an ein Mädchen)*		X4	
5†	20	3/4	C Menuett Trio from the Symphony No. 85 in B flat 'La Reine' 1785–86		X5	
6†	8	3/4	C Menuett *The Call of the Quail (Der Wachtelschlag)*	X2	X6	
7†	21	3/8	G Allegretto		X7	
8†	7	3/4	C Menuett	X3	X8	
9	22	2/2	C Allegro moderato (from the concluding passage of a set of variations for keyboard in C discovered in 1958)		X9	
10†	23	2/4	C Vivace (finale – rondo allegro — of a C minor symphony originally attributed to Dittersdorf).		X10	
11	9	3/4	C Menuett allegretto (opening two bars similar to start of string quartet Opus 54 No. 2 of about 1787)	X4	X11	
12	24	3/8	C Presto		X12	
13	1	4/4	F Allegretto (Opening two bars: Buonafede's aria 'La Raggazza col vecchione' from Act 1 Scene 7 of *Il Mondo della Luna* (1777)	X5		
14	2	3/4	F Vivace	X6		
15	3	2/2	F Andantino (Opening two bars: Symphony No. 53 in D major 'The Imperial' of about 1775)	X7		
16	4	2/4	C Andante cantabile (based on the melody 'Russian Dance' from the ballet *Das Waldmädchen* (The Forest Maiden) by Wranitzky and later used by Beethoven as the basis of a set of piano variations. The melody is by Giornovichi). It is nicknamed 'Die Dudelsack' ('The Bagpipe')	X8		
17	5	3/4	F Menuett	X9		
18	6	2/4	F Vivace (Finale — presto scherz — of Trio No. 3 for violin, viola and double bass (originally baryton)). Known to the Teubner family as *Die Kaffeeklatsch* ('The Coffee Party').	X10		
19	11	2/4	C Allegretto	X11		X1
20	12	2/4	C Andante	X12		X2
21	13	2/4	C Vivace	X13		X3
22	14	3/4	C Menuett	X14		X4
23	15	2/4	C Allegro ma non troppo	X15		X5
24	16	2/2	C Allegro (Fuga)	X16		X6
25	25	2/4	D Marche (Formerly believed to be by Beethoven after discovery of version on nineteenth century organ bearing the inscription 'Grenadier March arranged by Herr Ludwig v. Beethoven')			X7
26	26	2/4	E Andante (allegro)			X8
27	27	6/8	G Allegretto (Published by Haydn as 'Allegretto per il clavicembalo o piano forte' in Vienna in 1794)			X9
28	28	6/8	C Allegro (Finale of quartet Opus 71 No. 1 of the Apponyi quartets, 1793).			X10
29	29	3/4	C Menuett (Minuet from Symphony No. 101 in D major 'The Clock', 1794)			X11
30	30	2/4	G Presto (Finale of string quartet Opus 64 No. 5 'The Lark' c. 1793)			X12
31	31	3/8	C Allegretto			
32	32	2/4	F Allegro (Finale, in free revision, of Symphony No. 102, the London symphony, 1794–95, from preliminary sketches)			

} none of the three surviving organs make use of these two compositions

Variazioni, undated but apparently around 1793. The F minor variations, XVII: 6 of 1793, also shows some signs of this influence.

I believe it is fitting to conclude this resumé of the music by returning to the man who did so much of the original research, Ernst Fritz Schmid, and quoting *in extensis* his own concluding comments for which I offer a free translation:

> On the whole, the works of Joseph Haydn for the *Flötenuhr* afford us a particularly fascinating insight into his creations and we are obliged to the owners of the original manuscripts and original instruments for their friendly co-operation and also that they made it possible to present the hidden secrets to the great musical public on the occasion of the 200th birthday of the great master as a very special birthday present.
>
> May these exquisite little works of the science as well as the praxis be manifold stimulation, pure enjoyment and give us elation over the difficulties of our time which depress all of us today.

Those words were written as the world was coming out of the 1930s depression. Now, in the year of Haydn's 250th birthday, once again the world is emerging from a depression and the sentiments remain unaltered.

Primitivus Niemecz C^{mi}

Principis Esterhazy Bibliothecarius fecit in Esterhas Anno 1793.

Fig. 31. The inscription written across the width of the barrel of the third surviving Haydn/Niemecz organ. The surface of the barrel is paper covered and the ink, although somewhat faded, is still quite legible — see Plate 37 on page 65.

CHAPTER 5

The Creation of the Organs — A Summing up

We have seen that music for mechanical organ which was written by noted composers is far from unusual. We have already discussed the classical barrel organ works of Mozart, Beethoven, Cherubini, Handel and several others. All of these pieces were specially written for special instruments, yet none can be considered to be the result of circumstances as unique as those surrounding these Haydn works.

It is no doubt rather difficult at this time to appreciate the importance and the power of the Esterházy family. It was, for a start, the greatest of the many Hungarian noble families and successive members had distinguished themselves in the Imperial service.[1] This greatness stemmed from events in the year 1687 when Prince Paul Esterházy had conferred upon him the title of Prince of the Holy Roman Empire. This was in recognition of his efforts in securing the promulgation of the law which made the Austrian sovereign hereditary king of Hungary.[2] This title would be passed on to the Esterházy heirs. It was Prince Paul who was responsible for the construction of the family castle at Kis Márton (Kismarton, or, in German, Wenigmertendorf) which was Eisenstadt (literally the 'iron town'). The castle was completed in 1683.

The enormous fortune of the Esterházy family built up steadily over the years through a succession of successful marriages with the result that by the eighteenth century it was comparable only with the estates of Thököly and Rákóczi, but whereas the two latter fortunes dwindled even in that century, that of the Esterházys lasted until comparatively recent times. In 1938, the law which secured the hereditary title was abolished in Austria, and in 1946 Hungary confiscated the Hungarian estates of the Esterházys and incorporated them into the State.[3]

Haydn's involvement with the Esterházy family came about soon after he was dismissed as a choirboy from the choir of St. Stefan's Cathedral in Vienna. He took lodgings in a large house named the Altes Michaelerhaus. His room was in the attic, but the main part of the building — the ground floor — was the home of the Dowager Princess Octavia Esterházy. In the years to come,

[1] R. Hughes, *Haydn*, p 32.

[2] Hughes, *loc. cit.*

[3] H.C. Robbins Landon, *Haydn at Eszterháza*, p. 31.

Joseph Haydn was to serve her two sons (the brothers Paul Anton and Nicolaus) for almost thirty years.

It was in May of 1761 that Haydn joined the service of Prince Paul Anton. He was just twenty-nine years of age and as assistant kapellmeister he was responsible for 'everything appertaining to the music' although the ailing Gregor Joseph Werner remained the official Oberkapellmeister.

After several years of earning a living as a wandering street musician, Haydn now had a secure post although he was, to begin with at any rate, little more than a servant in the princely household. His first contract, dated 1 May 1761, contained wording which we would consider brusque in the extreme. There were clauses such as: '. . . he shall . . . take the more care to conduct himself in an exemplary manner, abstaining from undue familiarity and from vulgarity in eating, drinking and conversations . . .' and, elsewhere in the document, it stated that: 'The said Joseph Heyden (sic) shall appear daily in the antechamber before and after midday, and inquire whether His Highness is pleased to order a performance of the orchestra', and that he should 'take care to practise on all (the various instruments) with which he is acquainted'.[4] Even so, the contract, which is still in existence, placed him in relatively high social standing. He was to rank as a household officer and be maintained as such, but it also demanded that he compose whatever music the Court deemed necessary.

[4] H.C. Robbins Landon, *op. cit.*, p. 42.

A second contract dated 1779 was only slightly less demanding but still Haydn's duties remained both those of a servant and a gentleman, for he became a member of the Royal Household and was allowed to live in his own house.[5]

[5] H.C. Robbins Landon, *loc. cit.*

But if this was the type of allegiance demanded from an officer of the Prince of the standing which was accorded to Haydn, the position of the Court librarian Niemecz must have been appreciably lower and more rigidly controlled even though he himself was later to have an assistant (Joseph Gurck) and his duties multiplexed as musician, librarian and designer/builder of mechanical organs.

Less than a year after Haydn took up his employment with the Prince, Paul Anton died and his title passed to his younger brother Nicolaus who in the fullness of time came to be known by the soubriquet 'Nicolaus the Magnificent'.

The new Prince Esterházy, as was his predecessor, was a kindly employer to both men, yet he obviously ruled them rigidly and expected both hard work and devotion in return. On the one hand, sickness was always rewarded by the best medical attention available while on the other we find on record occasions where

Haydn was quite severely reprimanded for failing to attend to trifling details of his job, one menial aspect of which was keeping the music tidy and seeing that his orchestra and himself were always turned out smartly.

These early days of Haydn's employment were spent at Eisenstadt. Prince Nicolaus decided to create a new palace at a place where he might enjoy his favourite sport of hunting and the open air. A hunting lodge in the swamps at Süttör had long been an unofficial second residence (bills for alterations under the guidance of architect Anton Erhard Martinelli go back to the year 1721[6]) and now this was to be transformed into a palace on the grandest scale. This was to be named Eszterháza: today it is renamed Fertöd by the Hungarian authorities.

[6] H.C. Robbins Landon, *op. cit.*, p. 24.

Eszterháza was finished in 1766 and the Court moved in. The establishment at Eisenstadt was still maintained, however, and both seats continued in regular use by the prince and his household. In 1768 and again eight years later there was a fire at Eisenstadt which destroyed much of Haydn's music (H.C. Robbins Landon suggests that in truth little if anything was actually lost since Haydn had had his copyist — presumably Johann Elsser — at work to produce copies which were kept elsewhere and hence survived).[7]

[7] H.C. Robbins Landon, *op. cit.*, p. 150. The author somewhat contradicts himself in the same work on page 420 when, speaking of the fires of 1768 at Eisenstadt and Eszterháza in 1779, he suggests that Haydn lost many works in the fires, certainly most of the marionette operas.

After the seclusion of Eisenstadt, Eszterháza was an enormous building. It still stands today, restored by the Hungarians in the late 1950s, and reveals just how hard it must have been to maintain, to furnish and to live in. The building, thanks to its size, was virtually the domain of a self-supporting community within the framework of which the aspects which concern us here are the music and the organ-building activities.

The palace was, by all accounts, a pretty remarkable place. The Prince de Rohan commented in 1772 that in Eszterháza he had 'rediscovered Versailles'. On broadly Italianate style with imposing façade, the palace featured a frescoed hall, rooms panelled in rare woods and Japanese lacquer and furnished in gold-upholstered chairs, the whole illuminated by the finest crystal chandeliers. There was a picture gallery and, of course, the library which was to become the titular purpose of Niemecz's appointment to the Royal staff. Haydn, remember, was officially a member of the Royal household, a fine distinction as regards the employees of the Prince and one which placed him in a position far and away above that of the humble priest.

Eszterháza also had an opera house with a most elaborate stage upon which the finest operas might be performed before a capacity seating of 400 people. Besides that, there was a marionette theatre constructed in the form of a grotto and lined with stones and shells. These grounds, now mostly disappeared, were said to have been superior in every way to those of Eisenstadt in their richness and variety of style. Besides being stocked with game, the gardens contained temples, water cascades, courtly avenues, terraces and fine lawns.

In this atmosphere Haydn flourished and both he and his music were greatly appreciated by his employer. The environment was one certain to act as a stimulus to a creative musician and to spur him to explore all avenues in music and mechanical performance. He wrote widely for the marionette theatre, in itself a sort of mechanical, artificial world not totally removed from that of automatic musical instruments.

Haydn commented later to his biographer:

> My prince was always satisfied with my works; I not only had the encouragement of constant approval, but as conductor of an orchestra I could make experiments, observe what produced an effect and what weakened it, and was thus in a position to improve, alter, make additions or omissions, and be as bold as I pleased; I was cut off from the world, there was no one to confuse or torment me, and I was forced to become *original*.[8]

[8] *Grove's Dictionary of Music & Musicians*, 5th ed., vol. 4, p. 151.

While he was protected from outside influences, his music was far from insulated from the rest of the world and Haydn's fame spread far and wide, almost entirely without his knowledge. As early as 1766, an Austrian writer on music had compared his talents to those of the popular poet of the time, Gellert. Haydn knew nothing of the fact that his fame had extended beyond the immediate circle of the Esterházys and their very many friends who attended concerts. And yet even Dr Burney tried hard to find him when he travelled Europe in 1772 (the year of the 'Farewell' symphony), but while Burney was in Vienna, Haydn was out of reach at Eszterháza. When, by 1781, Haydn's music was being eagerly sought after way beyond the environment which nurtured him, and his Viennese publisher Artaria chose to have his portrait engraved for inclusion in a series of portraits of eminent musicians, Prince Nicolaus was almost as pleased and as flattered as was the master himself. From that time onwards, Haydn was unable to escape the knowledge that he was esteemed in circles far and away beyond Eisenstadt and Eszterháza. The days of what he thought to be isolation were over, if ever they really existed.

Always a religious man, it is thought that it was due to his friendship with Mozart that Haydn decided to take up Freemasonry in 1785. His close involvement with the Barmherzigen Bruder (Brothers of Mercy) led him to join the lodge *Zur Eintracht* and, as Rosemary Hughes suggests,[9] one of the main attractions for him must have been the emphasis placed

[9] R. Hughes, *op. cit.*, p. 58. The involvement with Freemasonry is indeed a complex one and, besides the connection with the Barmherzigen Bruder, affords us the probability of a direct link between many characters in the scenario surrounding the Viennese musical scene in the closing decades of the 18th century. There were eight Viennese 'Johannis' Lodges, the principal one being *Zur wohlthätigen Eintracht* (Beneficent Concord). Mozart was admitted to one of the minor lodges, *Zur Wohlthätigen* (Beneficence), in December, 1784. A year later, the

on the conception of universal brotherhood rather than on the repudiation of Christian teachings.

How it came to be that an obscure if talented monk should end up as a senior employee of the Prince of the Holy Roman Empire and become so closely involved with Haydn may at first seem something of a fortuitous piece of coincidence. However, I believe that it was no mere chance that this happened since Niemecz was virtually destined to meet with Haydn from the moment he took Holy Orders.

The link which made this possible was forged by the very first Prince Paul Esterházy to come to our attention. In the year 1679 he established a hospital for the poor at Eisenstadt[10] which, in keeping with the early concept of a hospital, was a strongly religious undertaking. Then, in 1760, Prince Paul Anton Esterházy founded the hospital of the Brothers of Mercy in Eisenstadt, thus enlarging the trust set up by the Palatine Paul.[11] When any member of the Eszterháza staff was ill, they received free medical treatment at the hospital under the munificence of the Prince. Indeed, the oboist Zacharias Pohl who was in Haydn's orchestra, died in the hospital in the year 1781[12] after twelve years of service.

Thanks to the researches of previous writers including Schmid,[13] we know that Niemecz was a member of the Order of the Barmherzigen Bruder and that, from the manner in which his indoctrination was completed, his treatment was different from that of the ordinary novice. Indeed, he was accorded some special privileges when he was ordained as a priest at the end of 1776. There can be no doubt that prior to this moment in his career he would have had no opportunity to practice organ-building of any kind.

It was in this year that Niemecz's predecessor as librarian at Eszterháza, Philipp Georg Bader, was at work with one of the novelties of the Prince — the marionette theatre. Bader wrote the libretto to Haydn's *Dido* in that year and in 1779 the words for another marionette opera of Haydn's called *Die bestrafte Rachbegierde*.[14] Bader died at the end of that year shortly after the fire of 18 November which totally destroyed the theatre, the music, musical instruments — and, according to the *Pressburger Zeitung* for 24 November 1779, 'two beautiful clocks'. Bader's position in the household is described in the surviving records as poet (playwright), librarian and, between the years 1778 and the time of his death, director of the theatre at Eszterháza. He was succeeded in these last-mentioned duties by Johann Peter Noethen (from 1 January 1780) who was also described as 'librarian'. It would appear that the duties of director of theatrical

Emperor Joseph decreed that the eight lodges should be amalgamated into a smaller number in order to make them easier to supervise. The particular Lodge which appears to have taken the initiative in instituting amalgamation discussions was Haydn's own lodge, *Zur krönten Hoffnung* (Crowned Hope) and, to mark the occasion, one of the brothers — none other than Paul Wranitzky — composed a special symphony which was performed at the meeting which was held on 9 December 1785. Wranitzky had been a member of Nicolaus Esterházy's orchestra under Haydn until earlier that year when he had left to take up a position as Musical Director to Count Johann Esterházy and leader of the Court opera. The discussions to unite the lodges were obviously successful. Three, namely Concord, Palm-Trees and Three Eagles, formed *Zur Wahrheit* (Truth) lodge on 6 January 1786. Haydn's lodge, Mozart's lodge and the Three Fires became *Zur neues-krönten Hoffnung* (New-crowned Hope) on 14 January 1786. In that year, Mozart's name appeared as a Master. However, this intermixing represents only the start of the story, for in 1790, Prince Nicolaus Esterházy himself was described as Master of this lodge, and one of his lodge brothers was Pasquale Artaria, a partner in the publishing business of Artaria who were Haydn's publishers. While very detailed records were not the policy of the Masonic Order, after the directive of the Emperor Joseph, the surviving records demonstrate increasing diffidence and brevity. See also Otto Erich Deutsch: *Mozart; A Documentary Biography*, A. & C. Black, London, 1965, particularly pp. 230 and 258.

[10] H.C. Robbins Landon, *op. cit.*, p. 32.

[11] H.C. Robbins Landon, *op. cit.*, p. 35.

[12] H.C. Robbins Landon, *loc. cit.*

[13] Ernst Fritz Schmid, 'Joseph Haydn und die Flötenuhr', *Zeitschrift für Musikwissenschaft*, January 1932, pp. 197–220.

[14] H.C. Robbins Landon, *op. cit.*, p. 38.

productions took up most of Noethen's time, for this was the year when Niemecz joined the Royal household with the official title of librarian. It was, let it be noted, 1780.

The practice of seconding dual or even multiple roles to servants and staff such as the examples described was not uncommon. Take the case of Prince Paul Anton's valet, Luigi Tomasini, who had come from Italy. He earned only 12 Fl. 30 Kr. a month in 1761, yet ascended to become leading violinist, earning 682 Fl. 30 Kr. by 1790.[15] And Haydn, who enjoyed children and had a lively sense of humour, almost ranked as a professional godparent for he was godfather to three of his six children, the Prince himself demonstrating the close-knit family atmosphere which he encouraged by being godfather to another. And Geiringer in his work on Haydn quotes an advertisment from the *Wiener Zeitung* for 1789: 'Wanted by nobleman. A servant who plays the violin well and is able to accompany difficult piano sonatas'.

This still leaves us with the question as to how Niemecz came to be chosen for this highly desirable job. Was it through the influence of Haydn or through the Prince himself?

An examination of the career of Haydn and the activities of Niemecz reveals some interesting points of concordance and it seems very likely that Niemecz came into contact with Haydn during the years of his early priesthood. Robbins Landon suggests[16] that the second known performance of the *Stabat Mater* took place at the Viennese Convent of the Brothers of Mercy and says that that institution, or its Eisenstadt branch, may have had something to do with the first performance in 1767.

An even more likely situation for a meeting concerns the composition of the *Kleine Orgelsolomesse*. Again Robbins Landon[17] suggests that it was probably during Haydn's annual stay with the Prince's Court at Eisenstadt in the winter of 1777–8 that he composed his *Missa brevis Sancti Joannis de Deo* for the chapel of the Brothers of Mercy. It is also thought that Haydn himself probably played the solo organ part and, of course, the continuo. This mass was also used by the Esterházy Castle Chapel. It will be recalled that the inscription on the 1792 Niemecz mechanical organ refers to 'S. Joan. de Deo'.[18]

It can only be conjecture but, suspecting that Haydn took an active part in selecting players for musical performances at which he officiated, and knowing that he held a position of trust with the Prince himself, had Haydn met Niemecz on one of these occasions, this could account for Niemecz being offered such a prestigious job at the Royal palace. Again, if Haydn had not been involved at this stage, at least perhaps not so directly, then there is

[15] H.C. Robbins Landon, *op. cit.*, p. 80.

[16] H.C. Robbins Landon, *op. cit.*, p. 144.

[17] H.C. Robbins Landon, *op. cit.*, p. 407.

[18] E.F. Schmid, *op. cit.*, p. 201.

still the likelihood that either the talents of Niemecz came to the attention of the Prince, or that he may even have canvassed the convents for a capable servant who could look after his books and manuscripts and, as in the old advertisement, make some music for his master. Convents were great sources of learning, music and literature, as were monasteries.

Since he already had a form of librarian to succeed the late Bader, did Prince Nicolaus create a position for Niemecz, or was that of Noethen the dubious one? The job title may indeed have been spurious, but it was Niemecz who wrote the anonymous history of the palace of Eszterháza and it was Niemecz who signed the last two surviving organs with his job title.

Although Haydn was largely a self-taught musician (this is clearly seen in the development of his music from the earliest through to the last, albeit the transformation was a gradual one as he gained the experience and confidence which he described earlier) he was not one for books. One can imagine that he probably had something to say on this subject to Niemecz who, we assume, spent at least some of his time working in the library. Giuseppe Carpani, the Italian poet and writer on music who knew Haydn well in later years and was an early biographer of the man, referred to him as 'an illustrious idiot'[19] in relation to all knowledge outside his art. It was said that his personal library comprised mainly technical works on music but this is not borne out by the inventory published by the Institut für Österreichische Kulturgeschichte in Eisenstadt.

A number of interesting questions are posed by the whole business surrounding Niemecz, Haydn and these mechanical organs. Why, for example, were they made? And who had the idea of making them? And, more to the point, for *whom* were they made? On a more mundane point, where were they made since presumably the Father was not to be found in his religious habit filing brass and shaping wood in amongst the Esterházy books!

First, it is worth noting the unique circumstances of their conception. While every other maker of mechanical organs in Europe — and there were many — was making instruments either for sale or for long-term monetary gain through exhibition (such as Mälzel, for example, with his Panharmonicon), Niemecz was already in a secure job with good pay and an assistant. One cannot help feeling that the assistant, Gurck, was probably left either to look after the books or perhaps served as an unofficial apprentice who helped to make the instruments. It is interesting to note that after the death of Niemecz Gurck described himself as able to make organs and to take orders for new ones. Niemecz, then, led a sheltered existence as far as his organ-building

[19] R. Hughes, *op. cit.*, p. 46.

activities were concerned. He was not under pressure to earn a living for himself with them and so one assumes that he could take his time over his work. Then there was the overriding consideration that as a priest he was an unlikely person to consider the building of mechanical organs as a purely entrepreneurial or speculative exercise.

So why did Niemecz take the apparently ultracrepidarian step of making these instruments? First, as 'a man of the Cloth' he was by no means the first priest to turn to organ-building and was equally not the first to look at the manufacture of mechanical musical instruments. In the first half of the last century, the Abbé Larroque taught himself organ-building having repaired a serinette, whereupon he conceived a grandiose plan for the construction of a new organ for the Madeleine which he planned to make out of the parts of a Mälzel Panharmonicon.[20] Although this can hardly be considered as an episode which bestowed credit on the organ-building clergy, the first treatises published on the arrangement of music for mechanical instruments came from two eminent men. The French priest Father Marie-Dominique-Joseph Engramelle published a book called *La Tonotechnie ou l'Art de Noter les Cylinders* in 1775. And a Benedictine monk, Father Dom Bedos de Celles, expanded on this information in his comprehensive treatise on organ-building, *L'Art de Factuer d'Orgues*, published in 1778. This work, a truly magnificent 'do-it-yourself' guide to the subject, provided exhaustive details with detailed illustrations for the manufacture of mechanical organs. These two books and their dates are significant.

Niemecz joined the circle of the Esterházys within which Haydn was very much a principle figure in the musical activities around which the family revolved. The Prince's love of good music and his fondness for Haydn was genuine (although it is known that they frequently had disagreements), but it was also a relationship which accorded the Prince considerable kudos. There was no other prince in Europe at that time who had at his disposal such a competent orchestra, and there was no other prince with so eminent a musician within his employ. The situation was unique.

Interestingly enough, when Korabinszky[21] compiled his Hungarian encyclopaedia in the year 1786, he included mechanical musical instruments manufactured by Niemecz in the entries concerning Eisenstadt and Eszterháza (see page 42). Since this pre-dates the earliest surviving Niemecz/Haydn organ as detailed and explained further on, it implies that Niemecz had already proved his ability to the Prince (if not to Haydn as well) and so the notion of a collaboration between Niemecz and Haydn

[20] Arthur W.J.G. Ord-Hume, *Barrel Organ*, p. 182–3.

[21] M. Korabinszky, *Geographisch-historisches und Produkten Lexicon von Ungarn*, Pressburg, 1786.

may well have come from the Prince himself.

When Nicolaus II realised just how talented Niemecz was, my belief is that it was entirely the Prince's idea that the talents of the two most interesting and important members of his household might be united to create a product which was truly Esterházy in concept, execution and repertoire. Do not forget that on the authority of Korabinszky we have references to Niemecz as a maker of musical novelties in the palace prior to the first of the three organs which we have today. Nicolaus II must therefore have encouraged Niemecz in his organ-building in the way that he encouraged Haydn in his composition. It could only have been a matter of time before their joint abilities developed to the point where Haydn agreed to provide special music. Both he and his prince had already heard the fruits of Niemecz's labours as a burgeoning organbuilder.

All this makes it more and more likely that during his time at the Brothers of Mercy he developed an interest in making clocks and organs. He might have had knowledge in a more practical way by the time he joined the employment of Esterházy but this is unlikely. One can be virtually certain that the works of Father Engramelle and Dom Bedos came under his scrutiny although this may not have been until after he came to Esterházy's library with its 75,000 volumes which its owner was proud to boast as containing a copy of every book published in Europe. The question almost becomes which provided the inspiration — Niemecz's training in the Brotherhood or his arrival in Esterházy's library!

As a musician and composer himself and with the collaboration of Haydn, Niemecz would have been ideally suited to utilise his spare time in what may initially have been seen just as a hobby to wile away the long winter evenings at the palaces.

What can be done, however, is to examine the literature available to Joseph Niemecz at the end of the 1770s and compare the details with the instruments which we still have today. It is here that some interesting similarities begin to be observed. I have already said that it is uncertain whether he built the entire instruments but this is not critical at this stage. Whether he built them or had them built, there is little doubt that he designed them and it is the inspiration for this design we have to find. First there is the idea of horizontal pipework under the baseboard. Dom Bedos shows a similar style in his four-volume book, Plate XCI. Details of clockwork motors with large-span flat-winged air-brakes and double spring barrels wound by fusees are illustrated in Plate XCVI while the barrel with many narrow strips forming its outer covering can be seen in Plate XCVII. In fact, although mechanical organs with clockwork motors proliferated at this period in their history, the detail similarities between the Niemecz machines and the plates cited are more than just a few. Each of these points does, however, add further evidence to the fact that the first organ cannot have been built in 1772.

These organs were built under the auspices of Nicolaus II, either for his own use in the palaces of Eisenstadt and Eszterháza as features, or for him to dispose of by way of gifts to very special friends. What greater gift might he give than an Esterházy musical machine created within his palace and playing music composed for him by his own and very talented kapellmeister! Such an instrument must truly have been the grandest gift of all!

Did Niemecz have a thriving 'production line' of mechanical organs under way in a workshop tucked away in the great palace? He may well have had just that and in which case this could imply that he had one or more assistants whose job was more organ-building than anything else.

The survival of organs from the Niemecz stable at Eszterháza is thus more certain than the survival of instruments built by other makers of mechanical organs. This can be deduced from the knowledge that they were very special instruments as regards all aspects of their creation and pedigree.

Fig. 32. This chart, facing, shows graphically how unlikely it was that Niemecz could have manufactured the first organ as early as 1772 and shows how the date of 1789, suggested by the surviving Haydn manuscripts, is both more logical and acceptable.

Niemecz did not join the employment of Nicolaus II until 1780. Four years later was published the anonymous description of the palace reliably attributed to Niemecz. This first book, let it be noted, bears no reference to Niemecz or his position. This first surviving mechanical organ similarly bears no name nor reference to his position. And the reference books by Engramelle and Dom Bedos were not published before 1775 and 1778 respectively. From the stylistic similarities already mentioned, these two works must have been his stimulus rather than the more improbable suggestion that he was a 'self-starter' and needed no such material.

The evidence of the music also suggests that 1772 is impossible. For this one must turn to the autograph of the piece listed in the conspectus as number 24 and entitled *Fuga*. This is in the former Czernin Castle of Jindrichuv Hradec (Neuhaus), CSSR, and is dated 1789. There is a copy of this in the Gesellschaft der Musikfreunde collection in Vienna which is entitled 'Acht Laufwerck Sonaten Komponiert von Herrn Kapellmeister Joseph Haydn, und in die Walze gesetzt von Primitiv Niemecz Bibliothekar zu Esterhas 1789 in December'.[22] Of course, Haydn could have composed the tune seventeen years earlier and given it to Niemecz (who would then at the most have been no more than a casual acquaintance) and not bothered to

[22] H.C. Robbins Landon, *Haydn in England*, p. 202.

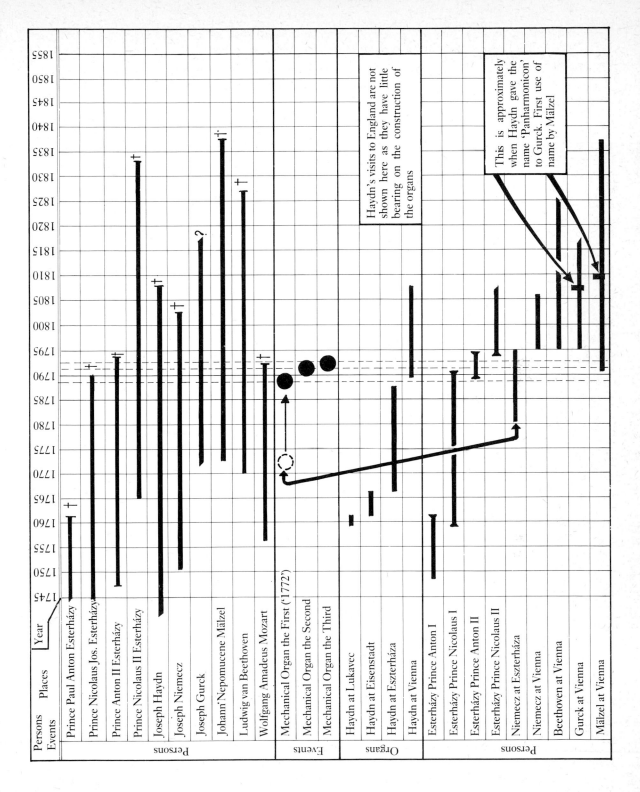

write it out again until 1789, but that is, I feel, stretching the imagination too far. This, then, virtually answers all the doubts, and places the three surviving mechanical organs very nicely into a four-year timespan — 1789, 1792 and 1793 — and allows us to postulate the existence of one or more other organs between the first two dates, and perhaps even one or more after the third date. Significantly, the thirty-second piece for which no organ has yet been found, was composed in 1793[23] and implies that there must indeed have been another instrument made. There are no Haydn autographs or copies which can be dated before December 1789, and the specimen which is the earliest and which bears that date is for the *Fuga*.[24]

I have left until now the question of the authenticity of the music — in other words is this all really Haydn's own composition, or is it a mixture of Haydn and one or more other and probably unknown composers. After all, there are many pieces in the repertoire for which no manuscript exists.

In recent years, doubts have been cast on the authenticity of those pieces which exist only on the organ barrels. These doubts have come from the Joseph Haydn-Institut in Köln and follow a discovery which Schmid himself announced in 1959. News of Schmid's find was published posthumously in 1970.[25] He made his discovery in October 1958 while on a study visit to the Mozart archives of the Schloss Neuhaus in Jindřichův Hradec in Southern Bohemia. He subsequently wrote that what he found 'casts new light on the legends which surround the origins and creations of these old Viennese instruments'. For here, in the collection of autographs formed by the Count Eugin (who died in 1868) lay two hitherto unknown autograph scores in the hand of Haydn. The first of these was for the piece Schmid listed as number 24 — the *Fuga* forming the last tune on the barrel of the so-called 1772 organ. But the whole discovery threw what had been taken as established fact and history into utter confusion, for the score was dated 1789. Schmid was faced with the legend of 1772 as the date of the organ construction on the one hand, and a dated score on the other. He suggested that the score must suggest that Haydn copied down the music which somebody else must have originated. However, when weighed in the light of the evidence of the several other pieces which post-dated 1772 *Il mondo della Luna*, Symphony No. 53 and the Opus 54 No. 1, &c), he finally began to question the Teubner/Reghem tradition.

It will be remembered by the Haydn scholar that Haydn made very many arrangements of popular songs from England, Scotland, Ireland and Wales such as the 150 melodies in the Napier collection.[26] These retained the familiar titles by which we

[23] H.C. Robbins Landon, *op. cit.*, p. 202.

[24] Ernst Simon, *Mechanische Musikinstrumente früherer Zeiten und ihr Musik*, p. 61.

[25] Ernst Fritz Schmid, 'Neue Funde zu Haydns Flötenuhrstücken' *Haydn-Studien* Vol. 2, December 1970, München-Duisberg. pp. 249-255.

[26] A selection of Original Songs in Three Parts. The Harmony by HAYDN, Dedicated by Permission to Her Royal Highness the Duchess of York . . . Printed for Willm Napier, Music Seller to their Majesties, No. 49 Great Queen Street, Lincolns Inn Fields'. These were published in 1792, the year after Napier became bankrupt (see Humphries & Smith: 'Music Publishing in the British Isles', London, 1970).

know them. As an arranger of such pieces, Haydn's stature as a composer was not diminished and it does not altogether come as a surprise to find that he made arrangements of then-popular pieces — number 16 is a good example. If this and other arrangements are his, then we do not disown his Scottish airs on the ground of authenticity.

But as regards the *Flötenuhr* pieces, the next consideration is, of course, are the pieces, arrangements or otherwise, Haydn's own? Here I revert to my earlier words that it is more likely that the circumstances surrounding the creation of these organs would have mitigated against the use of music other than that which Haydn had a direct hand in, either as composer or as arranger.

Following the Schmid revelation, the Joseph Haydn-Institut published some five years later a paper which reduced still further the number of pieces which were thought to be 'genuine' Haydn.[27] The conclusions in this paper were based apparently on the findings of the Haydn-Institut, but clearly were firmly founded on the acceptance of 1772 as the date of the first instrument. This document contains the statement:

[27] Sonja Gerlach, 'Haydn's Works for Musical Clock (*Flötenuhr*): Problem of Authenticity, Grouping, and Chronology', Haydn Studies, Norton, London and New York, 1982, pp. 126–129.

> The third clock (referring to the first mechanical organ) is not signed; perhaps, therefore, it was built not by Niemetz (sic) himself but by his apprentice Joseph Gurck . . . According to oral tradition it was built as early as 1772, but in fact it plays a fugue composed no earlier than 1789. Moreover it was probably built as late as 1796, to judge from the (somewhat hypothetical) dating of a spurious piece it plays (this refers to piece numbered 16 *AO-H)*. It therefore seems to be the latest of the three clocks (sic), not the earliest.

Elsewhere in the same paper, the author states:

> To judge from the pieces preserved in autograph Haydn used all the available pitches in most of the pieces, including the arrangements. There are only a few pieces in which one or two pitches are not used. On the other hand, in several doubtful and spurious pieces (Hob.XIX: 4, 26) from four to as many as nine pitches are missing. The absence of many pitches suggests that these works may not be authentic. In combination with stylistic and other types of evidence it serves to divide the doubtful pieces into those that are probably genuine and those that are probably spurious.

The 'stylistic and other types of evidence' are not offered in support of this somewhat confused reasoning which assumes that because an organ plays a set number of notes, then each piece of music should make use of each one. It also overlooks the fact that a small mechanical organ achieves its musical variety in the hands of a skilful barrel-pinner who will interlard simple pieces with more complex arrangements in the same way that an artist may choose to paint with only a few of the colours on his palette. Furthermore, it confuses the position of Haydn as a composer and arranger with Niemecz as an interpreter and mechanical creator. Once again, then, we have the old problem of a musicologist attempting to evaluate the mechanical musical instrument in terms of its music without being able to equate the development of the instrument itself. There can be no question that the unsigned instrument is indeed the earliest of the three.

Remember that the range of these organs (the gamut or, as Haydn-Institut prefers, the pitches) is limited. Haydn's use of the extremely limited range of Organ Number 2 — the Urban instrument — has already been commented on. If the first organ was indeed that (i.e. the very first Haydn/Niemecz production) – which on the face of it seems quite likely — then the mechanical musical experience was still being explored and developed. In general, however, even within these small organs, the tessitura remains remarkably constant, missing note opportunities or no.

If one now takes Schmid's findings of 1958 and the Joseph Haydn-Institut's 1975 interpretation on the one hand, and re-evaluates the evidence they jointly offer in the light of the first instrument being no earlier than 1789 (possibly even 1790 or 91), then the question of authenticity of the music is largely resolved. And if one investigates the dates when Niemecz, Haydn and Gurck were in concordance under the Esterházy roof, I believe that Haydn's contribution to mechanical music emerges unblemished. It all appears to be a case of trying to adjust the results to suit an incorrect 'fact' at the very foundation of the exercise. Haydn would not have had cause to present a mechanical organ to his prince that did not play music with which he had been actively involved.

It is probably worth putting on record that Anthony van Hoboken[28] was not at all clear in his mind about the dating of the music, although he seems not to have questioned the date of 1772 for the first organ pieces. He repeats the legend of the organ's presentation to Frau Barbara Gassmann on the birth of her daughter Anna which leaves one with a nagging suspicion that perhaps Mrs Gassmann maybe had a second, later daughter whose birthday she confused with that of Anna, or perhaps somewhere in the Gassmann home and its traditions there were *two* Haydn organs! The true explanation may never be known except that it is a safe bet that if there was a 1772 mechanical organ, then Niemecz did not build it and it could not be expected to bear any family resemblance to the organs we are talking about here.

Regarding the mechanical organs themselves, I have some doubts that they were the work of one man. Admittedly with a palace the size of Eszterháza it would be more than likely that the

[28] Anthony van Hoboken, *Joseph Haydn: Thematisch-bibliographisches Werkverzeichnis*, Schott's Söhne, Mainz, pp. 827–836.

household would include a cabinet-maker, possibly even a clockmaker. But for a man such as Niemecz to turn out instruments such as these three in so relatively short a period of time as a single-handed exercise in amongst other duties is unthinkable; they must at the very least have been the product of a dedicated team led by Niemecz whose main task was the setting of Haydn's music onto the barrel of the organ. Niemecz was, remember, still a priest and, of course, the extensive musical rehearsal and practice work demanded a very great deal of his (and everybody else's) time.

Ernst Simon[29] also gave this problem some consideration and formed the opinion that it was unlikely that the production of the instruments actually took place at the Prince's palace but that it evolved in collaboration with the Viennese mechanical organ industry which could supply all the components leaving Niemecz the job of arranging the music into a forest of tiny brass pins on the barrel surface. This suggestion is supported by a comment made by B.G. Chr. B. Busch in his *Handbuch der Erfindungen* published in Eisenach in 1817[30] when he says: 'Niemecz . . . built with the help of the instrument builder at Court (*Hofinstrumentenmachers*) Walter (Vienna) a self-playing organ . . . and sold it to England'. Even so, this seems to contradict what we know about the priest and it could be that the reference is more pertinent to the work of Gurck after the death of Niemecz. However, it might be more logical to assume that Niemecz acquired the parts he needed for his organs from established makers who worked to his designs and then assembled them in his own apparently unique manner, i.e. as very shallow instruments with horizontal pipework. He could even have commissioned complete instruments built to his specifications and delivered with blank barrels, although this seems somewhat contrary to the established reputation of Niemecz as an organ-builder. There is also the little matter of who paid for outside contract work; it would hardly have been Niemecz but it could have been the Prince.

The connection with Walter is proven. Anton Walter was the greatest builder of fortepianos of his age.[31] He was summoned to Eszterháza in February of 1781. He was known to Haydn since, after the fire of 1779 when his theatre harpsichord was completely destroyed, it was Walter who provided a replacement. On 3 March 1781, Walter, who was described as 'organ and instrument maker', was paid 24 Gulden for repairing the 'clavier and harpsichord instruments'. Walter might well have been the person who supplied components to Niemecz via Haydn, although whether Walter himself actually made the pieces or used his much closer contacts with the Viennese musical

[29] E. Simon, *loc. cit.*

[30] H.C. Robbins Landon, *Haydn at Eszter-háza*, p. 445.

[31] H.C. Robbins Landon, *op. cit.*, p. 749 –80.

instrument making industry to sub-contract their manufacture is unknown. There certainly was a great deal of sub-contracting between manufacturers and at that time there were, for example, men who specialised in the making of pipework and others who concentrated on *laufwerke* — the making of the clockwork or metal parts which made up the drive component of a clockwork instrument.

It seems more likely that Niemecz stumbled upon the book of Dom Bedos in the Esterházy library and, as enthusiasts are still to this day finding it, was captivated by its message and so began to design and experiment. Then I believe that Haydn also read this work and no doubt was particularly interested to see the set of finely-engraved plates illustrating how musical ornaments could be translated into barrel notation. These plates are reproduced in this book. And the instruments themselves were designed by Niemecz although probably not actually constructed by his hands.

This then would appear to answer most of the questions surrounding these intriguing mechanical organs. It offers an explanation as to how they came to be made, by whom and probably where. The big unanswered question, however, is how many were actually made? The three survivors are but part of the output of Prince Esterházy's enterprising duo — Franz Joseph Haydn and Joseph Niemecz. Somewhere there could well be more to be found and on one of these as-yet undiscovered organs will be found musical pieces numbered 31 and 32 — if the organs are still in existence, that is.

There does exist a very exciting and thought-provoking reference to a later instrument. In the *Wiener Hofzeitung* for 4 April 1798, there is a report of an intricate and outstanding instrument made by Niemecz which was demonstrated before a distinguished public in the aula of the Vienna University. Comprising 112 pipes, this organ played the overture to Mozart's *Die Zauberflöte*, three other orchestral pieces by Mozart, and two pieces by Haydn 'with the greatest precision, sounding like a big orchestra'. The organ was said to have been built for an Englishman. Were the two Haydn pieces on this instrument the elusive number 31 and 32? If this organ could be traced — and this must be considered extremely unlikely now — the enigma might be cleared up. The nearest we can get to these two pieces is this reference plus the informative passages from the manuscript diary of Beda Plank which have already been quoted.[44]

The three organs have experienced a chequered history since they were built about 190 years ago. At the time Schnerich wrote in 1924 he had knowledge of the existence of all three — '1772'/1789, 1792 and 1793. The one which had been examined in some detail was the 1792 instrument then belonging to Hans Urban, son of Dr Karl Urban. Soon afterwards, the instrument which was owned by Baron von Veyder-Malberg was examined and the music on both organs recorded. The mechanical organ of 1792 was at that time in a better state of preservation and the recording was issued in Germany, in America and then finally in Britain.

The first organ, '1772'/1789, had apparently disappeared from the scene although the name of its last owner was known. The successful location of that piece today was due to some careful detective work by William Malloch of California.

However, much of the delight and satisfaction in successfully locating the 'missing' and unrecorded instrument and locating the third one tended to be overshadowed when it became clear that the second and best-known instrument — the Urban organ (like Stradivarius violins, these organs are known by their owners' names) — had disappeared. The Urban organ was apparently sold sometime after the war and despite all efforts to trace it by the Gesellschaft der Musikfreunde and the Joseph Haydn-Institut, it so far remains elusive.

The actual date of disappearance even is uncertain but it should be remembered that Austria and Vienna in particular was Soviet-dominated until the signing of the so-called Vienna treaty on 15 May 1955. The Russians had already by this time burned the Eszterháza treasures. There is an uncorroborated suggestion that it might have been acquired by an American upon the liberation of the city. It would be extremely exciting if this unique piece were now to come to light again.

The history of the three instruments can be summarised as follows:

1772/1789 'Teubner'. Dedicated by Haydn to the wife of the Vienna Court choirmaster, Florian Leopold Gassmann at the baptism of their daughter who was later to become Anna Fux-Gassmann. Then the organ passed to relatives, the Teubner-Reghem family in Vienna. Today the property of Dipl. -Ing. Wolfgang Teubner, Vienna. Unrestored but in partial playing condition.

1792 'Urban'. Formerly the property of the House of Liechtenstein and then changed hands several times before passing into the hands of Dr Karl Urban in Vienna. Disposed of by his son, Hans Urban, sometime after the Second World War. Present whereabouts unknown.

1793 'Veyder-Malberg'. Haydn gave this organ to his Prince, Nicolaus Esterházy .the Second. It was ultimately disposed of by a descendant and subsequently travelled widely, visiting at

various times London, Merano, Vienna and Stuttgart. Finally
it went to Prien in Chiemgau where it became the property of
Baron von Veyder-Malberg. The instrument is now the
property of the Baroness von Veyder-Malberg and is on
indefinite loan to the musical instrument collection at the
Münchener Stadtmuseum.

Not only do these three mechanical organs represent one of the
most valuable documents of the music of Haydn, but they are also
among the most precious in the history of the instruments of
mechanical music. They have the ability to play for us today
exactly the performance which received the approbation of
Haydn which means that we can hear the music precisely the way
Haydn wanted it interpreted.

It is fortunate that in a war which destroyed many of the finest
musical instruments and automata in Europe, these three
survived along with a handful of other equally priceless
instruments from which our knowledge of musical styles of the
past is only just beginning to expand.

The instruments of Haydn's orchestra survived to be
catalogued but were then lost in the more horrifying and
unforgivable piece of vandalism. The Russians came to
Eszterháza in 1945 and, needing the palace as a hospital, they
took out all the furniture, the paintings and the musical
instruments, made a pile of them in the grounds and then set
them on fire. That evening, people in Oedenburg saw the sky
aglow with this gross and senseless expression of peacetime
barbarism; the next day a former Esterházy employee found the
neck of a violin in the smoking ruins.[32]

[32] H.C. Robbins Landon, *op. cit.*, p. 749
–80.

Haydn himself more than likely considered the mechanical
organ to be something of a whimsy — an amusing venture
bordering on the novelty. For him it must have been like
presenting a close friend with a personal gramophone recording
of a favourite work. Unlike the phonograph disc, however,
duplication of these instruments was a difficult and lengthy
process at the end of which each remained a unique work of
craftsmanship and musical art. One cannot help wondering what
Haydn would have made of our attitude towards these
instruments nearly 200 years on. He would probably consider us
somewhat odd to attach such importance to these novelties in an
age of computers, space travel and solid-state music. Whatever
the reaction, though, Niemecz must be accorded a place in the
history of music as well as a position of distinction alongside those
other master builders of mechanical organs such as the
Dutchman Winkel, the Swede Strand, and the Englishman
Charles Clay.

CHAPTER 6

Contemporary Haydn Clocks

Several other mechanical organs, invariably associated with timepieces, have been located with play music by Haydn. These range from the less important subsequent pieces to the much more important instruments of contemporary date, in other words instruments made within a few years of the originals.

One such instrument is in the collection of Dr. Franz Sobek which is housed in the Geymüllerschlössl at Potzleinsdorf, a

Plate 48. The musical clock in the Sobek Collection at the Geymüllerschlössl near Vienna which houses in its base a mechanical organ playing seven pieces of music. The instrument is said to have been constructed by the Viennese clockmaker Peter Rau on the strength of the strong similarity between this unsigned piece and another item in the same collection, a carillon clock, which bears the name of Rau. The two pieces do share some very marked points of similarity from the brass feet to the fish supporting the clock, the artistic pendulum and, above all, the allegorical bas relief panel along the bottom of the clock portion. On the second instrument, this panel is marked with the name of the artist Detler. While these two panels are not the same, the style and treatment is extremely similar.

suburb of Vienna. This instrument, inventory number 1608, catalogue number 36, is unsigned, plays seven tunes, one of which is by Haydn, and has a compass of twenty-five notes. The museum attributes the piece to the hand of Peter Rau of Vienna on the strength of various superficial similarities to another clock, this time with a carillon, which is signed 'Peter Rau in Wien'. Both pieces have a bas relief panel in the front bearing an allegorical scene. Each has a number of points of similarity and that used in the signed clock is itself signed with the name Detler. In the book *La Pendule Francaise,* Tardy (*alias* H. Lengellé) spells the artist 'Dottler' and variously spells the clockmaker as Pierre 'Rau' and 'Raus' ('Tardy', volume 3, page 659).

The organ in this instrument is of conventional layout with the pipework standing behind the barrel and arranged with the lowest notes nearest the clockwork motor (which still has its original gut-line fusee winding) followed by the remainder descending chromatically to the next lowest notes at the opposite end of the barrel. This style is similar to that employed by the English barrel organ builders in the eighteenth and nineteenth centuries.

The instrument has a bright and clear tone which lacks the mellowness of the Niemecz pieces. The musical arrangements are equally somewhat coarser although it must be said that they come over clearer thanks to their less-involved construction.

The museum catalogue dates the piece as having emerged between 1810 and 1820. This would appear to be correct from the musical standpoint since it is unlikely that Haydn (or Niemecz, come to that) would have passed over the special musical scores prepared for their own creations. What happened after both Haydn and Niemecz were dead is, though, another matter.

Of the seven pieces played, the last one is an arrangement of Haydn's *Flötenuhr* piece number 6, 'Der Wachtelschlag'. While the setting is very slightly different from the Haydn/Niemecz mechanical organs, it is obviously a contemporary variant and, with a compass of twenty-five notes upon which to draw, the barrel pinner has been able to follow the original notation. However, because the surface speed of the barrel is greater and the pinning somewhat coarser, it is abbreviated and so plays a shortened version.

The other pieces on the single organ barrel have not been identified but while at least one is by Mozart, the remainder is unlikely to be by Haydn.

What is unusual about this piece is that while automatic musical instruments playing the works of Haydn were far from uncommon, particularly in Austria, Berlin and London, the

Plate 49. Louis XV pillar clock with extensive clockwork organ in the base. Comprehensive repertoire of interchangeable barrels includes arrangements of Haydn works and a unusually expansive rendering of the piece with variations catalogued as Hoboken III: 76–3. The whole assemblage is undoubtedly French, the clock having Lepaute pinwheel escapement, sweep seconds and eight-day gong and striking trains chiming hours, halves and quarters on two bells. See also Plates 51 and 52 on page 130.

existence of a machine which plays an actual arrangement from a Haydn/Niemecz melody suggests some degree of closer-than-normal involvement with either the original instrument itself or with its creators — Haydn and Niemecz. The music the Esterházy organs played was, after all, rather special. Now if this musical clock with mechanical organ in the Geymüllerschlössl is indced by Rau — the evidence is circumstantial — then was Rau in some way connected with the Esterházy mechanical organs? Because the Rau(?) organ is definitely later than the Niemecz

Plate 50. The organ mechanism seen from the back of the 'Rau' clock. Note the arrangement of the pipework with the highest notes in open pipes in the centre continuing up the scale to the right in stopped pipework and concluding with four bass notes in mitred, stopped pipes at the left (viewed from the rear). The linkage which causes the organ to play by means of the timepiece can clearly be seen.

instruments (and displays somewhat cruder workmanship in the clockwork mechanism), the builder must have obtained the music either by sight of the score or copied the music with a well-trained ear.

There is, however, a further possibility and one which offers an elegant solution to several problems. There does not exist a manuscript score for the Haydn *Flötenuhr* piece which the Rau(?) organ plays. Could it, one wonders, somehow have passed into the hands of the builder of this organ? Of all the foregoing possibilities, this seems the most acceptable explanation for the fidelity of the performance and the absence of a surviving manuscript. Peter Rau was the son of Johann Rau of Vienna who became a master clockmaker in 1785 and who died in 1797. A manuscript might have come into his hands at this time and been passed to his son.

According to F.H. van Weijdom Claterbos (*Viennese Clockmakers and what they left us*), the Rau family were renowned Viennese clockmakers. Peter Rau was a master clockmaker in the Josefstadt and later a citizen of Neu-Lerchenfeld. He seems to have operated as master from 1811 until his death in 1829. See also Jürgen Abeller, *Meister der Uhrmacherkunst*, Wuppertal, 1977 (biographical details of the clockmakers named Rau).

Plate 51 (lower left). View on the front of the unsigned organ mechanism in the base of the pillar clock on page 128. The organ driving weight passes up to a pulley inside the top of the pillar. The organ has 29 notes plus two special keys for changing stops via additional pins in the barrel. Stops are 8ft stopped wood (continuous) and 8ft open principal plus 4ft chimney flute, both automatically selectable.

Plate 52 (below). The style of French clockwork and wooden pipework is seen here along with the grid-ruled barrel surface (also used by Bidermann). The air-brake wings have angular adjustment in the French style. Very high-quality workmanship is matched by an outstanding musical performance. Horological writer Tardy (see page 128) published drawings of this form of clock asserting that none had ever been made. This piece, dating from the 1790s and contemporary with Haydn, is a unique item in every way.

APPENDIX 1

Haydn and the Panharmonicon

When one considers the Panharmonicon or military band orchestrion, thoughts at once turn to Mälzel whose celebrated instruments secured much fame on account of an infamous involvement with Beethoven and a stolen composition. But there is a much closer connection between the Panharmonicon and Haydn as we shall see.

The existence of numerous references to Panharmonicon exhibitions which show the name of Gurk (or Gurck) as the owner/builder/exhibitor have confused many, myself included, in the past. Gurck, as we shall see from his own testimony, built an orchestrion in the early 1800s to which Haydn gave the name 'Panharmonicon' — another grandchild for the master who freely god-fathered the children of his orchestra musicians. Gurck was already in touch with Haydn through their joint employment with the Esterházys although where formerly Gurck had been library-servant, he was later to describe his position as that of 'landscape painter'.

While it was Mälzel whose name became inseparably associated with instruments *Panharmonica*, the first use of the name and, indeed, its dedication, point quite clearly to Gurck as being the originator of the first instrument so named. What is likely, though, is that in the same way as Flight & Robson's gigantic orchestral barrel and finger organ of the 1820s — the Apollonicon — found its name later used to describe similar contemporary instruments, Mälzel, who was not above acquiring other people's ideas for his own use, may have decided that Panharmonicon was a good name for the *genus* military-band orchestrion and so helped himself to whatever kudos surrounded Gurck's instrument and its patronage.

With the arrival of the second Prince Paul Anton Esterházy, there was a general running-down of not just the musical aspects of the royal palaces, but also of the office of library custodian. Freed or otherwise discharged from his palace duties, it was Gurck who officiated at the disposal of Niemecz's property on his death and who had the opportunity and facilities for making new organs. Perhaps Gurck and the young mechanician Mälzel may have met during this period and

exchanged ideas. What is an interesting thought, though, is that Gurck appears to have been associated with the construction of his Panharmonicon for seven years prior to its exhibition around 1810. Niemecz did not die until 1806. Who actually conceived of the idea of the instrument? Could the instrument have been one of the unfinished projects left behind when Niemecz went to join the Great Majority? And, if so, did Gurck assume the unfinished organ as his own work? It is interesting to note that it was not, apparently, finished for exhibition until after the death of Haydn who would have known its true origin. Niemecz built big organs (see the description of the instrument he had built to his plans by Anton Walter on page 43, although the character of these seems to have been biased firmly towards the orchestral rather than the exhibitionist orchestrion.

Gurck's Panharmonicon first appeared in London at Wigley's Exhibition Rooms, Spring Gardens, in November 1811, having earlier been seen in Germany the previous year. The best description of it was published in *The Times* on 28 November, albeit as an advertisement and prepared as a 'puff' for the show. The lengthy text is, nevertheless, the only description extant which tells us something of its building and, more particularly, its naming.

Panharmonicon
A brief account of the above extraordinary instruments (sic) which has for these few days only been submitted to public inspection in Spring gardens, will not be unacceptable to our readers, and especially to such as are prevented from witnessing its suprising (sic) construction and effects. Mr. G, a landscape-painter in the service of the Austrian Prince Esterházy, and, as to music, merely an amateur, had, it appears, for a long time applied his thoughts to the possibility of producing an instrument consisting of every wind-instrument employed in a full military-band, which should perform of of (sic) its own accord by means of interior mechanism. He communicated this idea to several celebrated professors at Vienna, who considered it impracticable on account of the widely different methods of

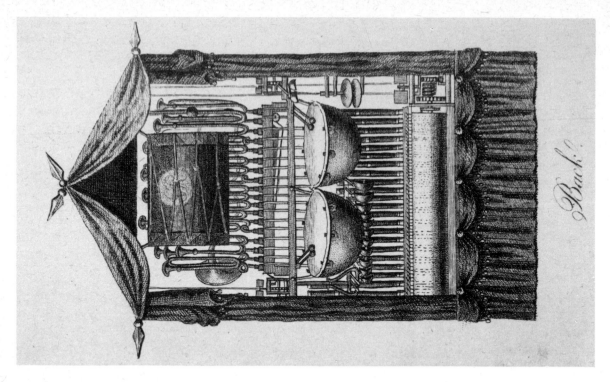

Plate 53. An engraving of Gurck's Panharmonicon presumably issued during the first showing of the instrument in London.

intonation every wind-instrument required; and, indeed, every one superficially acquainted with their various construction must be aware of the different mode of *embouchure* necessary to intonate a flute, a clarionet, an oboe, a bassoon, and above all, a trumpet or a French horn. To men of genius difficulties are but incitements! Partial success encouraged the German's perseverence. One instrument was conquered after another; and after innumerable experiments, his unremitting efforts were crowned by the discovery of a perfect artificial *embouchure* for his horns and trumpets. Undismayed, he now proceeded to the completion of his bold and laborious task, to which every moment free from his professional avocations as an artist, and many a long night, were sedulously sacrificed. Thus, after about seven years of incessant labour, he had the gratification of bringing his instrument to perfection just at the propitious moment for him, which preceded the great Haydn's last illness and death. That veteran *Orpheus*, the father of all that is good and great in music, was one of the first who viewed the result of Mr. Gurk's application and genius. He was delighted; and his applause Mr. Gurk appears to value above the aggregate approbation of all the Continental Sovereigns that inspected the performance. 'And what's to be the name of it,' asked Haydn, after minutely examining every part of the work. 'My child,' replied Mr. G, 'has no name as yet; might I presume to request the Father of Harmony to stand its godfather?' Haydn promised to think of the matter, and the next day sent a German note to the following purport:

Dear Sir, Call your instrument the PANHARMONICON; and, if any body ask you any question about it, tell him the name proceeds from old Haydn.

Your's, &c.

These few lines Mr. Gurk prizes beyond the value of the most precious relicks (sic).

Having thus briefly stated the pedigree of the instrument, we proceed to say a few words on its construction. The whole apparatus is contained in an elegant mahogany-frame, decorated with gilt carvings, and light blue silk curtains. This frame is about fourteen feet high, seven feet wide and four feet deep. Like a four-post bedstead, on removing the curtains, the whole of the interior mechanism is open to the view of the spectators. In front, stand 31 clarionets, behind those 20 flutes, and 20 German flutes; next to those is a set of wooden organ-pipes, then follow 18 bassoons: above these

are placed in a kind of second-story (sic), 14 brass trumpets, and four French horns: and in the back ground Mr. G. has ranged the more noisy instruments, viz. one pair of cymbals, two kettle-drums, one great drum, one smaller one, and one triangle. All these instruments are *real*, i.e. the same as are used in a band, except that each one is bored to produce one note only. They are set in play by a row of brass keys, raised by means of an endless number of small pegs, projecting on a revolving wooden cylinder of about five feet in length and one foot in diameter. This cylinder, as well as the main pair of bellows, is set in rotary motion by the principal clock-work; a second clock-work, on the right, acts by a smaller pair of bellows on the horns and trumpets; and a third clock-work, on the left, directs the drum, cymbals, etc. All the clock-works are wound up for every piece; an operation which takes but a few seconds, and the sufficiency of which is indicated by a whistling sound, a contrivance which precludes the possibility of overwinding.

As each of the different pieces (at present seven in number), performed on the Panharmonicon, equal in duration the length of a regular symphony, one cylinder is appropriated to each, which revolves, according to the extent of the composition, seven times round its axis, in such a manner as to bring, by an imperceptible shift, as many successive rounds of pegs under the same key as the cylinder moves times round its axis; a contrivance which must have required the most minute nicety to arrange. But Mr. G. is now diligently employed to set some popular English airs for his instrument; and that of 'God save the King', with variations, will be completed in a day or two; and others will successively follow from time to time. Of the compositions which the Panharmonicon now performs, the celebrated allegretto of Haydn's military symphony, a rondo by Romberg, and a set of German waltzes purposely composed for the instrument by Pechatscheck, seem to be the most popular.

As to the general effect of the music of this self-performing instrument, it is, as may be supposed, precisely that of a full band: it keeps the exactest time; and since every flute, clarionet, bassoon, etc. can be instantly lowered or sharpened by means of a screw, the whole harmony is clear and in perfect tune; although Mr. G. complains of the variableness and the damp of the English climate, which, he states, requires almost daily rectifications of the pitch and tone of

Fashionable Promenade,

MORNING AND EVENING,

AT THE

PANHARMONICON

Exhibition of Music

BY MECHANICAL POWER;

Equally Grand as a full Orchestra or Parade Band,

INVENTED BY

Mr. GURK from VIENNA,

NOW EXHIBITING

At the ROYAL GREAT ROOMS, SPRING GARDENS,

Charing Cross.

THIS PANHARMONICON consists of Two Hundred and Ten Musical Instruments; viz. frenchhorns, trumpets, kettle drums, oboes, clarinets, bassoons, cymbals, triangles, great drum, bells, and german flutes; performing the most select Pieces of Military Music, composed by MOZART, HAYDN, KRAMMER, &c.—From One o'clock until Four, and from Seven till Ten.—Admission 1s. 6d.

N. B. The whole of the Music is performed in each hour, concluding with God Save the King, or Rule Britannia.

Private Parties may command admission from Four o'clock until Six, PAYING DOUBLE PRICE.

A coloured Engraving of the Panharmonicon may be had at the Room, price 6d.

The Instruments will during the present Week, perform in each hour

Rule Britannia
1. Prince Regent's favourite March, by .... LOGIER.
   Duke of Gloucester's Volunteer quick Step, composed
   and arranged for the Panharmonicon, by ...... PERKIS.
2. Overture of Lodoiska, by .... KRRUTZER.
3. Allegretto of the Military Symphony by .... HAYDN.
4. Three Airs from the Zauberflute, by .... MOZART.
5. March with Trumpet Solo, by .... FR. STARKE.
   March with Trio, by .... FR. KRAMMER.
6. German Waltzes, by .... PECHATSCHEK.
7. Marquis Wellington's March : 1st. British Grenadiers ; 2d, Grand March ; 3d, Victory, closing
   with Bells, purposely composed for the Panharmonicon, by .... H. CLASING.
8. God Save the King, with Variations .... LOGIER.

Toppag, Printer, Playhouse-yard, Blackfriars, London.

Fashionable Promenade,

MORNING AND EVENING

AT THE

PANHARMONICON

Exhibition of Music

BY MECHANICAL POWER;

Equally Grand as a full Orchestra or Parade Band,

INVENTED BY

Mr. GURK from VIENNA,

NOW EXHIBITING

At the ROYAL GREAT ROOMS, SPRING GARDENS,

Charing Cross.

THIS PANHARMONICON consists of TWO HUNDRED INSTRUMENTS; viz. french horns, trumpets, kettle drums, oboes, clarinets, bassoons, cymbals, triangles, great drum, bells, and german flutes; performing the most select Pieces of Military Music, composed by MOZART, HAYDN, KROMMER, &c. Admission from One till Four 1s. 6d. and from Seven till Ten 2s.

N. B. The whole of the Music is performed in each hour, concluding with God Save the King.

An Engraving of the Panharmonicon may be had at the Room, price 6d.

The Instruments will during the present Week, perform in each hour

1. Overture of Clemenza di Tito .... MOZART.
2. Allegretto of the Military Symphony by .... HAYDN.
3. Hunting Piece, with an Imitation of a Thunderstorm
   purposely composed for the Panharmonicon .. FR. STARKE.
   Rondo, composed for the Instruments, by ..... ANDR. ROMBERG.
4. Three Marches, v.z. 1st. March of the Vienna Vo-
   lunteers ; 2d. March of Vienna Grenadiers, with
   Drum Solo ; 3d. Cavalry March with a Trio; the
   whole as performed on the Vienna Parade ..... FR. STARKE.
5. National Waltzes of Vienna .... PECHATSCHEK.
   Rule Britannia
6. Prince Regent's favourite March, by .... LOGIER.
7. Duke of Gloucester's Volunteer quick Step, composed
   and arranged for the Panharmonicon, by ...... PURKIS.
   God Save the King, with Variations .... LOGIER.

N. B. The Music is just published for the Piano Forte.

Toppag, Printer, Playhouse-yard, Blackfriars, London.

Fig. 33. Two surviving concert bills advertising two of the concerts given by Joseph Gurck's Panharmonicon when it visited London's Spring Gardens. Note that in deference to the English, Gurck modified the spelling of his name. Only one piece of music by Haydn features in these notices — the 'allegretto of the Military Symphony' No. 100 in G major dating from 1794.

his subsidiary instruments. The effect of the trumpets is the most surprising, especially in some solo passages of the military pieces, where it is scarcely credible but something more than mere wheels and pegs could produce flourishes so rapid and precise, as to resemble in all respects those produced by the breath of a human being, modulated by human intelligence. In some instances, however, the trumpets seemed too powerful for the delicate modulations of the clarionets and flutes, whose sound appeared greatly overpowered by their more boisterous neighbours in the upper story; but we profess our ignorance as to the practicability of diminishing the strength of the trumpets, or of increasing the power of the treble instruments. The swell, also, from the *piano* to the *forte* is another distinguished merit of the Panharmonicon.

Upon the whole, we confess, that both the sight of the complicated mechanism of this unique instrument, and the witnessing of its powers and effect, excited in us the strongest emotions of rapturous surprise. We could not help admiring a country, at the same time that we sincerely lamented its unfortunate lot, which, even in its present (we hope temporary) state of oppression, continues to delight surrounding nations by a multiplicity of pleasing as well as useful inventions, by its productions in the liberal arts, and by its literary works.

The concluding reference is to the Austrian–French conflict. Napoleon had entered Vienna in November of 1805, an event which while having little effect on the musical life of the city, seems to have been responsible for some of its artisans seeking refuge elsewhere. There was a number of comings and goings in Vienna at this time as truce was replaced by a short period of peace and then, as Haydn lay on his death-bed, Napoleon's troops again fought a conquering battle in Vienna.

Gurck's Panharmonicon performed in London throughout November and December of 1811 and into the following year. On 8 November 1813, notices for the performance, now at the new-styled Royal Rooms, Spring Gardens, stated that: 'Mr. Gurk from Vienna, respectfully informs the Nobility and the Public in general, that he has completed several New Pieces of Music, composed purposely for his extraordinary Instrument, called the PANHARMONICON.'

A notice which appears on 21 July 1817 is headed: 'PANHARMONICON EXHIBITION RETURNED TO LONDON' and continues:

Mr GURK, Inventor, from Vienna, with gratitude begs to acknowledge the great favours he has received from a British Public since his arrival in this country, at the same time he first exhibited at the great rooms, Spring Gardens. Mr. Gurk being on his way to Vienna, he will for a few weeks exhibit again his Panharmonicon at the above-mentioned rooms. This stupendous instrument, performing entirely by mechanical power, consists of a full military band, all in view to the spectators, performing ten pieces of music, composed by Mozart, Haydn, Bishop, &c. &c; the Battle of Waterloo by Bishop; the Trumpet-Solo sounding victory, and the French Horns, Kettle Drum, &c. &c, with Bells rejoicing, will be found gratifying beyond conception. Hours of Performance, at Eleven and Twelve in the Morning, and at Six, Seven and Eight in the Evening — Admission only 1s.

The reference to 'The Battle of Waterloo by Bishop' is misleading. This is more likely to have been the Beethoven work which was a feature of the Mälzel Panharmonicon. This particular title is the cornerstone of the confusion which exists concerning the instruments bearing the name Panharmonicon.

Those who composed for the Panharmonicon and whose music was pinned to the barrels are, in the main, different from those composers whom we have already encountered. With the exception of the continuing associations with Mozart and Haydn, it does seem that Gurck looked elsewhere for his music. For example, we find that the Panharmonicon which was shown in London played music by Krommer, Romberg, Pechatschek, Troppe and Kreutzer among others along with Logier and Purkis.

John Purkis, born London, 21 June 1781; was an organist of extraordinary ability. Blind from birth, he performed at the Foundling Hospital and was dubbed 'the young Handel'. At the age of nine he became organist at Margaret Chapel in Cavendish Square and later to St. Olave's in Southwark. In 1802 he took the organ bench at St. Clement's Dane in the Strand. Here he was close to the organ-building business of Flight & Robson in St. Martin's Lane and when that business built its giant Apollonicon, a barrel and finger organ of extraordinarily versatile capability, Purkis became its first performer in 1817. An enthusiast for mechanical music, he was obviously taken by Gurck's genius and wrote for it *The Duke of Gloucester's Volunteer Quick Step* (composed and arranged for the Panharmonicon by Purkis).

Johann Bernhard Logier, born Cassel 9 February

ROYAL GREAT ROOMS,
Spring Gardens, Charing Cross.

PANHARMONICON
Exhibition of Music,
BY MECHANICAL POWER,
EQUALLY GRAND AS A FULL ORCHESTRA BAND,
Performing the most select Pieces of Military Music,
COMPOSED
By MOZART, HAYDN, KROMMER, ROMBERG, &c. &c.

INVENTED BY

from

J. J. GURK,

Vienna.

THIS

Panharmonicon

CONSISTS OF

210

INSTRUMENTS,

VIZ.

French Horns,

Kettle Drums,

CLARINETS,

Cymbals,

GREAT DRUM

Trumpets,

BELLS,

OBOES,

BASSOONS,

Triangles,

Common Drum

AND

German Flutes.

Commences playing precisely at 1 o'Clock until 4, and from 7 to 10 in the Evening,
ADMITTANCE ONE SHILLING AND SIXPENCE.
N. B. The whole of the Music is performed in each Hour, concluding with God Save the King, or Rule Britannia.
Private Parties may command Admission from 4 to 6, paying 3s. each Person.

A coloured Engraving of the Panharmonicon may be had at the Rooms, price 6d.

TOPPING, PRINTER, Blackfriars, London.

Fig. 34.

1777; died Dublin, 27 July 1846, was a German pianist, pianoforte teacher and composer who is best remembered today for his invention of the 'Chiroplast', a device supposed to train the fingers of the hand as an adjunct to pianistic virtuosity. This gained him fame and wealth and considerable following for his piano-teaching system. Before he was twenty, he went to Ireland and married an Irish girl. He still worked in Berlin and elsewhere, including London, at odd times and made a name for himself in Britain with some pianoforte arrangements, one being the 'Prince Regent's Favourite March' and another being 'God Save the King with Variations', both of which were pinned to cylinders of Gurck's instrument.

Rodolphe Kreutzer, born Versailles, 16 November 1766; died Geneva, 6 June 1831, was a noted violinist and composer and went to Vienna in 1798. In 1791 while in Italy he composed two operas which, among his many operas, turned out to be the most successful. One was *Lodoïska*, first performed on 1 August that year and written in competition with his rival, Cherubini, whose own *Lodoïska* dates from the same year. Kreutzer's most popular music from this was the overture and the Tartars' March. The Panharmonicon played 'the overture or Les Tartares' from this work. Incidentally it was for Rodolphe Kreutzer that Beethoven dedicated his violin and piano Sonata in A major, Opus 47.

Franz Krommer was born in Kanenice near Třebíč on 27 November 1759, and died in Vienna on 8 January 1831. A violinist and composer of Moravian extract, he spent the years from 1794 to his death in Vienna where he attained some considerable status in music. He was deeply influenced by both Haydn and Mozart and his music was widely acclaimed. Gurck's instrument played Krommer's March and Trio (the handbills mis-spelled the composer's name as 'Krammer').

Andreas Jakob Romberg, born Vechta near Münster, 27 April 1767; died destitute in Gotha, 10 November 1821. A violinist and composer who was in Vienna in 1796–7 where his first quartet was greeted enthusiastically by Haydn. He wrote much music and many operas, and his 'Toy' Symphony was occasionally performed as an alternative to that of Haydn. He composed a Rondo especially for Gurck's instrument.

Franz Pechaček (Pechatschek) was a Viennese conductor and composer of operas and ballets as well as an arranger of Viennese waltzes. He was referred to as the Johann Strauss of his time although his reputation was later to be transcended by that of his child prodigy son, Franz (1793–1840). Arrangements of German and Viennese waltzes were set by Gurck on the Panharmonicon from the pen of Pechatschek.

Friedrich Starke was born in Elsterwerda, Saxony, in 1774 and died at Döbling near Vienna on 18 December 1835. A German instrumentalist and composer, he was extremely talented and soon after settling in Vienna, Beethoven entrusted the musical education of his nephew Carl to him. He wrote a good deal of military music, several marches by him being set on the Panharmonicon by Gurck.

The fate of Gurck and his Panharmonicon are unknown although it must be said that confusion between his instrument and that of Mälzel which bore the same name makes piecing together the events somewhat difficult.

Before taking a look at Johann Nepomucene Mälzel, we must consider the part played by the fake automaton chess-player of von Kempelen whose creation and exhibition is closely bound up with Haydn, Panharmonicon and even Niemecz.

In October of 1740, the Emperor Charles VI of Austria died and his daughter Maria Theresa assumed the Habsburg crown as Queen of Hungary and Empress of Germany. As a choirboy, Haydn sang before her Court and when later the Empress came to Eszterháza in 1773, Haydn presented himself to her. In 1769, she was resident at the Schönbrunn Palace and was being entertained by the French prestigiator Le Pelletier who was performing tricks using magnetism which, although new to the Viennese court, were common in Paris. For the occasion, the Empress had summoned a Hungarian nobleman called Baron Wolfgang von Kempelen to her palace. Von Kempelen was counsellor to the Royal Chamber of the Empress of Hungary and when she said to him that it was a pity that a Hungarian could not produce a clever and impressive display better than the French, von Kempelen found himself promising to produce something suitable within one year.

Von Kempelen's credentials for such a task were encouraging. Born at Pressburg (Bratislava) on 23 January 1734, he was just thirty-five years of age and ever since childhood he had displayed considerable mechanical genius. His knowledge of hydraulics had been put to good use in designing the cascades and fountains at the Schönbrunn Palace and he had also applied himself to the synthesising of the human voice using an artificial throat and hand-operated lips.

Von Kempelen chose for his masterpiece an artificial chess-player, a device which would apparently play a game of chess with a human opponent without a second human being present. In reality, only six months elapsed before its completion and it was on its way to Vienna. It is likely that, in view of the short time of execution, von Kempelen had been aware from the start that total automation was beyond his ability to create and that his machine must resort to trickery. In fact, the machine was worked by a small person who crouched hidden from sight within.

The chess-player was shown, demonstrated and then forgotten until soon after the death of the Empress in 1780 when her son and heir, the Emperor Joseph II, called his counsellor von Kempelen and asked if he would demonstrate the 'automaton' to the Grand Duke and Duchess of Russia on a forthcoming visit to Vienna. This took place in November of 1781 and was so successful that von Kempelen was persuaded to accept paid leave of absence from his post and take the device on a tour through England, France and Germany. The tour ended in 1785 and the chess-player was stored while its inventor busied himself back in Pressburg with the affairs of the Court and in the making of a fire-fighting appliance. Kempelen died on 28 March 1804.

Mälzel, who had settled in Vienna in 1792, had already heard of the chess-playing machine even if he had not actually seen it and he approached von Kempelen on several occasions to try to buy it. The high price asked — a massive 20,000 francs — prevented Mälzel from clinching a deal but, after the death of its builder, von Kempelen's son, who had no interest in it, agreed to sell it to Mälzel for half that figure.

At this time, Mälzel would have been thirty-four years old. He was born on 15 August 1772 at Regensburg (Ratisbon) and by the age of fourteen was an accomplished pianist and pianoforte teacher. Like von Kempelen, he was also something of a mechanical genius and, being the son of a father who was an organ-builder, he applied himself to constructing an orchestrion organ for the Archduke, Charles of Austria. This played music by Mozart, Haydn and Crescentini and cost its titled owner 3,000 Florins. It is reputed that the prince bought the thing solely for annoying his friends which either speaks badly of the musical taste of the Archduke and his friends or indicates that the mechanical organ was not entirely a satisfactory interpreter.

Mälzel then began the construction of another instrument, a veritable mechanical orchestra. At some time during its life, it became named the Panharmonicon although, unlike Gurck's instrument, this name did not, it seems, spring direct from Haydn. Since both instruments (Gurck's and Mälzel's) appeared to have a similar specification and goal in life, the name inspired by Haydn could well have been appropriated as a generic term for a mechanical military band. The new instrument which Mälzel built was an extended version of his first and besides clarinets, flutes, oboes, horns and bassoons included a serpent and a bass drum all operated mechanically. The wind instruments were arranged in two rows and its builder claimed that the method of blowing the reeds closely approximated the effect of the

tongueing of a human player. The entire instrument, with its triangular array of instruments (tallest in the centre, shortest to each side), was housed in a glazed cabinet six feet square and five feet high.

The orchestrion was first exhibited in Vienna in 1804 and was well received by all who saw and heard it. The instrument produced a powerful sound but was also capable of executing the quieter passages very well. In 1807, Mälzel took his instrument to Paris where it performed in the open on the Champs de Mars causing both astonishment and pleasure to the Parisians. As from the eighth of March that year, Mälzel gave daily recitals at two in the afternoon and at eight in the evening at the Hotel de Montmorency, Rue du Mont-Blanc, chausée d'Antin.

So popular were these recitals that in July Mälzel announced that thanks to public demand there were to be two more consecutive concerts, one at each of the advertised performance times. The admission was three francs for one show and six francs for the run-on. Later in the year, the concerts were shifted to a fresh location at No. 1, Cour des Fontainnes. For the opening at this new address, which took place on 12 December, the orchestrion featured a new work by Daniel Steibelt which portrayed in music the four turning points of the day.

Daniel Steibelt (born Berlin, 22 October 1765; died St. Petersburg, 2 October 1823) was a pianist and composer who was educated in an environment of mechanical music. He came under the patronage of the crown prince, later to be Frederick William II, and learned the harpsichord and composition under Kirnberger. When he went to Paris (the first of several visits) in August 1800, he took with him the score of Haydn's *Creation*. Besides operas, his main contribution among 110 opus numbers was piano music but there was also a number of so-called programme pieces (see Gottfried Müller, *Daniel Steibelt, sein Leben und seine Klavierwerke*, Leipzig and Zürich, 1933).

After these new concerts were under way, Mälzel returned to Vienna and left the day to day operation of the instrument, now advertised as the Panharmonicon, to the care of a manager. He returned to Paris the following October to première his latest novelty, an automaton trumpeter in the shape of a life-sized figure which from that time forward shared the concert programme with the Panharmonicon.

Mälzel's trumpeter, today standing in a glass cabinet at München's Deutsches Museum, was a clever piece of craftsmanship for the problems of sounding a trumpet artificially (i.e. without human lips) were solved mechanically. He achieved his musical feats through a sound knowledge of acoustics, engineering and applied

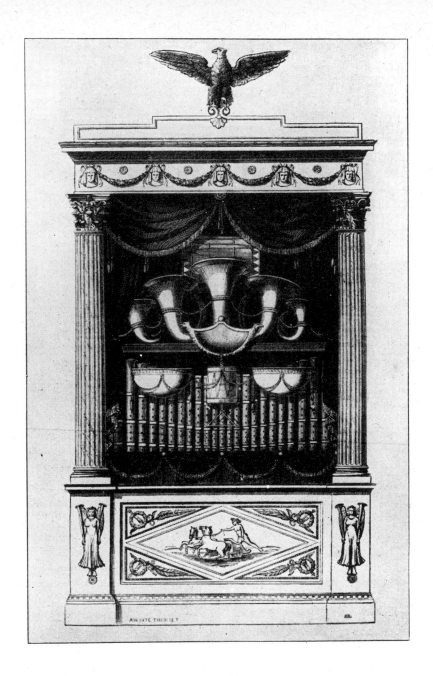

Plate 54. Although the Panharmonicons of both Gurck and Mälzel created considerable interest at the time of their exhibition in various parts of the world, illustrations of these progenitors of the orchestrion organ are few and far between. With their spectacular appearance and respectable repertoire, in an age when musical performances were social occasions it seems strange that so few pictures survive. This one, of an unidentified Mälzel Panharmonicon, is simply labelled 'German Musical Machine' demonstrating that, as with many writers of the time, the author did not recognise Austria as being any different from the many principalities which later came to make up Germany.

mechanics. Even so, many Viennese considered that he was in cahorts with the Devil and that he was practising Black Magic. In an earlier and less enlightened age, he would undoubtedly have been slain and his work destroyed like that of the Jaquet-Droz (the story of the destruction of *The Grotto* is related elsewhere).

But clever though Mälzel was, he was not totally respectable in his undertakings. While the usurping of the name Panharmonicon may not entirely have been due to his efforts (and may have been the work of the Viennese newspapers), he was, as we shall see, not above borrowing other peoples' ideas for his own monetary gain. But if he was less than honest, he was undoubtedly clever and, above all, a showman who was superbly capable of promoting his own inventions — or those of others — to the public.

Within a few months of introducing the automaton trumpeter, Mälzel began to tire of the Panharmonicon which he sold in Paris at the end of 1808 allegedly for 60,000 francs. He returned to Vienna where his reputation and talent had earned him the appointment of Mechanician to the Royal and Imperial Court — a post not entirely dissimilar from that which von Kempelen had held.

The emperor at that time was Francis I (Franz I) who had assumed the title of Holy Roman Emperor after the two-year reign of his father, Leopold II, the younger brother of Joseph II. With the final dissolution of the Holy Roman Empire in August 1806, Francis had become Emperor of Austria.

Mälzel had purchased the automaton chess-player in 1806 during the time when he was showing his orchestrion in Vienna.

During 1809, he was summoned as Court Mechanician to Schönbrunn to undertake some work and was indeed living in the palace when, after the Battle of Wagram, Napoleon arrived at the palace gates. Mälzel stayed put and, in fact, gave Napoleon a demonstration of the chess-player. Shortly afterwards, he moved into rooms at the piano factory of Matthäus Andreas Stein at the Red Rose, No. 301 in the Viennese suburb of Landstrasse. His connection with Stein no doubt was associated with parts for his Panharmonicon emanating from that maker.

Mälzel did not keep the chess-player for long, selling it for 30,000 francs (three times its purchase price!) by 1812. That was the year in which the industrious Mälzel was involved in making a diorama called *The Conflagration of Moscow,* and in the building of a new and larger Panharmonicon. This emerged as an orchestrion seven feet long, six feet wide and the same in height and produced the sounds of violins, cellos, trumpets, flutes, clarinets, drums, cymbals and triangle. As usual, it was operated by weight-driven clockwork.

Beethoven appears to have enjoyed Mälzel's mechanical contrivances and frequently visited him in his workshop at Stein's factory. The two became close friends and their acquaintanceship probably began in 1795 when Beethoven had written a letter of introduction for a 'Herr Menzel', apparently a misspelling of Mälzel. In this document, Beethoven extolled Mälzel's ability on the piano. Beethoven, less than two years older than the mechanician, and Mälzel had both come to Vienna in the year 1792 to seek their fortunes in music, the one from Bonn and the other from Regensburg.

But Beethoven had other reasons for being glad of Mälzel's friendship. He was going deaf and as his hearing became progressively worse, he turned to Mälzel for an ear trumpet. Six were subsequently made, but only the smallest and simplest offered any practical help. Beethoven made use of it for some years.

Mälzel's work on the new Panharmonicon was completed during the winter of 1812–13 and he began arranging and pinning music for the cylinders in preparation for a trip to London which he still planned to make. Beethoven was also to accompany him on the journey. The first barrels to be finished comprised Cherubini's *Lodoïska* overture, Haydn's 'Military' Symphony, and the overture and chorus from Handel's *Timotheus.* By the end of January he was working on a piece composed specially for him by Cherubini. This was the once-celebrated echo piece. As spring turned to summer, he began setting some special marches written for his instrument by the nineteen year-old Ignaz Moscheles.

Ignaz Moscheles, born Prague, 30 May 1794; died Leipzig, 10 March 1870, demonstrated very early on in his life that he was destined to be a musician. A compelling pianist, his name was established in 1815

Nouvelle Galerie des Panoramas
Boutique, N° 9.

J. MAELZEL,
Mécanicien, Inventeur du PANHARMONICON,
de l'AUTOMATE-TROMPETTE, etc.
Par Brevet d'Invention,
METRONOMES
ET
PETITS AUTOMATES PARLANTS

Fig. 35. Mälzel's visiting card used at the time of his Paris exhibition. Notice the reference to metronomes.

with his virtuoso *Variationen über den Alexandermarsch*. He studied with Albrechtsberger and Salieri. During the construction of the Panharmonicon, Moscheles was a frequent visitor to Mälzel's workshop and took a great interest in the way the barrels were prepared.

In the year 1814, Mälzel made his long-awaited visit to London bringing with him the Panharmonicon and the trumpeter as well as the diorama of the burning of Moscow, although the newspaper notices avoided identifying the particular city to be burned every day. The following notice regarding this exhibition is of particular interest in that it refers to the instrument as 'his grand panharmonicon' which implies a generic term rather than a specific name and adds weight to the conjecture that Mälzel took the name 'panharmonicon' from the instrument named by Haydn and built by Gurck.

Mr. Mälzel begs leave to inform the nobility, gentry and the public in general that he will have the honour to exhibit every day (except Friday) at eight in the evening, his *grand panharmonicon* and his *Automatic Trumpeter* which have never yet been seen in this country, and of which he is the inventor. The Trumpeter plays: 1 The Signals of the Cavalry. 2 A March composed by Mr. Hummel. 3 An Allegro by Mr. Pleyel. The two latter with accompaniments.

He will further represent to the views of the public, *a Hebe, a sublime picture* made transparent by a double effect of light; after which the Panharmonicon will execute, 1st The Overture to Lodoiska, by M. Cherubini, 2nd A Military Symphony by Mr. Haydn.

Afterwards will be seen *a great city on fire*. The view is taken from the citadel, between which and the city the spectator observes several military corps filing off with their military music, which is executed by the mechanism. In the left side is very distinctly to be seen the progress the fire has made, and the natural motions of men, horses, carriages, etc, etc. The representation is faithful, and accompanied with appropriate music.

The whole will terminate by, 1st The Grand Symphony of Mr. Beethoven, so well known and admired in London. 2nd An Echo by Mr. Cherubini. 3rd Two French Marches, by Mr. Moscheles, which will be executed by the Panharmonicon.

Gradually, the showman side of Mälzel took the upper hand and soon he began to regret parting company with the automaton chess-player. By 1817, he had managed to secure its return although whether by re-purchase or

other arrangements seems uncertain. From 1818 to 1821, he toured England, Scotland and elsewhere with it but finally, after several people had published the secret behind its operation, the thing ceased to be of great interest to the wide-eyed public at large. Mälzel tried to sell it to no avail and finally took it to America where it toured with moderate success. His death in 1838 effectively marked the end of the story, the actual chess-player device meeting its end in a Philadelphia museum conflagration in 1854.

Mälzel visited Amsterdam somewhere between 1805 and 1806 and there met the Dutch organ-builder and inventor, Diederich Nicolaus Winkel, who had been

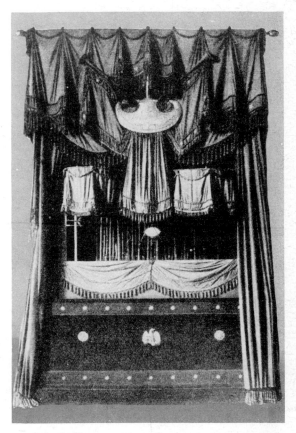

Plate 55. Possibly the most well known of the small clutch of surviving Panharmonicon illustrations is this one, reputed to represent the one formerly in the Stuttgart museum and destroyed during the Second World War. It does, however, bear little resemblance to the surviving museum pictures which show the mechanism less drapes. The strong Turkish influence of the decoration reflects the styles of the time but the draped drums and heavy curtains must have either muted the sound or helped to conceal imperfections. The original negative for this much-copied picture was lost in the War.

experimenting with a prototype metronome. Mälzel saw this, took the idea home with him, produced an improved version and began marketing it under his own name. Winkel was allowed no redress until the damage was too late to repair. In 1821, Mälzel again visited Amsterdam and Winkel justifiably tried to prove his claim to the invention. This he did and secured official verification of his invention, but to no avail. It is considered that this rebuff was the force which motivated Winkel to manufacture the Componium, a twin-cylindered orchestrion which could produce endless variations on a theme pinned to one cylinder via the aegis of a complex clockwork computer and random analyser.

Johann Nepomucene Mälzel's brother, Leonard, was also involved in making orchestrions but little is known as to the part he played in the proceedings. In 1829 he built one which 'produced an orchestra of forty-two automata which play together'.

The fates of several of the Mälzel instruments are known but only one survived into recent times. This was one which was kept in the former Industrial Museum in Stuttgart. There it perished in the Second World War. Fortunately, however, twelve of its barrels survived in a basement store and are still extant. They measure 1.25m long by 24cm in diameter (50¼ in. x 9 in.).

In the same way that Winkel's entitlement to the title of metronome inventor was denied to him by Mälzel, so Gurck's entitlement to be recorded as the person to whom Haydn gave the name Panharmonicon has been usurped by Mälzel. Neither Winkel nor Gurck had the ability to capitalise on their inventions adequately and neither had the talent for self-promotion that Mälzel possessed. Perhaps history will now adjust itself to the facts.

For expansion of the association of Haydn and the Court of Austria, see Christopher Dies, *Biographisches Nachrichten von Joseph Haydn,* Vienna, 1810 (there is a revised edition by Horst Seeger published in Berlin, undated, but 1959). For the story of von Kempelen's chess-player, see Bradley Ewart, *Chess: Man vs Machine,* A.S. Barnes, New York, 1980 (a most valuable documentation). For a description of some of the London shows, see Ord-Hume, *Clockwork Music,* 1973, also *Barrel Organ,* 1978, both published in London by George Allen & Unwin. There are also references in Richard D. Altick: *The Shows of London,* Harvard University Press, 1978 (this author confuses the terms

Fig. 36. The foundation of Niemecz and Gurck, exploited by Mälzel, led to the development of the mechanical orchestras which achieved their zenith of perfection in Leipzig, Berlin and the Black Forest early in the present century. Frederick Theodore Kaufmann built his Orchestrion, seen here, and showed it to Queen Victoria in 1851, a massive yet impractically fragile demonstration that miniature musical perfection had inexorably progressed into the mass media and the desire for the spectacular.

'orchestrion' and 'panharmonicon' and is not always to be relied upon). A fine study of the life of Daniel Steibelt is Gottfried Müller, *Daniel Steibelt: sein Leben und seine Klavierwerke,* Leipzig and Zürich, 1933. The story of the Componium of Winkel and its method of working is set out in the work *Histoire de la Boite á Musique* by Chapuis (in translation as *The History of the Musical Box,* published by the Musical Box Society International, United States, 1979), and in *Barrel Organ,* already cited.

APPENDIX 2

Making Mechanical Organs and Arranging Music

On the following pages are reproduced the detailed plates from the book *L'Art du Facteur d'Orgues* by Dom Bedos de Celles which was published in 1778. These plates provide the most graphic demonstration of the art of mechanical organ construction and additionally instruct on the arrangement of music for the barrel of the mechanical organ.

This series is prefaced by a reproduction of the title page of Father Engramelle's 1775 book *La Tonotechnie ou l'Art de Noter les Cylindres.* Then follows six plates. In the first three are given drawings for making a hand-cranked model while the next two show a clockwork version. The final plate in this section shows how to form the barrel from many strips of wood. The similarity between the first Haydn/Niemecz organ and these plates is striking. Note particularly that the keyframe of the serinette is shown with the keys, which are here made of wood, each mounted individually on separate pivots — exactly the principle used on the first of the three organs.

The plates which follow show the tools which Dom Bedos recommended for mechanical organ barrel-pinning. Note the four pairs of stepped pliers for making staples of flat-sectioned brass wire of varying lengths according to the value of the note they were to produce. This could then be checked on pinning with the special gauge seen on the third plate.

Then follows a plate showing the so-called dial method of dividing the barrel into component parts, normally the length of the smallest note to be played. The dial — virtually a micrometer — is fixed to the organ case and a pointer attached to the winding handle. By stepping round a pre-calculated number of divisions, various measures can be catered for by using a number of discs and numbered wheels.

The next illustration comes from Engramelle and shows several tunes marked for barrel-pinning. The symbols above the notation indicate the form of *martellement* or cadence which, although not written out, the pinner will arrange on the barrel.

The extensive section of 14 plates, which follows is without much doubt the most important guide to

mechanical organ making which has come down to use today. The first nine plates show various types of cadence, or appoggiatura and how this should be written in barrel-noter's shorthand, how it should be translated into barrel pinning — and what the result will sound like when the organ is played.

The final five plates in this set show a simple tune of the period marked as for a barrel organ playing thirteen notes, chromatically from G to g.

LA TONOTECHNIE

O U

L'ART DE NOTER

L E S

CYLINDRES,

Et tout ce qui est susceptible de Notage dans les Instrumens de Concerts méchaniques.

OUVRAGE NOUVEAU,

Par le Père ENGRAMELLE, Religieux Augustin de la Reine Marguerite.

_____

.... Ego , cur acquirere pauca
Si possum , invidear?... *Horat.*

_____

A PARIS,

Chez P. M. DELAGUETTE, Libraire-Imprimeur, rue de la Vieille Draperie.

M. DCC. LXXV.

Avec Approbation & Privilège du Roi.

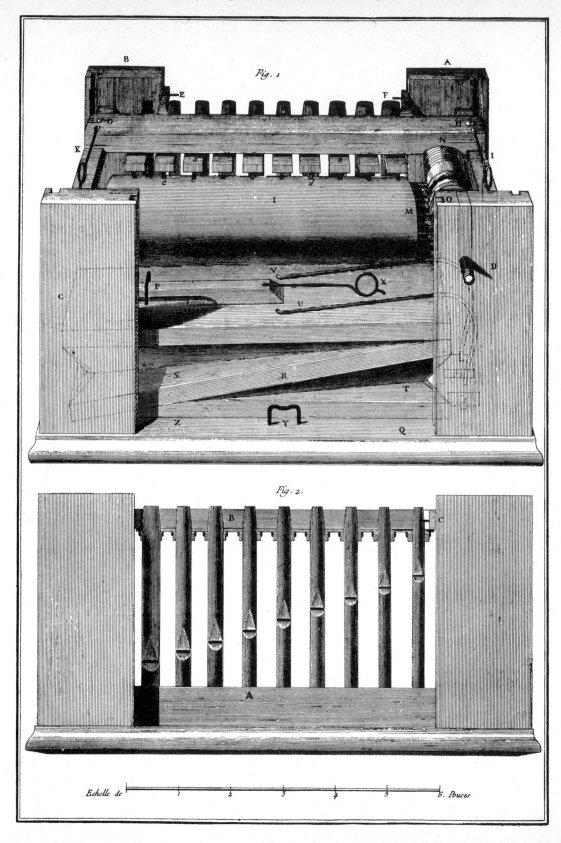

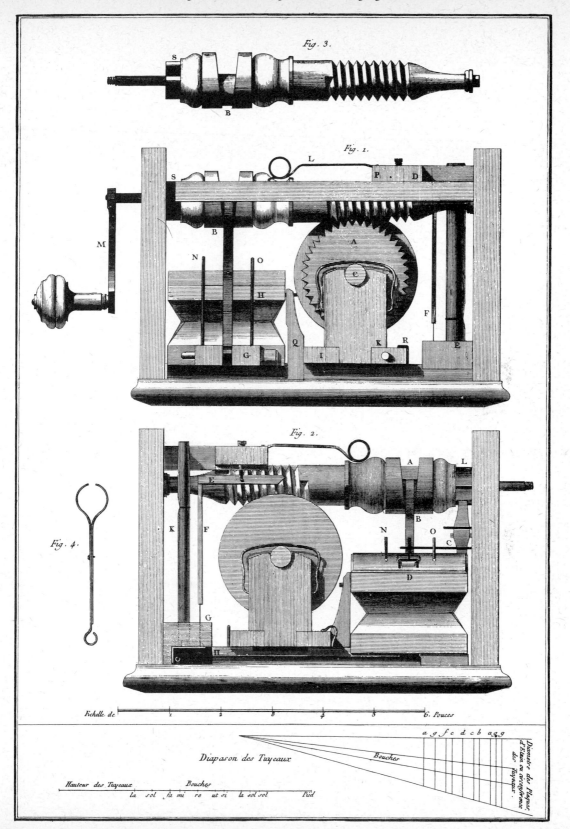

Fig. 3.

Fig. 1.

Fig. 2.

Fig. 4.

Echelle de 1 2 3 4 5 6. Pouces

Diapason des Tuyeaux

Bouches

a g f e d c b a g g

Diametre des Plaques d'Etain ou circonference des Tuyeaux.

Hauteur des Tuyeaux Bouches

la sol fa mi re ut si la sol sol Pied

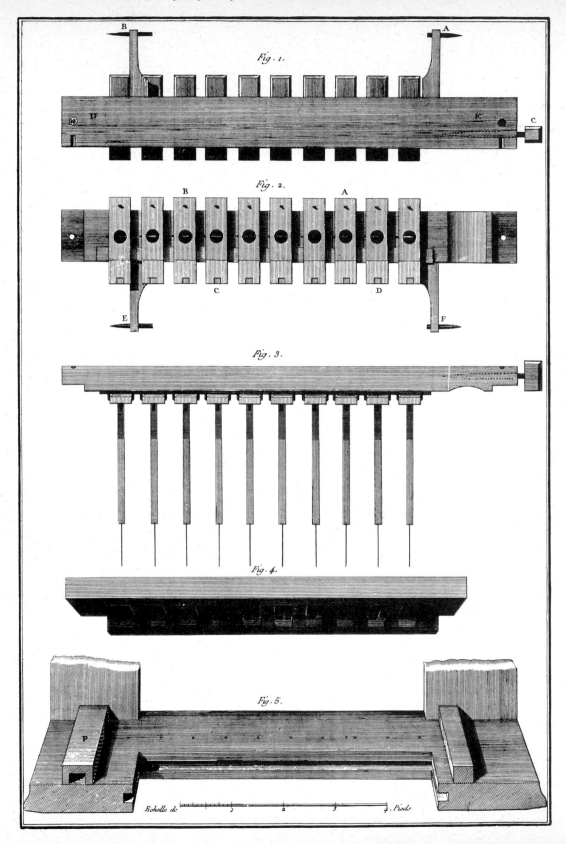

Fig. 1.

Fig. 2.

Fig. 3.

Fig. 4.

Fig. 5.

Echelle de: 1   2   3   4. Pieds

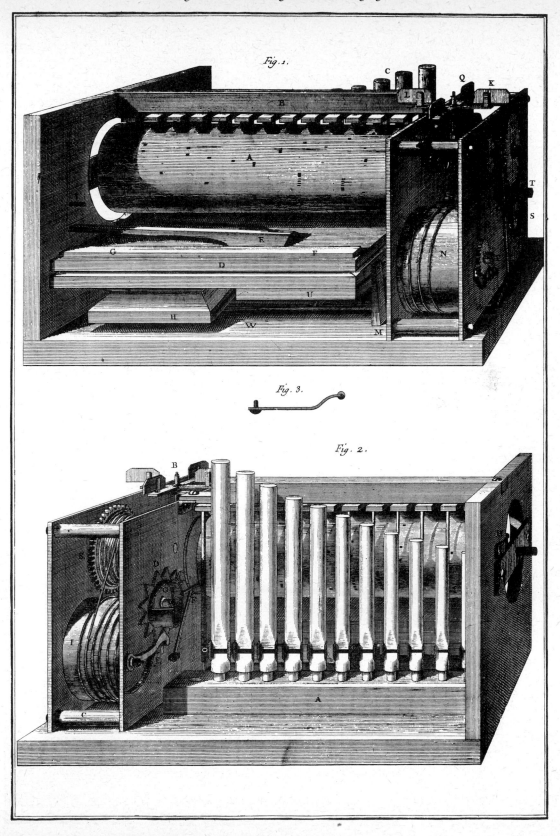

Fig. 1.

Fig. 3.

Fig. 2.

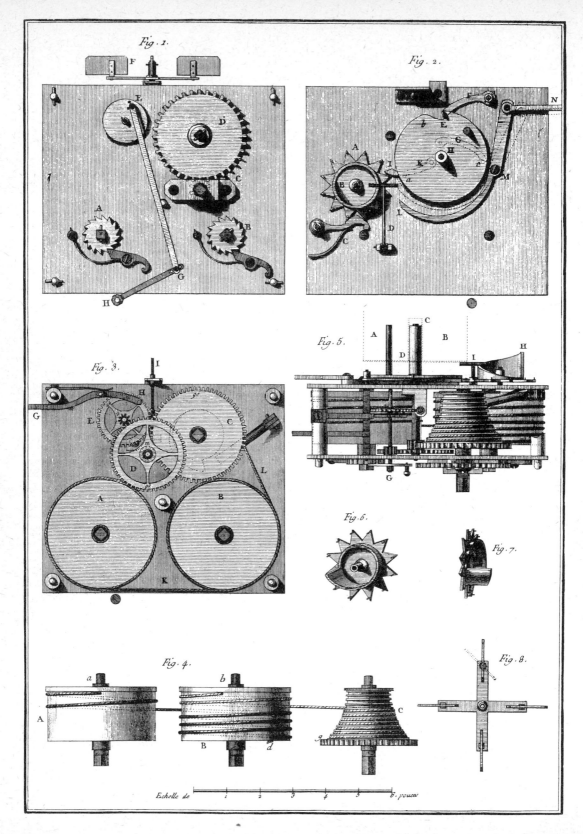

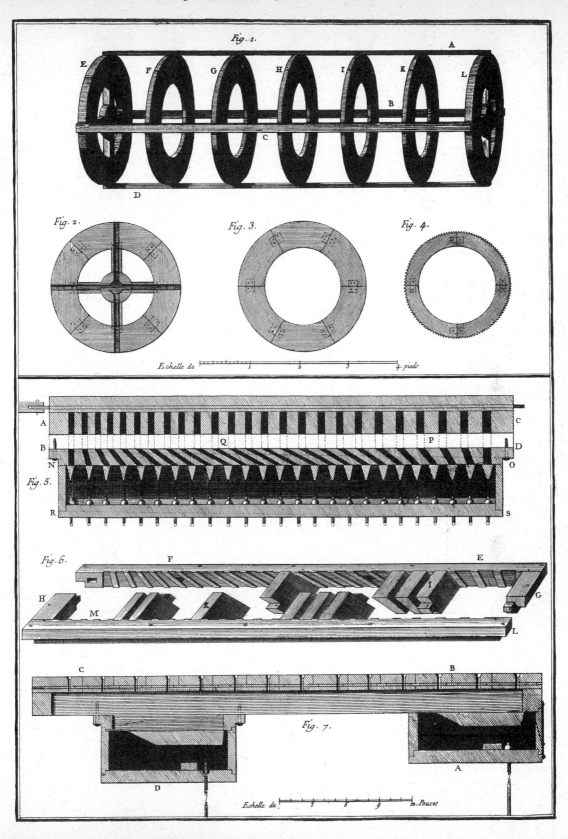

Fig. 1.

Fig. 2. Fig. 3. Fig. 4.

Echelle de 1 2 3 4 pieds

Fig. 5.

Fig. 6.

Fig. 7.

Echelle de 3 6 9 12 Pouces

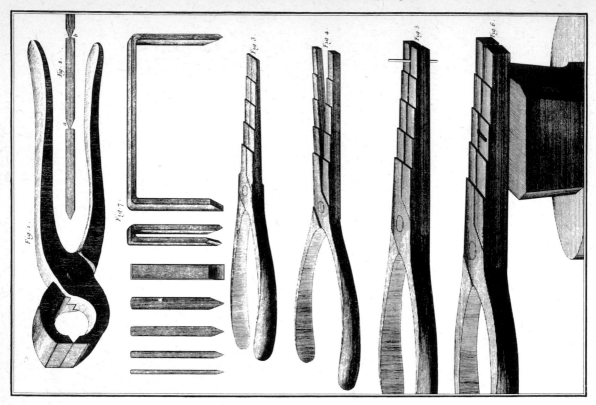

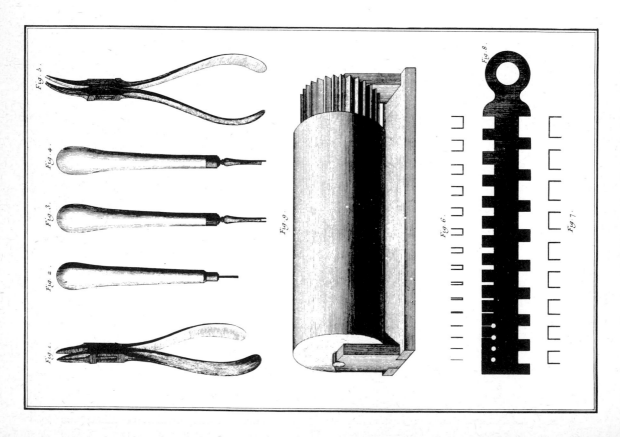

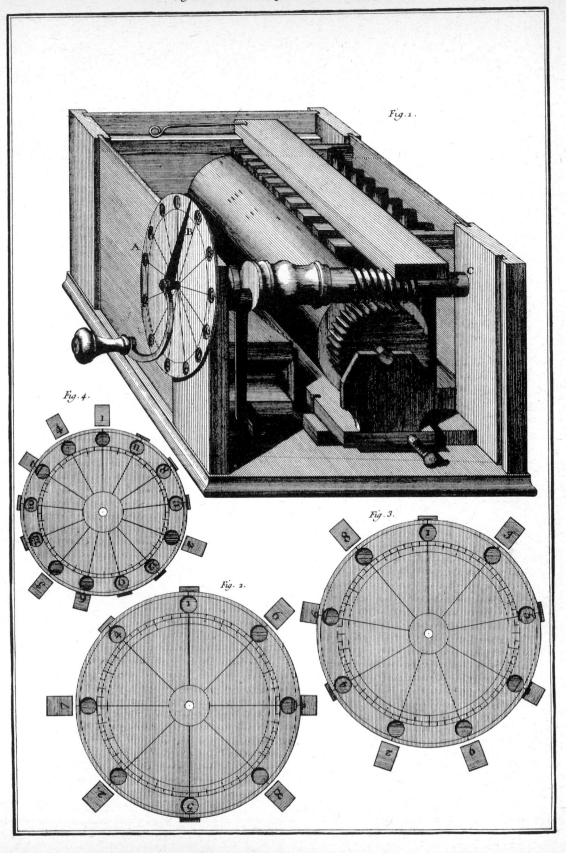

Fig. 1.

Fig. 4.

Fig. 2.

Fig. 3.

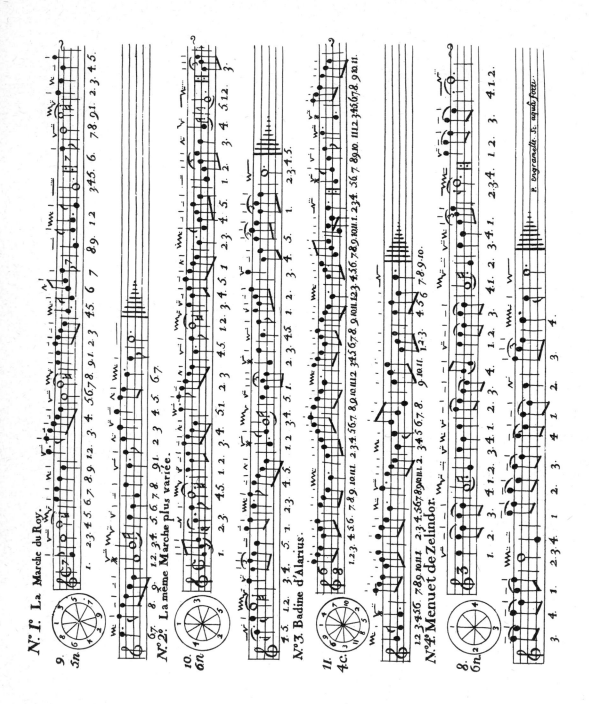

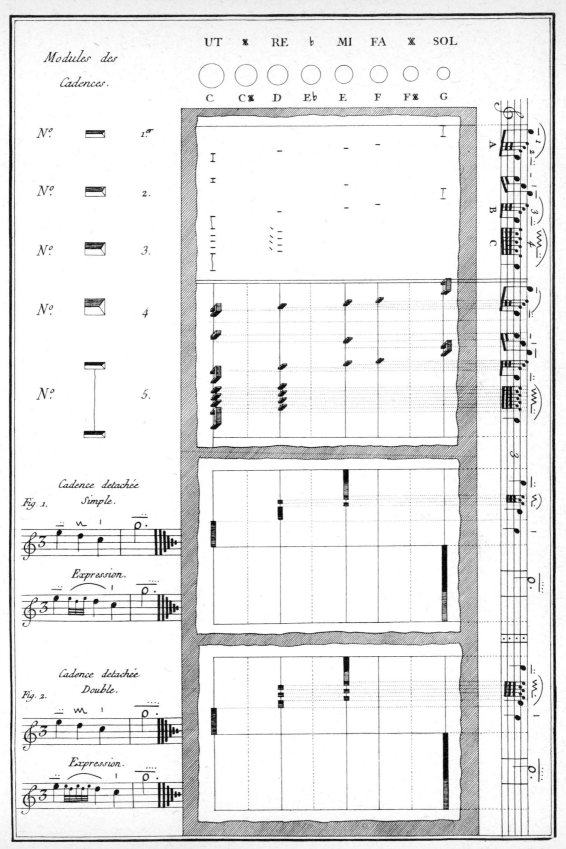

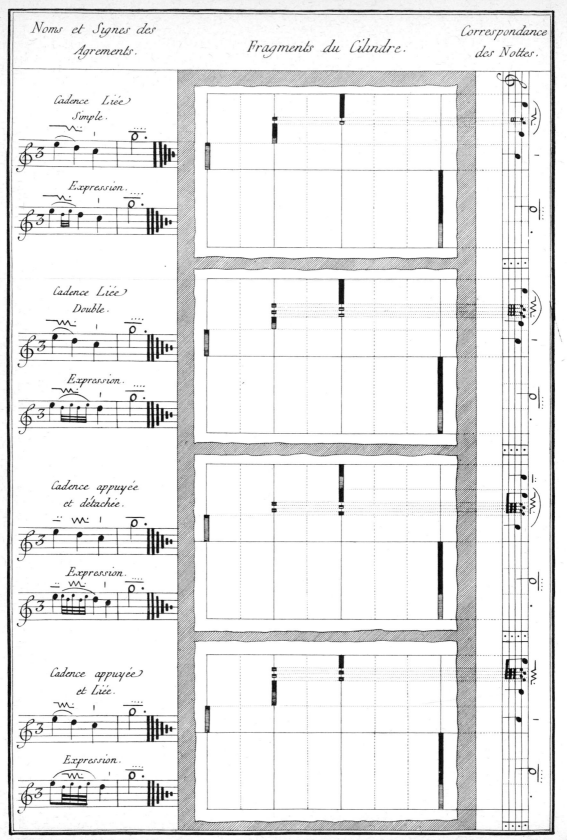

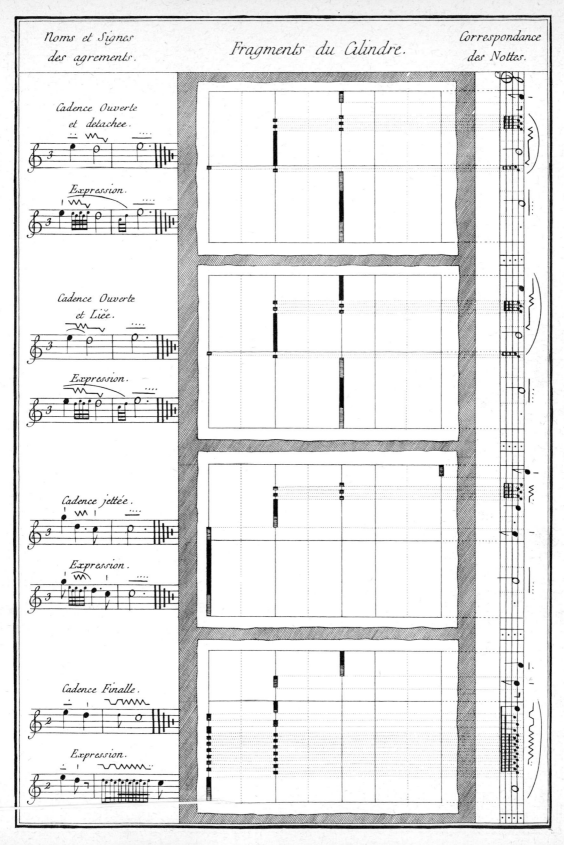

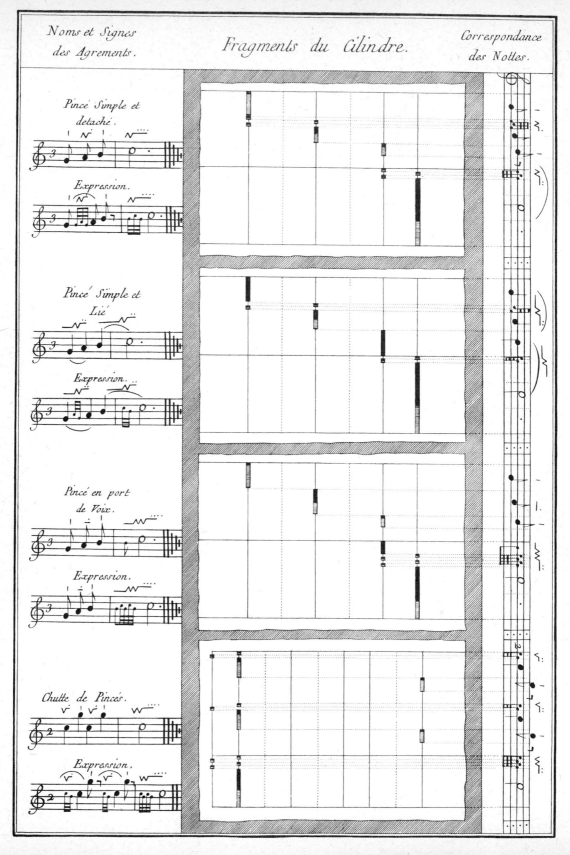

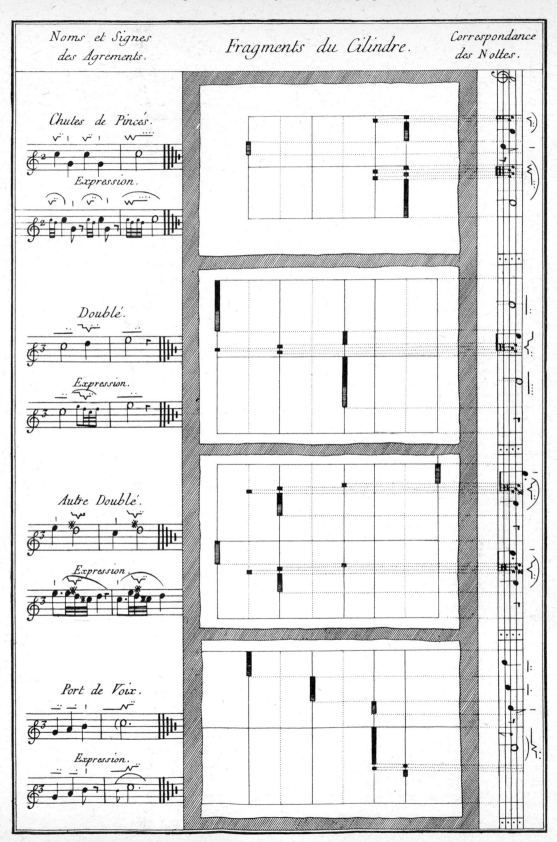

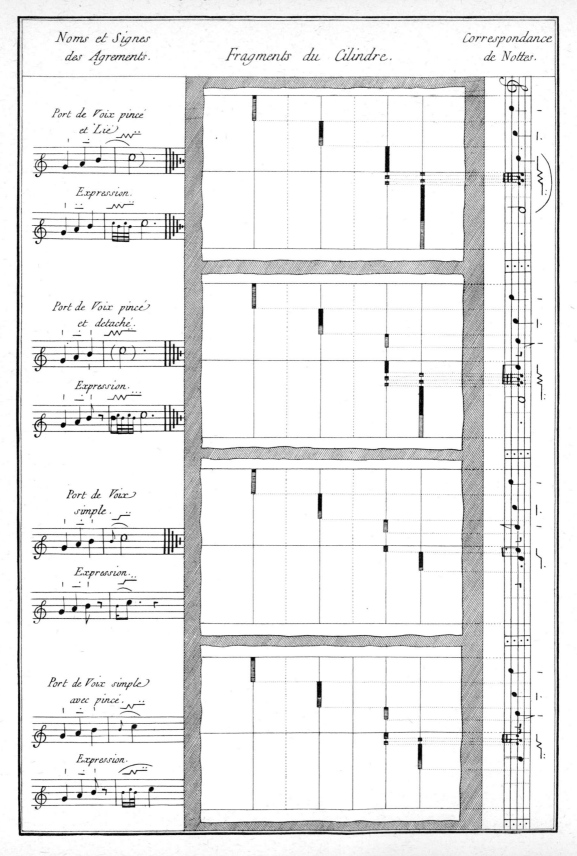

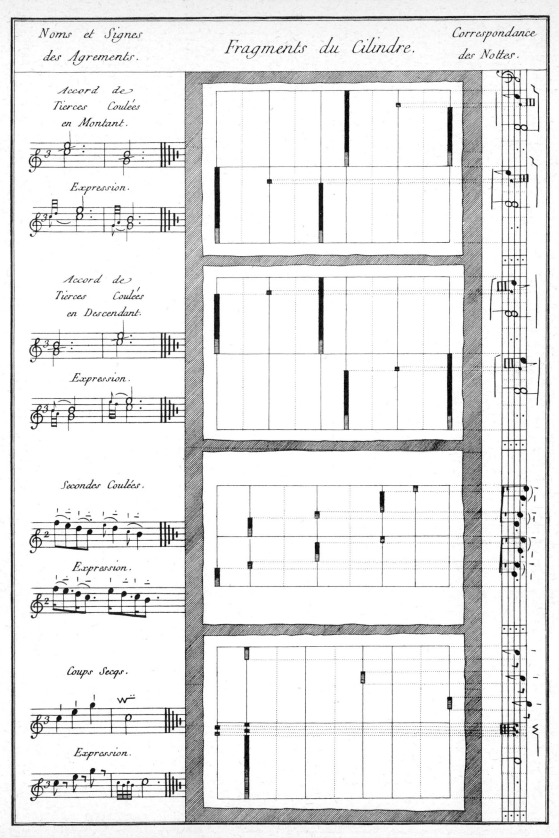

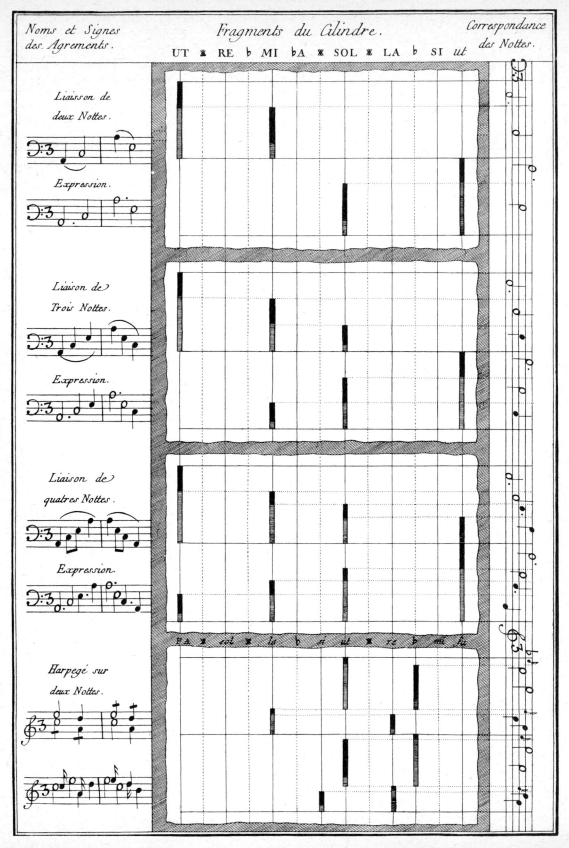

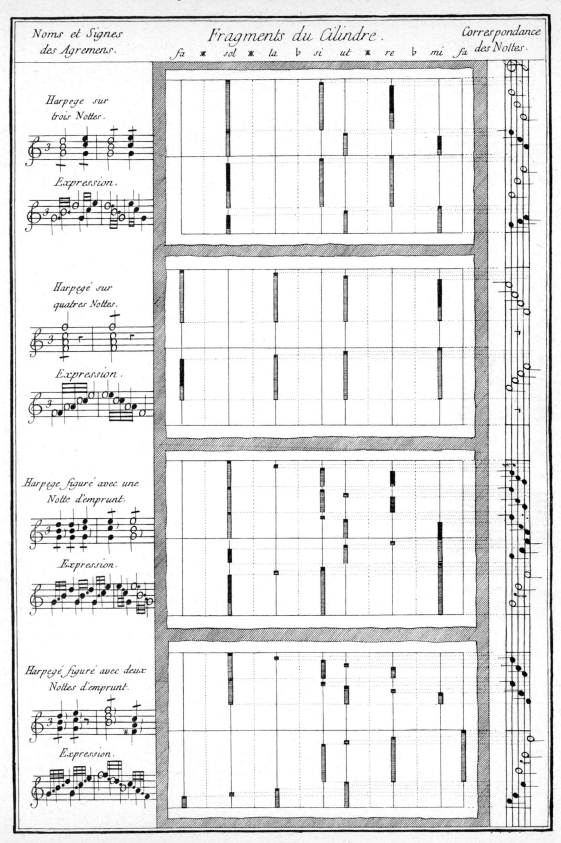

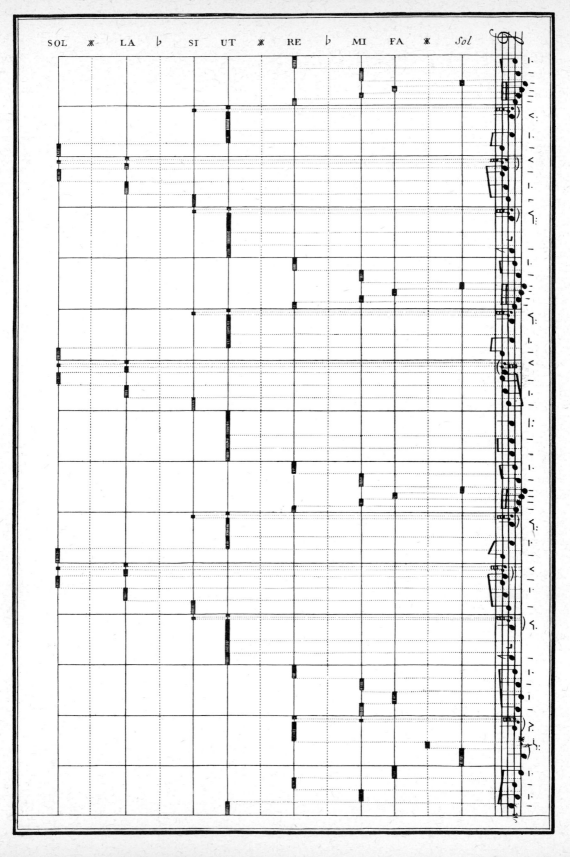

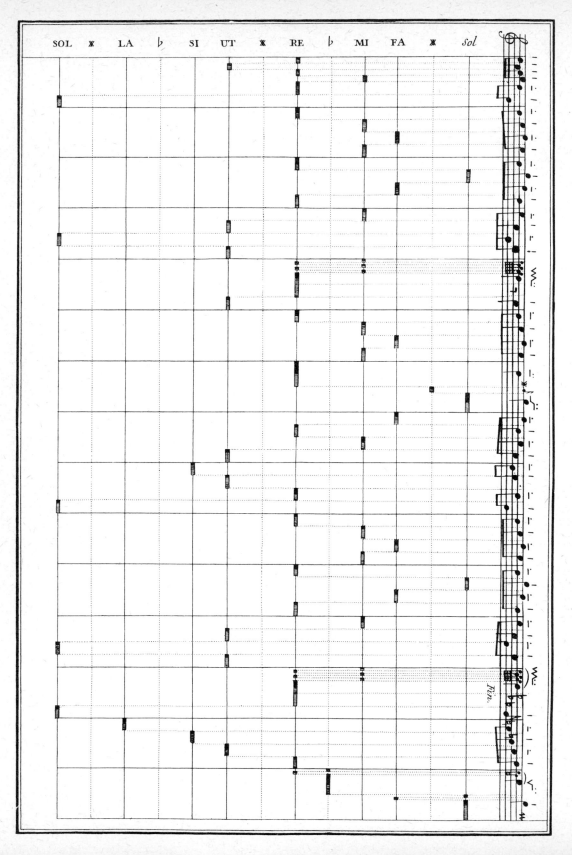

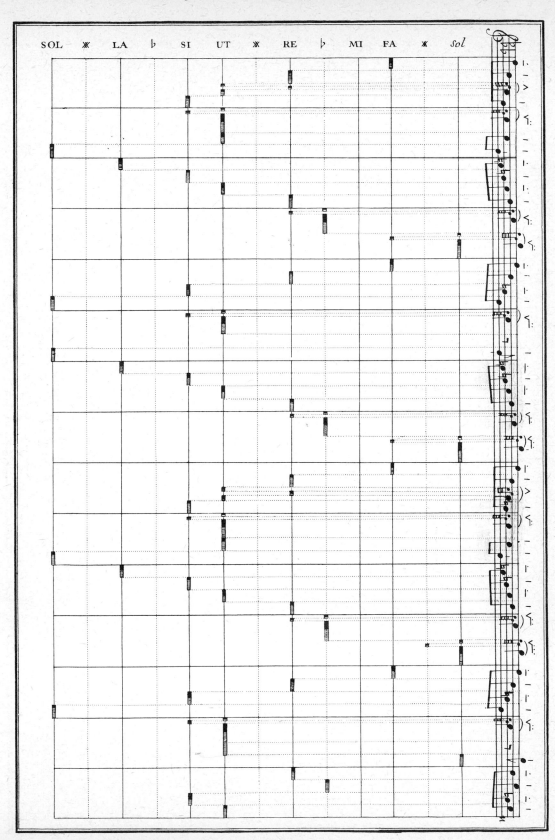

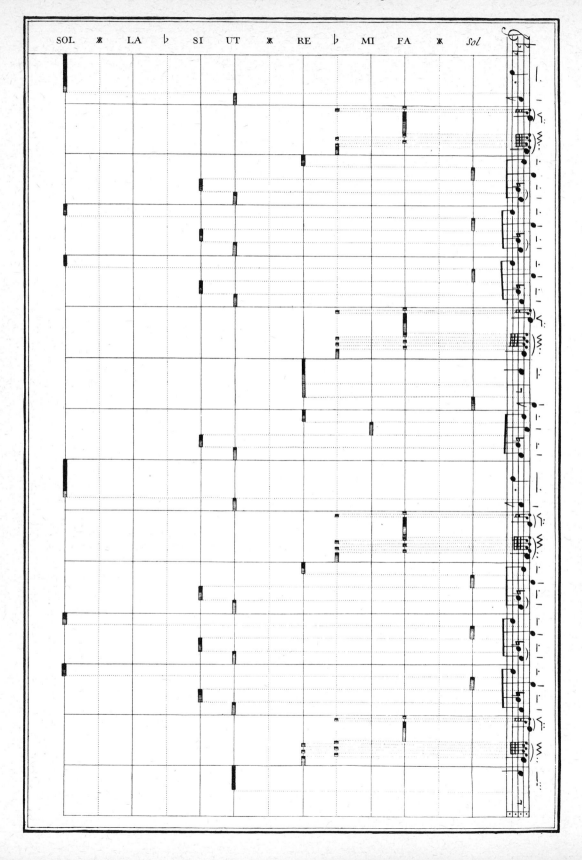

Biography

On the following pages are presented brief biographical details of the more important names which appear in the foregoing and in particular details of the composers who wrote for mechanical organ and the clockmakers and musical instrument makers who made the mechanisms which played their music. This section is to be used as a quick-reference source for basic information.

Arzt, Franz Egydius. A maker of large musical clocks of exceptional quality. Little is known of Arzt and he is remembered by only a few surviving pieces. It is believed that he was born in München in 1757, the son of Johann Martin Arzt. He became a master clockmaker and worked in München between 1779 and 1781 in which year he moved to Vienna where he died on 3 March 1812. Besides organ-playing clocks, he also perfected a machine for spinning silk thread for which he received an award of 1000 Fl. in 1802. He was succeeded by his son Josef who was also a master clockmaker between 1824 and 1857. One Arzt organ clock playing the 'Grenadiers' March' arranged by Beethoven was formerly in the Heyer Museum, Cologne, and is now in Leipzig.

Bach, Carl Philipp Emanuel. Born Weimar, 8 March 1714; died Hamburg, 15 December 1788. The second son of Johann Sebastian Bach, C.P.E. Bach left behind him a considerable number of pieces for mechanical instrument. This included four pieces marked 'für Flötenuhr', three marked 'für Flöten und Harfe' (for organ and harp or dulcimer mechanism), five for '2 Flöten' (a *Flötenuhr* with two registers gedackt and open), two for '2 Clarinetten' (a mechanical organ with two clarinet registers), two simply marked 'für eine Drehorgel' (for a hand-turned barrel organ), and fourteen for 'eine Harfenuhr' (for mechanical dulcimer). These can be found itemised in Alfred Wotquenne, *Catalogue thématique des oeuvres de C. Ph. Em. Bach*, published in Leipzig in 1905 (page 67).

Bach, Wilhelm Friedemann. Born Weimar, 22 November 1710; died Berlin, 1 July 1784. The second child and eldest son of Johann Sebastian Bach. Was interested in the harp-playing clock and composed several pieces for this instrument. Wolfgang Schmieder (*Themat.-Systemat. Verzeichnis der Werke Joh. Seb. Bachs*, Leipzig, 1950, p. 632 *et seq.*)

lists one of these as *Stücke für eine Spieluhr nach dem Musikspielwerk einer aus dem Schloss in Köthen stammenden Wanduhr.*

Bader, Philipp Georg. Described as a poet, playwright and librarian, Bader was employed by Prince Nicolaus Esterházy sometime before 1776 and remained in the household of the prince until his death in 1779. He was director of the theatres at Eszterháza and prior to that position was assistant to the organisation of the marionette theatre. With the official job description of librarian, he was the direct predecessor of Joseph Niemecz (q.v.). Bader also wrote the *libretti* for Haydn's opera *Dido* in 1776 and at least one other marionette opera for which Haydn composed the music. H.C. Robbins Landon comments that: 'Bader's libretti show that he was a highly educated man with a dry sense of humour'. After his death, his duties were officially taken over by Johann Peter Noethen, described as 'librarian and assistant at the Marionette Theatre', a position inferior to that subsequently taken by Niemecz.

Balbastre, Claude. Born at Dijon, 8 December 1729; died Paris, 9 April 1799. French organist and composer who produced a piece of music which he named *Romance* and which Dom Bedos (q.v.) identified as eminently suited to being pinned on an organ barrel. Consequently, Dom Bedos made a graphic arrangement of this music which he expressed both in staff notation and in mechanical notation and published in his treatise on barrel organ construction. This music has been seen as a fine example of mechanical music and in recent years it has been arranged for much later instruments.

Bauer, Johann L. Berlin. Chancellor to Frederick William the Great, he built small mechanical organs one of which was presented to the Czarina Catherina II in 1784. He exhibited organ clocks and an orchestrion in Leipzig in 1829 in collaboration with another maker of these instruments named C. Heinrich.

Bedos de Celles. A Benedictine monk at St. Maur in France, Dom Bedos de Celles was born in 1706 and died on 25 November 1779. Between 1776 and 1778 he compiled a monumental reference work entitled *L'Art du Facteur d'Orgues* which comprised a lavishly detailed and well-illustrated four-volume treatise on the construction of the pipe organ. A definitive work for many years and still sought after by builders who seek to remanufacture the classic type of instrument (it is available today as a facsimile edition), a large section of one of the volumes (the facsimile is in three) is devoted to the mechanical organ and there is a long treatise on the art of arranging music for barrels and actual barrel pinning. This text stands to this day as the only complete reference source on this complex task. Parts of this work appear in Appendix 2.

Beethoven, Ludwig van. Born Bonn, 15/16 December 1770; died Vienna, 26 March 1827. German composer of Flemish descent who studied for a time with Haydn who nicknamed him 'the great Mogul'. From an early age he was exposed not just to mechanical music but also to those who wrote for the mechanical instrument. Besides Haydn, he studied with Johann Schenk, Antonio Salieri and Albrechtsberger, all of whom at some time or another were involved with automatic organs. But above all Beethoven was in Vienna where many builders of the instruments lived and worked. He knew Mozart who composed for Müllers Art Cabinet (see under Mozart) and he himself arranged some music for the mechanical organs which the eccentric Count Deym owned. He wrote some music especially for them including some settings which give us an idea how big these instruments must have been. One piece, an *adagio assai* in F major, was arranged for seventy-nine notes, another was for eighty while a third was for 102. Besides these and other small pieces, Beethoven's major contribution was the so-called 'Battle' Symphony ('Wellington's Victory'), *Wellingtons Sieg, oder die Schlacht bei Vittoria*, Opus 91, written for Mälzel's Panharmonicon to celebrate the victory achieved in 1813. The saga of this piece and the manner in which its score was obtained by Mälzel and passed off as his own work is recounted in Ord-Hume, *Barrel Organ*.

Benda, Frantisek (Franz). The Bohemian family of Benda was almost as famous as were the Bachs and their musical activities spanned an almost identical period. There were many fine musicians and composers but it is Franz Benda, born in Stáre Benátky, 24 November 1709; died Potsdam, 7 March

1786, who is notable in our context. Among the music which he left was a manuscript entitled *1 Stück zur Harpfen Uhr* and there were other small works which he wrote for the so-called harp-clock or mechanical dulcimer.

Bidermann, Samuel. Augsburg, Bavaria, Germany. Born in 1540, Bidermann made mechanical spinets which could be operated either from a small keyboard or from pinned wooden barrels powered by a clockwork motor. He built a mechanical organ for a clock made by Matthais Rungell. Fine quality early work, several examples of which survive.

Bidermann, Samuel (the younger). The son of Samuel (above), he made organ-playing mechanisms to be fitted into artefacts such as sewing baskets.

Cherubini, Maria Luigi Carlo Zenobio Salvatore. Born Florence, 14 September 1760; died Paris, 15 March 1842. Son of a harpsichordist at the Teatro della Pergola, Cherubini became a distinguished Italian composer. His music became popular with the builders of automatic musical instruments. In July, 1805, he visited Vienna and appears to have made friends with both Beethoven and his predatory friend, Mälzel, very quickly. Within a short space of time, Mälzel's Panharmonicon was performing Cherubini's music. The *Zeitschrift für die elegant Welt* for 21 August 1806, refers to one of Mälzel's instruments playing Haydn's 'Military' Symphony, Mozart's Fantasie in C minor, and Cherubini's overture to the opera *Medea* which was first performed in Paris in 1797. Another popular piece was the so-called 'echo tune' of Cherubini which was played on at least one Panharmonicon. He also composed at this time a piece entitled *Air pour le Panharmonicon* which was published in Paris in 1806 and the manuscript for which is preserved in the Deutsche Staatsbibliothek in Berlin. The year before this, he composed his *Sonata per l'Organo a Cilindro situato nel Tempio della Notte del Giardino di Schönau presso Vienna*. This has recently been arranged for manual organ by Wolfgang Stockmeier (published Fr. Kistner & C.F.W. Siegel & Co, Cologne, 1968). In the winter of 1812/13, Mälzel exhibited an impressive 'art cabinet' containing an organ which played among other works, the overture to Cherubini's *Lodoïska* dating from 1791.

Cimarosa, Domenico. Born Aversa, Naples, 17 December 1749; died Venice, 11 January 1801. The son of a poor working-class family, Cimarosa grew up to be an extraordinarily talented composer. Although he never wrote specifically for mechanical organ, his music was popular for this idiom. The *Wiener Zeitung* in 1801 (page 3993) described a large automatic organ for sale by the art dealer Karl Mechetti which had twelve barrels, one of which was devoted to the music of Cimarosa.

Clay, Charles. Born Stockton, 1716; died London, 1740. A maker of very fine quality musical clocks incorporating mechanical organs or carillons of bells. In his short life, Clay produced a number of fine monumental instruments and is best remembered outside horological circles for his involvement with Georg Friedrich Händel who composed or arranged some of his other compositions for him. The collection *Ten Tunes for Clay's Musical Clock* is well known and dates from about 1736.

Csatkai, Endre (Andrew). Born Darufalva, Hungary (now called Drassburg in Austria), 13 August 1896. Art historian and writer on music who made an early and valuable study of Haydn and his music.

Dandrieu, Jean François. Born Paris, 1682; died Paris, 17 January 1738. Court composer and organist, Dandrieu was one of the fathers of French organ music. He also found time to compose for the mechanical organ which was allegedly used for teaching caged birds to sing — the serinette. One work has been traced, a short piece for this instrument.

Eberl, Anton. Born Vienna, 13 June 1766; died Vienna, 11 March 1807. Austrian pianist and composer who once enjoyed great popularity. His music is now largely lost. He composed music for Johann Nepomuk Mälzel's large mechanical orchestras and for a similar instrument made by Strasser (q.v.) he composed an *Adagio, Allegro et Rondeau* specially for the organ.

Eberlin, Johann Ernst. Born Jettingen (nr. Günzburg, Bavaria), 27 March 1702; died Salzburg, 19 June 1762. Organist and composer who became chief organist at Salzburg in 1729. He was Court Organist to Archbishop Franz Anton, Graf von Harrach when he was twenty-five years old. A fluent composer whose work was much admired by W.A. Mozart. Eberlin provided Leopold Mozart with five pieces for the *hornwerke* barrel organ in the Hohen-Salzburg when the barrels on this 1502-vintage organ were re-pinned in the eighteenth century.

Ehrbar, Conrad. Berlin. One of the group of outstanding makers of mechanical organs and musical clocks in the period c. 1780–90.

Eisenburger, K. See under Hassler.

Elffroth, Carl Ludwig. Also spelled *Elfroth*. Berlin. One of the small group of outstanding makers of mechanical organs and musical clocks which flourished in the period 1780–90.

Engramelle, Marie Dominique Joseph. Naturalist and mechanician, Father Engramelle was born in Nedonchel, France, in 1727. He built organs as a spare time occupation and devoted a great deal of his time to contemplating the question of the mechanical playing of music. He devised a notation system for mechanical music and designed a set of tools for barrel pricking and pinning. In 1757 he built an automatic instrument which could 'record' keyboard music in a form which could be worked into a pinned barrel so that the original music could be played back. In 1775 he published a work called *La Tonotechnie ou l'Art de Noter les Cylindres*. His work was subsequently expanded by the Benedictine monk, Dom Bedos de Celles (q.v.). Engramelle died in 1781.

Erbach, Christian. Born in Hesse, 1573; died Augsburg, 1635. German organist and composer. Succeeded Hassler (q.v.) as town organist of Augsburg. He composed music for Langenbucher's *Pommerische Kunstschrank* (Pommeranian Art Cabinet). See also under Hainhofer.

Esterházy. One of the most famous and wealthy of the noble families which were dotted about Europe. It was Paul Esterházy (1), Palatine of Hungary (born 1636; died 1713) who built the palace at Eisenstadt in 1683. He was succeeded by Joseph (2) who died in 1721. His successor was the ten-year-old Paul Anton (3), born in 1711; died 18 March 1762. His reign did not actually begin until he came of age when he was twenty-four in 1734. Nicolaus (Miklos) (4) was the grandson of Paul (1) and was born in 1714. He was Paul Anton's (3) brother and was forty-nine years old at the time of his accession in March of 1762 (the actual ceremony was held in May that year). He earned the nickname 'the magnificent' and was responsible for building the palace of Eszterháza into which he moved in 1766 before it was fully completed. He was Haydn's employer and benefactor and was also to be responsible for hiring Joseph Niemecz (q.v.). Nicolaus (4) married Maria Anna Franziska Weissenwolf on 3 August 1777. He died at the age of 77 years on 28 September 1790, and was succeeded by his son Anton (5), born 1738, then in his fifty-fifth year. Anton had married Countess Maria Theresa Erdödy on 11 January 1763, in celebration of which occasion Haydn composed the opera *Acide*. The death of his wife in 1782 was followed in 1785 by his marriage to another Maria Theresa, this one being the Countess Hohenfeld. Anton (5) died in 1794 and was succeeded by his own son Nicolaus II (6) who was the grandson of Nicolaus 'the magnificent' (4). He was born on 12 December 1765, and died in 1833. He was Haydn's last employer within the Esterházy family and paid him the honour of visiting him in his own home when Haydn was a sick and frail man approaching the end of his days. Nicolaus II (6) married Maria Josepha Hermenegild, the Princess Liechtenstein (born 13 April 1768) on 15 September 1783. She was a woman of particularly striking beauty and Haydn became specially friendly with her in a spirit of what seems to have been mutual admiration. In later years she used to run errands for Haydn, taking his manuscripts to Artaria, his Viennese publishers. The Esterházy wealth and treasures were dispersed during the nineteenth century and the final break-up came with the restructuring of Central Europe after the First World War. Although the palaces of Eszterháza and Eisenstadt survive as museums, gone long since is Haydn's own opera house and theatre, and following the mass destruction of family treasures by the Russians in 1945 few if any of the possessions and artefacts remain. One of the numerous Esterházy palaces — the one in Bratislava (formerly Pressburg and now capital of Slovakia) — is now an infant's school.

Gassmann, Florian Leopold. Born at Most in Brüx, May 1729; died Vienna, 20 January 1774. A respected Bohemian conductor and composer who studied at Bologna with Padre Martini. He lived for a while in Venice in the service of Count Leonardo Veneri where he achieved his first successes as an opera composer. So esteemed was he in this capacity that he was summoned to Vienna to take up the position of ballet composer as successor to Gluck. In 1772 he succeeded Reutter as Court conductor. He was the founder of the oldest Viennese music society, the Tonkünstler-Societät, which later became the Haydn Society (after 1862). He left two daughters, Maria Anna Fux (1771–1852), and Maria Theresa Rosenbaum (1774–1837) who were opera singers of some standing before they married. An extensive autograph/commonplace book belonging to the Rosenbaum family during this period is preserved today in the documentation of the Teubner instrument. Gassmann was killed falling from a carriage. He left more than twenty operas and a great deal of other music.

Giornovichi, Giovanni Mane. Also known as Jarnowick. Born Palermo either in 1735 or 1740; died St Petersburg, 21 November 1804, apparently at the age of sixty-nine and during a game of billiards. A talented violinist and composer, he was a pupil of Lolli and played in Paris until some misbehaviour forced him to leave town. He joined the orchestra of Prince Rohan-Guémené as *konzertmeister*. His employer was French envoy at Vienna from 1772 to 1774. After that, Giornovichi joined the orchestra of Friedrich II, King of Prussia. A conceited and argumentative man, he repeatedly fell out with people and even his first concert in London in May of 1791, although a great success on the surface, resulted in his being summoned to a duel by Johann Baptist Cramer — which he did not attend. He composed the so-called Russian Dance theme used in Wranitzky's ballet which Haydn used as the basis for number 16 in the thirty-two mechanical organ pieces. Beethoven also used this theme for his twelve A major piano variations, Opus 182.

Gurck, Joseph. Also spelled 'Gurk'. Assistant to Joseph Niemecz in the library of the Princes Esterházy from 1795. Collaborated in the manufacture of mechanical organs and after the death of Niemecz was responsible for disposing of his property, completing unfinished instruments and creating more instruments and touring Europe, finally coming to London with his Panharmonicon *(see Appendix 1)*.

Hainhofer, Philipp. Augsburg, Germany. A patrician organist and composer who, in the year 1617, composed several canons for the mechanical organ built by Achilles Langenbucher into the *Pommerisches Kunstschrank* which was destroyed during the Second World War. For details of this instrument and transcriptions of the music, see Protz, *Mechanische Musikinstrumenten.* For an earlier account and the only source of information on Hainhofer, see John Böttiger: *Philipp Hainhofer und der Kunstschrank Gustav Adolfs*, Stockholm, 1909.

Handel, Georg Friedrich. Born Halle, 23 February 1685; died London, 14 April 1759. Although of German birth, Handel became a naturalised Englishman and was a composer of considerable standing. Around 1740 or earlier, he came into contact with the London clockmaker Charles Clay (q.v.) who was a noted maker of musical clocks. Out of this meeting came the composition of a number of pieces of music — some were arrangements of existing pieces — in two distinct groups. The first collection was called *Ten Tunes for Clay's Musical Clock* (in actual fact there are *eleven*), and a second group of seven making eighteen in all. The eleven pieces in the first set are all for an organ with twenty-nine notes while those for the second are for a fifteen-note instrument. The music of Handel was popular with other English makers of mechanical organs and both Clay and George Pike (Pyke) used pieces of his music in various arrangements. Some of these have survived in copyists' notation and one is reprinted in Ord-Hume, *Mechanics of Mechanical Music*, p. 66–7.

Hassler, Hans Leo. Born in Nürnberg, 25/26 October

1564; died Frankfurt, 8 June 1612. German organist and composer. Played in Augsburg where he met an inventive weaver named G. Heinlein. Together with K. Eisenburger they built a mechanical organ which, in the words of its builder, 'had no equal'. Hassler composed the music for this instrument and took it on a tour of several German towns and then went to Prague and to the Court of Rudolf. Rudolf was delighted with the instrument, purchased it and somewhat rashly awarded Hassler the monopoly of production of mechanical organs. However, another builder was also at work — Eisenburger — who made a similar mechanical organ which was hidden in an exquisitely carved writing desk. Hassler promptly saw this as an infringement of his monopoly and took court action against Eisenburger, his former collaborator. The legal wrangle went on for a number of years and involved the intervention of the Elector of Bavaria and Emperor Rudolf II himself. It seems that Hassler's instrument was the better since it had a greater number of registers and could play 'very short notes'. The outcome of the case is not known as it seems to have become a morass of legal confusion. Eisenburger continued making instruments but no sooner had Hassler concluded the legal suit on that count when we find him involved in a far more serious piece of litigation. The Emperor had commissioned from him another mechanical organ for which Hassler composed new music and requested Heinlein to pin these compositions on the barrel. Unfortunately, Heinlein was without the necessary finance to see the job through and was forced to borrow money from various other sources. Before he could complete the work, though, he fell ill and died and at once all his possessions were seized by his creditors. Hassler managed to secure much of the organ which Heinlein had in his possession but without the rest of the pieces it was impossible to complete. Again Hassler went to the courts: this time Fate intervened and he died before final judgement could be given. The organ appears never to have been finished and the parts were lost.

Haydn, Joseph. Born Franz Joseph Haydn at Rohrau, Lower Austria, 31 March/1 April 1732; died Vienna, 31 May 1809. The elder of two sons born to a wheelwright. Both sons transcended their humble beginnings and both became great composers, Michael Haydn became the teacher of Weber and musical director to the Archbishop of Salzburg, while Joseph Haydn went on to become one of the greatest of all composers. He is often referred to as 'the father of the symphony', yet he also laid the foundation of the string quartet and of chamber and instrumental music. A deeply religious man, his musical output extended from the sacred oratorio (*The Creation* and *The Seasons* being the best examples), through brilliantly-scored choral works such as the *Theresienmesse* to no fewer than 104 symphonies. He entered the cathedral school of St. Stephan in Vienna at the age of eight and by the age of ten had amassed a wide knowledge of church music. Dismissed from the school at seventeen through a silly prank, he took to playing in street bands while studying seriously. At the age of twenty-seven he joined the household of Morzin at Lukavec, a position he only held a short time as Count Morzin was forced to disband his orchestra within little more than a year. In 1761 he entered the household of the Prince Esterházy at Eisenstadt and began a long and fruitful association with no fewer than four of the princes, Nicolaus II being his prime inspiration and whose Court he served the longest. With the arrival at Eisenstadt of the monk, Joseph (Primitivus) Niemecz, Haydn embarked on a deep and sincere involvement with mechanical music, composing no fewer than thirty-two pieces for the mechanical organ. Three of the organs which are the outcome of this association and which together represent thirty of these pieces are preserved today as is a number of manuscripts some of which are annotated with information concerning the way in which Haydn wanted the barrels pinned. The music in this present study is those pieces catalogued by Anthony van Hoboken as Group XIX 'Pieces for Musical Clocks' or 'mechanical clocks', neither description being correct. Haydn's patronage of the mechanical organ emerges as having been very important and his ability to understand its advantages and limitations ranks him foremost among the many who composed for this medium.

Heinlein, G. See under Hassler.

Heyer, Wilhelm. Born Cologne, 30 March 1849; died Cologne 20 March 1913. There were two great collectors of musical instruments in the nineteenth century. One was Paul de Wit in Leipzig and the other was Wilhelm Heyer in Cologne. De Wit was also notable for his erudite editing of the *Zeitschrift für Instrumentenbau*, later to become the *Zeitschrift für Musikwissenschaft*, as well as the famous German music trades directory, *Weltaddresbuch...* De Wit died in 1905 and his collection was dispersed. Two earlier de Wit collections had already been acquired by the Berliner Musikinstrumenten-Sammlung — one in 1888 and another in 1891. The majority of instruments left at his death went into the Heyer Collection housed in the Musikhistorisches Museum Wilhelm Heyer in Cologne. The curator was the distinguished Georg Kinsky (q.v.) who held office from 1909 until 1926 when the whole collection was presented to Leipzig University by the owner of the C.F. Peters music publishing house, Dr Henri Hinrichsen. Heyer was the founder of a famous paper manufacturing business. See also under Kinsky.

Hoboken, Anthony van. Born Rotterdam, 23 March 1887. Dutch musicologist who became a pupil of the historian Heinrich Schenker in Vienna. He became the cataloguer of all Haydn's music, his monumental work being *Joseph Haydn: Thematischbibliographisches Werkverzeichnis,* within which the mechanical organ pieces are listed as XIX: 32.

Hofhaimer, Paul. Born Radstadt (Salzburg), 25 January 1459; died Salzburg, 1537. A composer and organist of reputedly outstanding ability. Most of his music is now lost. Largely self-taught, he was court musician to the Emperor Maximilian I. In the closing years of the nineteenth century when the organ barrel of the Salzburg Castle 1502-vintage barrel organ was repinned, Hofhaimer's *Hymne* was set as the third tune. One wonders if it might not have been one of the tunes set on the original 1502 cylinder. (See Rudolf Quoika: *Altösterreichische Hornwerke,* 1959, p. 45 and 75 *et seq.* and also Joh. Ev. Engl: *Das Hornwerk auf Hohensalzburg,* Salzburg, 1909, in which is reproduced the musical score of this, Joseph Haydn's 'Österreichische Volkshymne' of 1797 and the other music used in the re-pin of 1893).

Huguenin, Abram Louis. Born Neuchâtel, Switzerland, 1733; died Berlin, 1804. Son of Moise Huguenin, clockmaker to the King of Prussia, Abram Louis came from a long line of famed clockmakers. In 1765 he went to Berlin to direct the royal clock factory and worked on the mechanical organs in clocks which played the music of Carl Philipp Emanuel Bach (q.v.). Was responsible for the making of a number of outstanding instruments.

Jaquet-Droz, Henri Louis. Born 1752; died 1791. The son of Pierre Jaquet-Droz (q.v.) he created many fine automata with music, perhaps the most notable being *La Musicienne,* a female android seated at a small organ which she played by the actual articulation of her fingers and hands to depress keys on a keyboard. This piece has always been considered to play music which Henri Louis Jaquet-Droz himself composed — he was also a fairly successful musician and composer. However, it was not until the restoration of the piece to playing order in 1978 that it became possible to hear this music properly and the present author was at once able to identify one of the melodies played as *Fischer's Minuet* and has cast doubts that the other pieces are by the builder (see

The Music Box, vol. 8, 1980).

Jaquet-Droz, Pierre. Born 1721; died 1790. A maker of superb automata and clocks incorporating organwork. Of Swiss origin, he worked at various times in Paris, Geneva and Madrid and the family had a subsidiary operation in London where fine automaton clocks were crafted for the lucrative export market to China.

Kaufmann, Johann Gottfried. Born 1752; died 1818. Served an apprenticeship as a stocking-knitter in his native town of Siegmar, Saxony. After three years he went to Dresden where he began making mechanical musical instruments. He was succeeded by his son Friedrich (born 1786; died 1866) who built an orchestrion which he called the Belloneon in 1805. This had twenty-four free metal reeds with trumpet resonators as well as two kettle drums and was made for the King of Prussia. It played regimental marches of the Prussian Cavalry. He also made a mechanical trumpeter in 1810 which is now in the Deutsches Museum in München. As well as automatic instrument-playing androids, the Kaufmanns also made orchestrions, one of which was the Salpingion which played the 'Hallelujah Chorus' from the *Messiah* of Handel on reeds, trumpets and kettledrums. His own son was Friedrich Theodore, born 1823; died 1872.

Kinsky, Georg. Born Marienwerder, West Prussia, 29 September 1882; died Berlin 7 April 1951. German musicologist who was entirely self-taught in music. He became a scholar of some considerable importance and was curator of the Heyer collection, originally housed in the Musikhistorisches Museum Wilhelm Heyer in Cologne until 1926 when it was moved to Leipzig (see entry under Heyer). While in this position, Kinsky endeavoured to purchase for the museum the 1793 Haydn/Niemecz mechanical organ (now in the Veyder-Malberg collection and on loan to the Stadtmuseum in München). It seems that the impending transfer of the museum may have been the reason why this deal never went through.

Kircher, Athanasius. Born 1601; died 1680. A Jesuit priest who was among the earliest in recent times to identify the capabilities and potential of the concept of mechanical music. In his book *Musurgia Universalis* published in 1650 he devoted considerable space to establish the capabilities of the mechanical organ, Kircher's writings have largely been discredited in recent times due to their containing a high proportion of speculative writing; in one book, for example, he writes about the music then in current use to relieve the effects of the bite of the tarantula.

Kirnberger, Johann Philipp. Born Saalfeld, 1721;

died Berlin, 1783. An eminent Thuringian theorist who studied music with Bach and played in the Court orchestra in Berlin, later becoming musician to the Princess Amalia. Author of a valuable work on equal temperament and composer of a considerable amount of music, he is also known to have written a piece entitled *Allegro für die Singuhr*.

Kleemeyer (Kleemayer), Christian Ernst. A Berlin maker of first-class, fine-toned mechanical organs which operated in conjunction with timepieces. One was bought by Frederick William III in 1825 and now stands in the Potsdam marble hall. One clock with mechanical organ made by Kleemeyer is in the museum of the Leipzig University. Another, apparently made in 1797, played the overture to Mozart's *Die Zauberflöte* to great perfection. Kleemeyer seems to have been active between 1766 and 1805.

Langshaw, John. A London maker of barrel organs who was employed by Handel's amanuensis, John Christopher Smith (1712–95) in about 1761 in setting music upon the barrels of a large mechanical organ which was being constructed for the Earl of Bute, a task which he apparently completed 'in so masterly a manner that the effect was equal to that produced by the most finished player'. Langshaw died in 1793.

Liechtenstein. Like the Esterházys, the Liechtensteins were among the richest and the noblest families in Central Europe during the seventeenth, eighteenth and nineteenth centuries. The relationship with the Esterházy family through marriage is referred to under Esterházy (q.v.).

Mälzel (Melzel, Mäzl), Johann Nepomucene. Born Ratisbon, 15 August 1772; died at sea, 21 July 1838. The son of an organ builder, he settled in Vienna in 1792 and soon gained fame for his invention of the Panharmonicon orchestrion organ which, among other orchestral instruments, could imitate string tones. He appears to have made a number of instruments with the name Panharmonicon and for one of these he offered to provide Beethoven (q.v.) with an ear trumpet in exchange for a suitable piece of music. Beethoven produced the 'Battle Symphony' and Mälzel tried to pass it off as his own composition which started a fierce feud between the two men. By all accounts, he made some fine instruments and it is regretted that his professional life was marred by his stealing the Dutch organ-builder Winkel's idea of the metronome which he then manufactured under his own name. He also went on tour exhibiting a fake automaton chess-playing machine. His brother, Leonard Mälzel, was also an eminent builder of

mechanical instruments. Eleven years younger than Johann, he made a number of instruments which ultimately earned him the title of Court Mechanic to the Imperial Physical and Astronomical Cabinet in Vienna. He died in 1855.

Möllinger, Christian. Berlin, fl. 1784–1826. Court clockmaker to Frederick William II (nephew of Frederick the Great). Made some outstanding timepieces with mechanical organwork, one of these pieces being dated 1791.

Mozart, Wolfgang Amadeus. Born Salzburg, 27 January 1756; died Vienna, 5 December 1791. Arguably the most important composer of all time, Mozart was greatly admired by Haydn and indeed they became close friends. It is thought that Haydn took up Freemasonry due to the influence of Mozart. On his return from London in 1791, Haydn was bitterly upset to learn of Mozart's death. Mozart wrote three pieces of music for mechanical organs in the collection of Count Joseph Deym von Stritetz, the Bohemian soldier who later fled to Holland under the assumed name of Müller. These pieces are Köchel-catalogued as K. 594 Adagio and Allegro in F minor 'A Piece for a Mechanical Organ in a Clock'; K. 608 Fantasy in F minor 'Organ piece for a Clock'; and K. 616 Andante in F major 'For a Cylinder in a small (mechanical) Organ'. The first two of these appear to date from 1782, but it is known that the last piece carries the date 4 May 1791. All were written in Vienna. Another piece, K. 617, written on 23 May 1791, for a small group of instrumentalists led by the blind virtuoso Marianne Kirchgässner and first performed by her at the Vienna Opera on 19 August that year, is thought possibly to have been reworked as a fourth piece for one of the Müller/Deym automaton organs (see *Count Deym and his Mechanical Organs* by O.E. Deutsch in *Music & Letters*, vol. 29, 1948). A more likely contender for the supposedly forgotten fourth mechanical organ piece is an Adagio in C major, K. 356, catalogued by Einstein as 617a and written during the first half of 1791. This piece, brimming with arpeggios and written, apparently, as a solo for glasharmonika, is far closer related in style to the other three. A hitherto unknown work of Mozart (an arrangement of a Tyrolean melody) was discovered and identified on the barrel of a small mechanical organ now in the Nationaal Museum van Speelklok tot Pierement, Utrecht. For the story of this and its builder, D.N. Winkel who also built the Componium, see Ord-Hume, *Barrel Organ*.

Mozart, Leopold. Born Augsburg, 14 November 1719; died Salzburg, 28 May 1787. Father of Wolfgang Amadeus Mozart. Composer of music for mechnical organs at various times and best known of these works are the six pieces which he wrote for the 1502-built barrel organ in Salzburg Castle when its barrels were re-pinned. These pieces date from 1759.

Niemecz, Joseph. Born Vlašim (near Benesov in Bohemia), 9 February 1750; died Vienna, 9 January 1806. Studied Philosophy until joining the *Barmherzigen Bruder* (Brothers of Charity, or Brothers of Mercy) in 1768. Took his vows on 29 August 1769, and was ordained as a priest in 1776, taking the name of Father Primitivus Niemecz. In 1780 was appointed successor to Philipp Georg Bader (q.v.) as librarian to Prince Nicolaus Esterházy. In 1795 he moved with the royal household to Vienna. Built at least three mechanical organs pinned with music which was provided by his friend and tutor, Joseph Haydn. Niemecz also played in Haydn's orchestra at the royal palaces besides attending to the library which was reputed to have one copy of every book ever published and totalled 75,000 books and manuscripts.

Schmid, Ernst Fritz. Born Tübingen, 7 March 1904; died 20 January 1960. Germam musicologist who graduated at the University of Freiburg. Lectured at the University of Graz where he also conducted concerts. Was president of the German Musical Society and a prolific and respected author on music and musical history. He lived his closing years in Vienna at Belghofergasse 7, XII/2 and made a detailed study of Haydn's involvement with the mechanical organ which was published in 1932.

Schnerich, Alfred. Born Tarvis, 22 October 1859; died 1944. Austrian musicologist and specialist in the history of church music. Published a valuable book on the life of Haydn (*Joseph Haydn*, 1922) in which he first drew attention to Haydn's involvement with mechanical music.

Specht, Christian. Engaged in the choir and orchestra of Eszterháza, Specht was a bass singer possessing a remarkable range from F at the bottom of the bass clef to a'. Haydn was particularly friendly with this man and so when, in 1778 and for some quite unaccountable reason, Specht lost his voice, Haydn was partly responsible for keeping him in the musical scene by engaging him as a viola player. This was something of a comedown for the former artist and his salary was finally reduced accordingly. However, in 1781 a fresh contract was drawn up for him which allowed him a number of benefits in the way of victuals and this was worded as follows:

'For his part he agrees to keep in good order, to string, to quill and to tune all the clavier in Esterház, also those clavier belonging to the singers, and under which it is understood are included the musical clocks

in Esterház and Mon Biyouz (Monbijous was a hunting castle nearby), to which end he is to procure at his expense the strings and raven's quills' (from Robbins Landon: *Haydn at Eszterháza*, p. 62).

Specht died at Eisenstadt on 21 February 1809, shortly before Haydn's own death in May of that year.

Strand, Petter (Per). Stockholm, Sweden. Born 1756; died 1826. Maker of outstanding mechanical organs with timepieces. His instruments are quite as individual as those of Niemecz, displaying a characteristic style that is possibly unique in that the pipework is not arranged in the normal way solely above the organ table, but extends above and below it to form a mechanism which is shallow in depth (front and back) but needing a large case to enclose the symmetrical triangular display of pipework above and below. Britten (*Old Clocks & Watches & Their Makers*) gives Strand dates of 1791–1815, but these are only *floruit* dates. Five Strand clocks are known: three in a private museum in Stockholm and another in the Nordiske Museum, and one which the author acquired on the sale of the Mekanisk Musik Museum, Copenhagen, for the Utrecht Museum in 1981.

Strasser, Johann Georg. Born in Baden near Vienna, Strasser was responsible for setting Haydn's music on organ barrels. Likely to have been known to the 'Vienna Circle' of Niemecz and Mälzel, &c, he appears to have moved to Russia. Valentin L. Chenakal (*Watchmakers & Clockmakers in Russia*) traces his first musical clocks made in St. Petersburg in 1792. Strasser flourished to about 1801. Possibly of Russian descent since there was already a maker of travelling clocks there at the beginning of the eighteenth century called J.P. Strasser. In the nineteenth century, Strasser was a notable name in clockmaking in the Glashütte/Sachsen area. Johann Georg Strasser made outstanding mechanical organs including one with barrels including music by Haydn.

Vaucanson, Jacques de. Born 1709; died Paris, 1782. Famed engineer who devoted much of his life to mechanisms, machines and automata. Produced several remarkable pieces including two androids exhibited in Paris in 1738. One was a flute-player, the other a Provençal shepherd playing twenty airs on a *galoubet*. Most renowned for his automaton duck which ate food, digested it and then excreted it in a lifelike manner.

Walter, Anton. Born in Vienna in 1752 and died there in 1826. A maker of pianofortes and organs who also made harpsichords. He worked for the Esterházy family and rebuilt Haydn's harpsichord after it had been burned in a fire at the theatre in Eisenstadt.

Even so, Haydn did not think greatly of Walter's work saying that he was too expensive and that few of the instruments he made were entirely satisfactory. Walter is thought to have been involved in supplying components to Niemecz for the making of the Haydn/Niemecz organs.

Werner, Gregor Joseph. Born Ybbs an der Donau, 28 January 1693; died 3 March 1766 in Eisenstadt. Employed by Prince Paul Anton Esterházy as musical director. His musical compositions were a source of inspiration to Haydn who was subsequently to succeed him as *Capellmeister*. His influence on Haydn, certainly during the early period of Haydn's time with the Esterházys, was undoubtedly great.

Wranitzky, Paul (Pavel Vranický). Born Nová Rise, December, 1756; died Vienna, 28 September 1808. Of Moravian origin, he was a violinist and composer who went to Vienna in 1776 and studied under Joseph Kraus. In 1780 he joined the orchestra of Prince Esterházy at Eisenstadt and became friendly with Haydn. He later (in 1785) became leader of the Court Opera in Vienna and stayed in this position until he died. A prolific composer who was held in high regard by Haydn and who was a member of Haydn's masonic lodge for which he wrote a symphony. See reference under Giornovichi.

PICTURE CREDITS

An important part of this book is the photographic illustrations which make up its pictorial content. Grateful thanks are thus due to the museums and archives which have supplied material and permitted reproduction. The following is a list of sources of pictures used. Unlisted pictures are either the work of the author or are untraceable.

Plate 2 — Berlin Museum archives; **3** — Ilbert Collection, British Museum, London; **4** — Colin Futcher, Surrey; **5, 6** — Museum of London Collection; **7, 11, 14, 49, 51, 52** — Nationaal Museum van Speelklok tot Pierement, Utrecht, Netherlands; **8** — Howard Fitch, New Jersey; **10** — Christie's South Kensington, London; **13** — Karl Marx University, Leipzig; **42, 45, 46, 47** — Berlin, Staatsbibliothek Preussischer Kulturbesitz, Musikabteilung; **43, 44** — Státní Oblastní Archiv v Třeboni, Jindřichův Hradec, Hungary; **48** — Österreichisches Museum für angewandte Kunst, Vienna, Austria; **53, 54** — Westminster Music Library, London; **55** — Bildarchiv preussisches kulturbesitz, Berlin.

The following line illustrations are reproduced with grateful acknowledgement: *Fig. 33* — Westminster Music Library, London; *Fig. 34* — Helga Froschmeier; *Fig. 35* — *Illustrated London News*, London.

Select Bibliography

Bedos, Francois (Dom Bedos de Celles), *L'Art du Facteur d'Orgues,* Paris, 1778 (facsimile, Kassel, 1977).

Bobinger, Maximilian, *Alt-Augsburger Kompassmacher,* Augsburg, 1966.

Buchner, Alexandr, *Mechanical Musical Instruments,* London, c. 1954.

Dies, Albert Christoph, *Biographische Nachrichten von Joseph Haydn,* Vienna, 1810 (revised edition by Horst Seeger, Berlin, 1959). See also *Griesinger.*

Engramelle, Marie Dominique Joseph, *La Tonotechnie ou l'Art de Noter les Cylindres,* Paris, 1775 (facsimile, Geneva, 1971).

Fuchs, Aloys, *Handschriftlicher Thematischer Katalog von Haydns Werken in der Preussischer Staatsbibliothek Berlin,* vol. 15, no. 6 (facsimile published in Wilhelmshaven, 1968, as *Thematisches Verzeichnis der sämtlichen Kompositionen von Joseph Haydn 1839*

Griesinger, G.A. and **Dies,** A.C., *Biographischen Nachtrichten von Joseph Haydn* (trans. Vernon Gotwals as *Joseph Haydn, Eighteenth Century Gentleman and Genius,* Wisconsin, 1936)

Hoboken, Anthony van, *Joseph Haydn: Thematisch. -bibliographisches Werkverzeichnis,* Mainz, 1957–71

Jöde, Fritz, 'Joseph Haydns Flötenuhrstücke', *Zeitschrift Schulmusik,* vol. 5, 1932

Nowak, L., 'Esterhazy', *Die Musik in Geschichte und Gegenwart,* vol. 5, Kassel, 1956

Ord-Hume, Arthur W.J.G., *Barrel Organ,* London, 1979

Ord-Hume, Arthur W.J.G., *Clockwork Music,* London, 1975

Ord-Hume, Arthur W.J.G., *The Mechanics of Mechanical Music,* London, 1973

Perragaux, Charles/**Perrot,** F-Louis, *Jaquet-Droz et Leschot,* Neuchâtel, 1916

Pohl, C.F/**Botisber,** Hugo, *Joseph Haydn,* Leipzig 1927

Poppe, Johann Heinrich Moritz von, *Geschichte aller Erfindunger und Entedekkungen . . .,* Stuttgart, 1837

Protz, Albert, *Mechanische Musikinstrumente,* Kassel, 1940

Quoika, Rudolph, *Altösterreichische Hornwerke,* Berlin, 1959

Robbins Landon, H.C., *Haydn: the Early Years 1732–65,* London, 1980

Robbins Landon, H.C., *Haydn: the Late Years, 1801–80.* London, 1977

Robbins Landon, H.C., *Haydn in England, 1791–1795,* London, 1976

Robbins Landon, H.C., *Haydn: the Years of 'The Creation', 1796–1800,* London, 1977

Robbins Landon, H.C., *Haydn: the Late Years, 1801–80. London, 1977*

Roth, Friedrich, 'Der Gross Spieluhrprozess Hans Leo Hasslers von 1603–11', *Sammelbände der Internationalen Musikgesellschaft,* vol. 14, 1912

Schmid, Ernst Fritz, 'Hans Leo Hassler und seine Bruder', *Zeitschrift der Historisches Vereins für Schwaben,* Augsburg, 1941

Schmid, Ernst Fritz, 'Joseph Haydn und die Flötenuhr', *Zeitschrift für Musikwissenschaft,* vol. 14, January, 1932

Schmid, Ernst Fritz, 'Joseph Haydn, Werke für das Laufwerke (Flötenuhr)', Hanover, 1931 (facsimile with additions, Kassel 1954)

Schnerich, Alfred, *Joseph Haydn und seine Sendung,* Vienna, 1922

Simon, Ernst, 'Friedrich der Grosse und die mechanischen Musikinstrumente', *Zeitschrift für Instrumentenbau,* vol. 32, Leipzig, 1912.

Simon, Ernst, *Mechanische Musikinstrumente früherer Zeiten und ihre Musik,* Wiesbaden, 1961 (2nd edition, 1980)

Index

Note: Generally speaking, quoted authors only are itemised, not the titles of their works. Newspapers and periodicals, however, are named either in full or in acceptable abbreviation. Plates are indicated in **bold** type indicating the page upon which they appear. Line drawings are similarly indicated with a page number, this time in *italic*. The main list of illustrations at the front of the book shows Plate and Figure numbers with page references. Key character references, i.e. those referring to Haydn, Niemecz and Esterházy, are restricted to salient entries.